The Dynamics
of
America's Housing

The Dynamics
of
America's Housing

James W. Hughes
George Sternlieb

CENTER
FOR URBAN
POLICY RESEARCH

Published by the Center for Urban Policy Research
Building 4051—Kilmer Campus
New Brunswick, New Jersey 08903

Library of Congress Cataloging-in-Publication Data

Hughes, James W.
    The dynamics of America's housing.

    Bibliography: p. 215
    Includes index.
    1. Housing—United States. I. Sternlieb, George.
II. Rutgers University.   Center for Urban Policy
Research.   III. Title.
HD7293.H826   1987   363.5′0973   87-4515
ISBN 0-88285-122-5

Contents

IV. Market Relationships

Exhibits

II. Housing Demand

Chapter 2. Housing Demand: The Population Baseline

Chapter 3. The Household Revolution

Chapter 4.   The Maturing Society and Market Segmentation

Chapter 5.   Future Households: Scale and Shape

Chapter 6.   Income: Accelerator and Brake

III. Housing Supply

Chapter 7. Housing Supply: The Potent Baseline

Chapter 8. Housing Production Cycles

Chapter 9.   Regional Shifts Revisited

Chapter 10.   Housing Cost Structures

Chapter 11.   Financing Costs: New Mortgage Realities

Chapter 12.   Components of Inventory Change

Chapter 13.   Scale, Condition and Amenity Level

IV.　Market Relationships

Chapter 14.　Market Barometers: Demand–Supply Interrelationships

Preface

After a far from auspicious debut, the 1980s turned out to be another decade of American housing abundance. While certainly not benefitting all strata of society, nor all geographic subsectors, the nation's shelter system soared from the trough of the 1981–1982 recession. Housing triumph supplanted housing crisis. While most forecasts suggested a docile, cyclical shelter recovery, the mid-decade production record more than matched that of any comparable time period of the 1970s.

But the underlying forces and parameters were quite different from the predecessor decade. It is the purpose of this book to isolate the market dynamics which gave shape to the 1980s, and which will provide the foundations for the housing realities of the balance of the century. America of the 1980s is far different from the America of the 1970s. The dimensions of the 1990s will be equally at variance from either of these decades.

The book is partitioned into four broad sections: Overview, Housing Demand, Housing Supply, and Market Relationships. Section I provides an overview of our conclusions of housing realities to come. The second—Housing Demand—comprises five chapters, focusing on demographics, future households, and income parameters. The third section consists of seven chapters concerned with the supply of housing. It evaluates the patterns and forces of production cycles, inventory adjustments, cost structures, financing, and regional variation. The two chapters of the fourth section isolate the intersection between supply and demand as they are reflected in market relationships, and then target guidelines on housing to come.

The principal dynamics that will define "the final housing era" of the century are overviewed in Section I starting with the broad demographic and economic frameworks. The detail of the matrix which, in our opinion, will shape America's housing follows. But the primary target is to secure a grasp of the future.

James W. Hughes
George Sternlieb

I

Overview

1

Overview of the Coming Era

The Demographic Framework

Changing demographics will dramatically alter America's housing future, continuing, though in a markedly different fashion, the interaction and evolution of the past four decades. Demographics and housing in the last half of the twentieth century can be viewed as a three-act play. The first-act theme was set in the immediate post-World War II period: the nesting generation and its offspring—the baby boom—transformed not only shelter configurations, but housing geography. Tract-house suburbia dominated America through the early 1970s.

The second act features a new cast of characters. The coming of age of the baby boom, and the household revolution it helped fashion, redefined the housing market. Family-raising imperatives were joined by the need for alternative housing formats. Singles, mingles, lofts, conversions and condos were just a few of the market partitions which emerged.

This book emerges from a "pause between the acts." The conclusion of our play is quite different in themes from its start, though it follows their logic. Our cast now is aging—and this is reflected by the actions we forecast.

For the balance of this century, maturing housing demand will characterize America. Yuppies (young upscale professionals) and Dinks (dual income, no kids) were key merchandising meccas of the 1980s. But this is waning, with Grumpies (grown-up mature professionals) or some other yet-to-be devised acronym destined to represent the "1990s" marketing phase. A revised housing calculus will emerge, reflecting the relentless progression of age. This will mark the third demographic shelter era of the second half of the twentieth century.

3

Act One

The Post-World War II Nesting Generation (1945–Early 1970s)

Conceptually, two of our "acts" can be partitioned out of the period between World War II and the mid 1980s. The first was defined by the nesting generation—the original "Levittowners"—whose aspirations and family-raising requirements dominated America's housing markets from 1945 to the early 1970s. Housing was shaped by the requirements of child rearing. The baby boom roared, and tract-house suburbia was born.

But the era of the American dream house was more than the product of demography. It also fed back on the post-World War II demographic pattern, facilitating the emergence of the nesting generation. Without the "nests," and their ready availability, the baby boom probably would have been a much more modest phenomenon.

Expanding and maturing families, aided by the long sweep of post-World War II prosperity, began to further change the housing market. The middle class began the era in a house that Levitt and a great many other builders made famous shortly after the war—an 800-square-foot tribute to modesty. Standards racheted upwards. The nesting generation moved from a house that was "stripped-down" to one that was continuously refined as amenity followed amenity during the 1950s and 1960s.

Thus the evolution of shelter expectation, and realization, paralleled the economic advances of the era. But the modest housing beginnings often have been forgotten. The frame of reference for shelter-seeking baby boomers was not their parents' first house, but the more expansive dwelling that was achieved in later years.

Act Two

Baby-Boom Housing Demand: Early 1970s–Mid 1980s

By the beginning of the 1970s, the baby boom began to enter the housing market directly in full force. The second post-World War II housing act was powered by the offspring of the first. The "boomers" impacted the market in a far different fashion than did their parents.

Their values and life-style aspirations produced an eclectic mix of household configurations. Shelter formats were revised to accommodate a changing demand profile.

The homogeneous mass middle market of the previous act was supplanted by a segmented shelter marketplace no longer dominated by the imperatives of child rearing. Empty-nesters, singles, mingles (unmarried couples) and yuppies are only a few of the demographic–market partitions which emerged. And condominiums, loft conversions, patio-houses, townhouses, and zero-lot-line configurations were just some of the supply variations which arose, set in an environment of economic uncertainty and change.

Act Three

Maturing Housing Demand (The Balance of the Century)

The final years of the "American Century" will be marked by maturing shelter markets, driven by the "middle-aging" of the baby boom. In the preceding shelter period, this generation blazed new, and revolutionary, paths to first-time household formation and then to first-time homeownership. In the final demographic housing period of the century, their maturing housing demands will present a two-edged sword. On the positive side will be the huge web of trade-up markets that will emerge—accommodations appropriate in scale, amenity, and ingenuity to a populace in its peak-earning years. On the negative side will be the voids forming in the markets vacated by the aging baby boom. The baby-bust generation will prove far too small a replacement cohort. First-time household formation, entry-level shelter, and first-time homeownership therefore will diminish in scale through the turn of the century.

Despite potential market gaps, the demographics of affluence will hold sway. The inevitable maturing, pairing, and nesting of Americans offer the potential of far more potent *individual* household shelter demand. America in the 1990s will be a nation of experienced middle-aged homeowners attempting to ascend the higher rungs of the housing ladder. The less fortunate will be left to inherit the leftovers. As a function of declining household formation, these will be more plentiful than in the earlier periods.

The Economic Matrix

Three broad economic eras—roughly corresponding to the preceding demographic partitions—also have defined America's housing dynamics since World War II. The *first* was the post-war drive to affluence, beginning in 1945 and lasting until 1973, the year of the energy revolution. America's international economic hegemony drove the standard-of-living escalator seemingly inevitably upward; median family incomes doubled in real terms during this period. Widespread prosperity created an unprecedented mass middle market and rising shelter standards. Demographically inspired housing aspirations were realized via the sheer power of the American economic machine. They were aided by a sheltered housing finance system born during the depths of the Great Depression and continually refined to meet the needs of an expansive shelter industry. Long-term, single-digit, fixed-rate, self-amortizing mortgages were viewed as a keystone of the American economic order.

The *second* economic era was heralded by the 1973–1974 oil crisis and lasted through the 1981–1982 recession, the worst since the Great Depression. The period was defined by unprecedented economic and political shocks, accelerating inflation, the beginnings of a redefinition of the world economic order, and an American living-standards escalator seemingly under constant repair and suddenly reversed in direction. The median family income in the United States ended the period at far lower levels than at the beginning. With the fading of the casual prosperity assumptions of the earlier era, Americans sought refuge from the economic uncertainties—and found it in housing. A post-shelter-society mentality developed. Housing investment became a means of coping with inflation, taxation and the need for personal saving.

But as the era came to a close, the housing finance system that powered America's shelter bounty was virtually dismantled. The instrumentalities designed to function in stable low-inflation economic environments simply could not continue. Homogenized financial markets replaced sheltered housing credit. With full exposure to the economic elements, America's system of shelter provision fell into severe disarray as the period came to a close.

Disinflation emerged as a key parameter marking the beginning of the *third* economic era. It was joined by other attributes characteristic of the recovery and expansion phases of the business cycle. Typical among these was the resumption of income growth between 1982 and

1986. The period was also initially characterized by the seeming disappearance (or remission) of the sharp economic shocks and dislocations of the preceding era and—budget and trade deficits notwithstanding—the return of economic confidence.

The new homogenized financial world, with lending for housing merely one of its components, proved adequate to the task of supporting housing in America. Indeed, as the nation moved deeper into the second half of the 1980s, America's housing barometers began to indicate market conditions thought to be relics of the past. National rental vacancy rates began to approach double-digit levels, mortgage rates trended into single-digit ranges, and homeownership affordability thresholds again began to include the majority of American families. The economic environment of housing had seemingly come full circle, suggesting the baseline for the post 1990 era.

One future certainty will be the continuing presence of the *business cycle*. Within its swings, long-term demographic, economic, and housing-production forces are subject to all manner of short-term distortions. But housing demand and supply parameters have predictable longer-term dynamics.

The Dynamics in Force

Within the context of the broad demographic and economic frameworks, America's housing dynamics are many in number, but they *are definable*. The first organizing partition is the population baseline.

The Population Baseline

- The monolithic, mass middle market of the immediate post-World War II era has given way to highly differentiated nodes. As we close the century, America's population reflects a vast array of life-style alternatives, consumption patterns, shelter desires, and specialized needs.
- This sustained market partitioning and segmentation will not be the result of explosive population growth. Immigration shifts aside, America will continue to experience declining overall population growth rates and modest absolute growth increments.

- The internal structure of the nation's population will, however, experience sharp changes. Virtually all of the positive age-structure shifts will be secured in the life-cycle span of peak housing consumption (35 to 54 years). The negative shifts will be centered in the years of first-time household formation and first-time homeownership (20 to 34 years). Two major forces will drive these events: the baby boom explosion of the late 1940s through the early 1960s, and the baby bust which followed.
- The former will fully mature into the 35- to 54-year age span by the year 2000, making this the largest and most dynamic age sector. The baby-boom cohort will continue to define—if in an increasingly mature fashion—the most significant market partitions.

America's Households: Market Segmentation

- The baby boom-spawned household revolution transformed the demand for shelter in America. The generation that brought with it the world of singles and near-singles has set in motion forces that will pattern the 1990s and beyond.
- The new "reduced-scale" household became the American norm by the 1980s. Underpinned by the "new empire" of singles, marriage and divorce patterns, and reduced fertility, the classic American family of the 1950s shifted from mom and pop—and two or three children—to one- and two-person configurations.
- The classic progression of life-cycle stages—from first-time household formation, to family raising, to empty nesterhood—has become far more complex. Alternative stages and paths—permanent singles or resingled (uncoupled) status, mingles (unmarried couples), never-nesters (permanently childless couples), and single-parent families—define new shelter preferences and needs.

Detailed Future Demand Parameters

- The future of housing demand will be quite different from the two eras following World War II. It is a scenario of slower household growth mirrored by a decline in the absolute level of housing starts. But as a function of age and household type, demand will be skewed upscale.

- The 1970s may have been the era of the revolutionized household; the 1990s represent a return to a somewhat more conventional pattern, with the vast historical family "middle" securing some level of revitalization. The future portends more modest housing production numbers, but at higher levels of amenity—and cost.
- Shelter-demand realities to come will be driven by the phenomenon of demographic aging. The projected future central housing path is defined by the following parameters:

Between 1970 and 1980, the number of households in the United States increased by 1.7 million per year. A massive retrenchment took place in the early 1980s due to worldwide recession. Between 1980 and 1983, the average annual gain in households barely exceeded one million, virtually equivalent to the 1960s' experience.

The 1984 to 1990 projections show annual average household increases shifting to 1.3 million. A further diminishment in the 1990s is also projected. Between 1990 and 1995, the annual average gain in the number of households should retreat toward one million, i.e., the equivalent of the disaster years of the early 1980s. A much more mature America of nearly 100 million households will be dominated by those "settled in" to their middle years. By the last five years of the century, the shrinkage accelerates, with household growth averaging only 900,000 annually.

Homeownership will increase its share of shelter. During the 1970s, 70 percent of the household gain comprised owner households. Between 1984 and 1990, ownerships are projected to account for over 72 percent of household growth, with a further surge to 85 percent in the 1990 to 2000 era.

However, with overall household-growth increments contracting, this sharp marginal increase in proportion will boost the total share of homeownership by 2000 to only 67.2 percent, as compared to 64.4 percent in 1980 and 62.9 percent in 1970.

Housing producers will have to be wary of the potentially modest scale of housing requirements. For example, even though ownership will account for over 83 percent of the tenure selections of the 1990–1995 household increment, this translates in absolute terms to 883,000 owner households annually, fully one-quarter lower than the 1.2 million yearly average of the 1970s.

And suppliers of new rental accommodations face even more drastic adjustments. Renter households in the 1970s grew by more than one-half million annually. Their projected yearly increment in the 1990 to 1995 period will fall below 170,000.

The future age partitions of America's households accentuate the probability of these dynamics. Through the balance of the 1980s, households 35 to 44 years of age dominate the growth profile, but in the 1990s, they will be supplanted by (i.e., they will progress into) the 45- to 54-year-old sector. Mature adulthood, however, brings with it increasing rates of homeownership. Householders at their fiftieth birthday approach an 80-percent homeownership rate.

Rentership rates, in contrast, are highest in the younger age brackets, and the latter will decline. Contraction is the rule in the under-25-years-of-age sector during the balance of the 1980s and will be reflected in the number of 25- to 34-years-old householders in the 1990s. The latter will increase by almost two million in the five years between 1995 and 2000 (renters and owners combined); but this age sector will still remain the largest rental target, accounting for nine million out of 34-million renter households.

And in the 1990s, the seemingly relentless growth of the elderly will begin to abate. The demographic cohort produced by the birth dearth of the 1920s and 1930s (which, in turn, as it helped form the "nesting generation" of the 1960s, spawned the baby-boom eruption) will have begun to settle into their retirement years. Households over 65 years of age will secure their smallest growth contingents in more than half a century. But because of the reduced scale of overall growth, they will maintain their market share. The focus of housing for the elderly will be more a tribute to their increased age than their growth in number.

Coinciding with the overall aging tendencies will be more changes in the configuration of America's households. Although not sufficient to resurrect the American family norm of the 1950s, married-couple families will make a decided comeback. Between 1970 and 1984, married couples increased by about 5.5 million, barely 25 percent of the total household increase. The 1984 to 1995 projections, however, indicate married couples increasing by almost 8.3 million, representing 63 percent of the 13.1 million total household increment. This penetration increases from 1995 to 2000, with married couples responsible for two-thirds (3.1 million) of the total household growth of 4.7 million.

In contrast, the explosive growth of both family and nonfamily-female householders should abate. For example, female householder families increased by more than 3.2 million between 1970 and 1980; between 1984 and 1995, they will increase by less than 1.6 million. Since this is a lower-incomed household configuration, one of the nation's more potent shelter dilemmas may be mitigated.

The diverging growth projected for married-couple and female-householder families, respectively, underscores our vision of a tilt toward a more upscale market climate. In particular, the bulk of the growth in married-couple families will be married-couple owners between the ages of 35 and 54 years, historically the most affluent household sector.

Income: Dynamic Versus Constraint

- Income, translated into housing-buying power, will provide the locomotive of the future housing-demand train. The demographics of tomorrow are income-favorable and represent potentials not evident for more than a generation.
- The household age and configurational dynamics of the 1990s will generate a burgeoning of these demographic sectors— married couples 35 to 54 years of age—that traditionally inhabited the upper rungs of the income ladder. Incomes peak at middle age and are highest for married-couple household configurations.
- By the 1990s, virtually the entire baby-boom generation will have moved en masse into the 35- to 54-year-old span, the classic peak-earning years. The majority will have "paired and nested," many of them privileged "super couples" of two working professionals. The resources that they command will be fully brought to bear on housing. The future of housing demand will largely be the future of the baby-boom generation.
- But the latter has never been, nor will it ever be, a monolithic whole. There will be demographic sectors of less-than-affluent financial capacity—single parent families key among them. Not everyone will be able to secure adequate accommodations on the "express"-housing train.
- The notion of middle-class shrinkage—of a bipolar society of rich and poor—will not be borne out. The upscale market will expand due to the rising affluence of the middle; this will be a much more significant shift than any "lower-class" expansion.
- There are two major codicils to the thesis of demographically driven affluence to come: the United States's economic performance in the 1990s is the first. The engine of economic growth must have sufficient capacity to power a huge demographic "load" up the income-growth/shelter-demand track. Secondly, America's minority population is growing. A solid national housing market will depend on their becoming full economic citizens.

The Forces of Supply

- Despite being characterized as the decade of economic "shocks," the 1970s turned out to be America's housing decade. Following a disastrous start, the mid 1980s brought forth one of the best production periods in the nation's history. America's supply system has demonstrated the capacity to adapt to change and seemingly surmount any obstacle in its path. Resiliency will continue to mark America's "shelterers" in the 1990s.

- But the housing industry rides a perilous economic roller coaster. Housing is subject to a continuous boom–bust cycle. During a severe recession, when GNP declines by less than two percent, housing starts can plummet by half from peak levels. When the economy surges, production can double from recessionary lows. Such cyclical swings will persist in the future; the business cycle will determine short-term housing-supply patterns.

- Production also responds to other market forces, cyclical and long-term. When affordability levels decline during business-cycle downturns, attached dwellings increase market penetration. The latter also respond to the demographically linked demand for entry-level or non-family-raising shelter. Future demographics, however, portend a long-range shift to a trade-up market. Prestige upscale housing will power the 1990s' markets.

- Future federal tax legislation will also define housing production to come. The generous provisions of the 1981 tax act stimulated the multifamily-rental market sector. The revisions of the 1986 tax act subsequently placed a damper on it. The actions of America's lawmakers, as well as the laws of cyclical economics, will shape the scale and composition of production.

- Regional economic fortunes will define one geographical dimension of future supply activity. The rise of the Sunbelt and stagnation of the Frostbelt were marked by the increased critical mass of housing secured by the South and West during the 1970s. In contrast, a resurgent Northeast economy in the 1980s helped fashion renewed levels of production.

- A second dimension of the locational calculus is implicit in the rise of the suburban/exurban fringe as job locus. In our estimation this ensures an equivalent areal expansion of housing location.

- Within the changing reservoir of housing, large-scale buildings remain the exception rather than the rule in America. Small-scale residential environments predominate. However, while structure size remains modest in unit count, individual single-family dwelling units, with only recessionary setbacks, demonstrate sustained growth in size. This trend line will extend into the future, with only business-cycle variations.

- The shelter infrastructure of America continues to be upgraded; substantial infusions of resources provide improvements in its quality and physical attributes. The scale of the process, however, contributes to increasing costs.

- The pool of housing will stay continuously in flux, with new construction, inventory removals, and conversions changing the composition of the stock. In general, removals systematically delete the supply of its low-cost, least-attractive accommodations. From the viewpoint of the nation as a whole, this is a reflection of, and serves as a stimulus for, new additions to the inventory that are far superior in quality. But from the perspective of low-cost shelter, this process has a negative impact on the supply available to the least fortunate in our society. The dilemma this process engenders will be significant to America's housing future.

- Real-income increases will be almost instantaneously reflected in a surge of housing amenity. The kinds of housing that Americans buy, and their amenity levels, respond to the depths of consumer pockets. The long-term trend, though interrupted by recession, is one of increased housing quality and appurtenance.

- America's unparalleled exposure to inflation and income lags in the 1970s changed the cost calculus of shelter. Affordability levels plunged as the decade closed. But by the mid 1980s, the long inflationary cycle of housing was redressed by disinflation and income growth. Affordability soared. The inflation–affordability linkage will remain critical in the future.

- American fiscal policy in the early 1980s, after nearly a century of making special provisions for housing through low-interest-rate mortgages, essentially homogenized the financial markets. Mortgage interest rates are drastically affected by mainstream markets and have become essentially interchangeable with, and subject to, the broad needs of general financing for corporate and governmental use.

- The new system, with enhanced securitization and secondary market activity, proved adequate to support the mid-1980s

housing boom. It has yet to be tested in a more austere or tax-
ing economic/fiscal environment. But housing production sur-
vived high single-digit and even low double-digit interest rates.
Consumer acceptance of such thresholds is a 1980s'
phenomenon which will persist in the 1990s.

Market Foundations

- Americans will use their housing stock less intensively. Shrinkage in household size coinciding with increasing unit sizes, and
  an overall housing inventory expansion in excess of household
  growth, will generate rising quantities of housing per occupant.
- The overcrowding concerns of a generation ago largely abated
  by the 1970s. They will not totally disappear by the 1990s; residual problems will remain. But overcrowding is largely a problem
  of the past.
- Americans of means will continue to shift to homeownership.
  Within the renter pool, the burden of rents on income will grow
  more stressful. The problem will be most severe for female-
  householder families, much less so for married couples. A
  demographically linked rental-market problem will characterize
  the 1990s.
- For the broad pool of owners, the scale of the housing-cost burden will continue to be modest. Those at the margin—first-time
  buyers or trade-up buyers—will devote larger shares of income
  to housing. But because the overall *scale* of demand (the level of
  the net household growth) in the 1990s will shrink, the market
  will become more competitive, with affordability levels improv-
  ing.
- The post-shelter society of the 1970s—of housing as investment
  as well as shelter—will not return. But the dreams and aspirations of ownership will continue unabated, whatever the shape
  of the economic matrix to come.

II

Housing Demand

2
Housing Demand: The Population Baseline

People—their number, characteristics, and choice of groupings—represent the initial baseline in understanding the demand side of the residential market. From a broad housing-demand perspective, there have been three sweeping demographic tendencies that dominated post-1960 America. The first of these has been the decelerating rate of population growth in the United States linked to evolving age structure and fertility patterns. A second, but countervailing trend, has been a rising rate of household formation, i.e., more households generated from a given number of people of specific ages. Crosshatching these events has been a rapid change in the configuration of America's households: once "atypical" life-style formats have assumed much great prominence in the nation's shelter arena.

Housing marketers, in common with other consumer merchandisers, are faced with bewildering market partitioning and segmentation; the monolithic, generation-long, mass middle market has given way to highly differentiated nodes requiring equally stratified development tactics. Public policymakers, too, confront new housing challenges. America emerged from World War II with a common set of widespread shared values; as we close the century, America reflects a vast array of life-style alternatives, consumption patterns, shelter desires, and specialized needs.

These are just some of the parameters which must be explored. Our practice, wherever possible, is to provide long-term data baselines. The future is far from immutably tied to the past, but the latter still yields the foundations of projection. Yet also crucial are crest-of-the-wave variations which may be particularly pertinent signals to the near-term future, and therefore must be given equal attention.

Total Population

The rapid population growth *rate* of immediate post-World War II
America was short-lived (Exhibit 2-1). It has been replaced by a virtual
absolute growth plateau lasting for a quarter of a century. In the decade
of the 1950s, there was an increase in resident population of 18.5
percent, reflecting the surge of births now popularly known as the baby
boom. (By our definition, the baby boom took place between 1946 and
1964.) During the 1960s, the equivalent gain was less than three-
quarters that rate—13.4 percent—with the 1970s continuing the
downward-rate momentum. During the latter decade, the nation's
population grew by only 11.4 percent, less than two-thirds that of the
1950s. And the rate for the first half of the 1980s fell to only 5.2 percent.

But the sheer scale of growth in America is still worthy of note.
The population base expanded so very rapidly—from 150-million people in 1950 to 238 million in 1985, an increase far in excess of 50
percent—that even relatively small percentage changes represent massive numbers of individuals. The 1980s' scale of absolute annual growth
has been on the order of 2.3-million individuals. Despite declining
rates, the absolute magnitude of annual population increases virtually
stabilized in the 1960 to 1985 period at the 2.3- to 2.4-million-person
level.

EXHIBIT 2-1

Resident Population of the United States: 1950 to 1985

		Increase Over Preceding Census	
Year	*Number*	*Number*	*Percent*
1950 (April)	151,325,798	19,161,229	14.5%
1960 (April)	179,323,175	27,997,377	18.5
1970 (April)[1]	203,302,031	23,978,856	13.4
1980 (April)	226,545,805	23,243,774	11.4
1985 (July)	238,291,000	11,745,000	5.2

Note: 1. Figures corrected after 1970 final reports were issued.

Sources: U.S. Bureau of the Census, *Statistical Abstract of the United States: 1986*
(106th edition), Washington, D.C., 1985; U.S. Bureau of the Census, Current Population
Reports, Series P-25, No. 977, *Estimates of the Population of the United States to August 1,
1985*, Washington, D.C., 1985

Changing Age Distributions

Even more significant for housing than total population is the evolving pattern of age distribution within it. An age-structure profile dominated by pre-school and school-age children—the 1950s and 1960s, for example—will have quite different housing-demand ramifications than one dominated by young and maturing adults (the 1980s) or by full-scale maturation (the 1990s). And age-structure distortions do not disappear quickly, but mature, setting the stage for a future whose probability of realization is far more secure than in other forecasting areas. The data in Exhibit 2-2 are illustrative.

Dominating America's age-structure shifts are three major forces: the baby boom spawned in the 1950s, the baby bust of the 1960s and early 1970s, and the sustained growth in the ranks of the elderly. The largest absolute and relative changes in the 1970 to 1984 period reflect these phenomena (Exhibit 2-2), as do the changes projected for the closing years of the century.

EXHIBIT 2-2

Total Population Age Structure, U.S. Total Population
(Including Armed Forces Abroad):   1970 to 1984
(numbers in thousands)

Age	1970	1980	Change: 1970-1980		1984	Change: 1980-1984	
			Number	Percent		Number	Percent
Total	205,052	227,704	22,652	11.0%	236,681	8,977	3.9%
Under 5 years	17,166	16,457	(709)	−4.1	17,816	1,359	8.3
5 to 13 years	36,672	31,080	(5,592)	−15.2	30,165	(915)	−2.9
14 to 17 years	15,924	16,139	215	1.4	14,707	(1,432)	−8.9
18 to 24 years	24,711	30,347	5,636	22.8	29,375	(972)	−3.2
25 to 34 years	25,324	37,593	12,269	48.4	41,107	3,514	9.3
35 to 44 years	23,150	25,882	2,732	11.8	30,718	4,836	18.7
45 to 54 years	23,316	22,737	(579)	−2.5	22,436	(301)	−1.3
55 to 64 years	18,682	21,756	3,074	16.5	22,316	560	2.6
65 years and over	20,107	25,714	5,607	27.9	28,040	2,326	9.0

Sources: U.S. Bureau of the Census, *Statistical Abstract of the United States: 1986* (106th edition), Washington, D.C., 1985; U.S. Bureau of the Census, Current Population Reports, Series P-25, No. 965, *Estimates of the Population of the United States, by Age, Sex and Race: 1980 to 1984*, U.S. Government Printing Office, Washington, D.C., 1985

While America's total population grew by 11 percent in the 1970s, the number of individuals in the crucial household formation, first-time-homebuyer age sector—those 25 to 34 years of age—grew by more than four times that rate, or 48.4 percent. (In 1970, the first baby boomers reached the age of 24 years and by 1980 had become 34. In the latter year, the youngest members of the cohort were 16 years old.) When to this group is added a 22.8-percent gain in the 18- to 24-year-old category, the full scale of the maturing baby boom is evident. It was marked by the comparative vigor in the 1970s of garden apartment development and other physical symbols of new household formation. Nearly 18-million people out of a total population growth of 22.7 million were in the 18- to 34-year-old sector. They may have stressed the labor-force absorption capacity of the nation's economy, but from a housing perspective they provided an enormous market base.

The baby-bust cohort, impacting the youngest age sectors in the exhibit, also exerted widespread influence throughout American society. The so-called "birth dearth" introduced the reality of school shrinkage during the 1970s, but it only tangentially impacted the housing-demand equation. While it had far less impact (at least as of this time period) than the baby-boom generation on the *quantum* of housing required, the baby bust influenced the *shape* and *scale* of individual dwelling units.

The sustained growth of the elderly within the national age profile also generated demand implications not revealed by total population aggregates. The 27.9-percent increase in the number of individuals 65 years of age and older was exceeded only by the growth rate of the 25- to 34-years-of-age sector; an additional impetus was provided for further segmentation within America's housing system.

The age structure visibly shifted in the early 1980s. As indicated in Exhibit 2-2, the continued aging of the baby boom moved the growth "bulge" to more mature age sectors; the 35- to 44-year-old bracket accounted for more than half of the total population increase of the 1980 to 1984 period. And this age span represents a stage in the family life cycle that is particularly potent in terms of the acquisition of single-family shelter. What is evident was the early realization of a maturing America, whose feedback on housing will strongly influence the American market through the rest of the century.

The early 1980s also marked the beginning of a more direct housing-demand impact arising from the first stages of the baby-bust generation. While the shrinkage of this cohort centered on the high school-age population—14 to 17 years olds—the "baby busters" began to influence the size of the 18- to 24-years-of-age sector. It is in the older segments of this group that household formation first begins to take place en masse. But by the 1980s, it had become an age sector starting to contract in size.

While the elderly continued to expand their ranks, growing at more than twice the national rate, a new phenomenon emerged at the other end of the age spectrum. The under-5-years-of-age population began to increase, reflecting *not* changes in fertility, but rather the sheer number of individuals—the baby boomers—in their prime childbearing years. Their progeny, the baby boom echo, is setting the stage for housing demand requirements to come, particularly the configuration and scale of individual dwelling units.

Age-Dependency Ratios

An additional perspective on shifting age composition is illustrated in Exhibit 2-3. Age–dependency ratios are defined for those too young to be accorded independent economic status (i.e., youth—persons under the age of 18 years per 100 persons 18 to 64 years) and those who by demographic convention have passed out of it (i.e., old-age—persons

EXHIBIT 2-3

Age–Dependency Ratios, U.S. Total: 1970 to 1984

Year	Total[1]	Youth[2]	Old Age[3]
1970	78.0	60.6	17.5
1975	71.3	53.3	18.0
1980	64.6	46.0	18.6
1981	63.7	45.0	18.7
1982	62.8	44.0	18.8
1983	62.2	43.3	18.9
1984	62.1	42.9	19.2

Notes: 1. Sum of youth and old-age ratios.
2. Persons under 18 years per 100 persons 18 to 64 years.
3. Persons 65 years and over per 100 persons 18 to 64 years.

Source: U.S. Bureau of the Census, Current Population Reports, Series P-23, No. 145, *Population Profile of the United States: 1983-84*, U.S. Government Printing Office, Washington, D.C., 1985

65 years old and over per 100 persons 18 to 64 years). Strictly speaking, the age–dependency ratio is a measure of age composition, not of economic dependency, but it does reflect the latter in a general way. Thus, in broad summary fashion, the ratios provide some insight into the changing demographic stresses of American society.

First, and perhaps most important, is the scale of shrinkage in the dependency ratio over time. In 1970, for every 100 people within their nominal "working-age" years, i.e., 18 to 64, there were 78 outside it. By the mid 1980s, the ratio had declined to the 62-percent level—fully 16 fewer "dependents" for every 100 persons in their working years. All of the decline was accounted for by youth, as the baby boom matured. The specific youth–dependency ratio declined from over 60 in 1970 to below 43 by 1984. Concurrently, the old-age ratio stayed close to the 18- to 19-percent level.

By the mid 1980s, America's age-defined working population had far fewer age dependents than held true fifteen years earlier. From a housing-consumption perspective, the pattern implied the potential of a high level of discretionary housing expenditures.

Fertility

The maturing process that is evident when viewing America's population–age structure has a powerful secular dynamic behind it. But a crucial and potentially volatile variable is fertility. A basic measure of the phenomenon is the total fertility rate, i.e., the number of births a woman would have by the end of her child-bearing years if, during her entire reproductive period, she were to experience the age-specific birth rates for the given period. While all those individuals who will form households throughout this century are presently alive, it is the future pattern of reproduction which will ultimately determine the actual size of households and, with the latter, the shape of specific dwelling-unit demand.

The dramatic fertility shifts which have taken place are evident in Exhibit 2-4. Some of the factors that influence this key to the future— and may well have the capacity to alter it in the future—are clarified. A longer overview yields some perspective. The years of post-World War I prosperity, from 1920 to 1929, showed a relatively high but downward-trending fertility rate (approximately 3.0, i.e., the average

EXHIBIT 2-4

**Total Fertility Rate: 1920 to 1984 by Five-Year Periods and
1970 to 1984 by Year, U.S. Total**

Period	Total Fertility Rate
1920–1924	3.248
1925–1929	2.840
1930–1934	2.376
1935–1939	2.235
1940–1944	2.523
1945–1949	2.985
1950–1954	3.337
1955–1959	3.690
1960–1964	3.449
1965–1969	2.662
1970–1974	2.094
1975–1979	1.774
1980–1984 (Preliminary)	1.809

Year	Total Fertility Rate
1970	2.480
1971	2.267
1972	2.010
1973	1.879
1974	1.835
1975	1.774
1976	1.738
1977	1.790
1978	1.760
1979	1.808
1980	1.840
1981	1.815
1982	1.829
1983 (Preliminary)	1.789
1984 (Preliminary)	1.804

Note: The total fertility rate indicates how many births a woman would have by the end of her childbearing years if, during her entire reproductive period, she were to experience the age-specific birth rates for the given period.

Source: U.S. Bureau of the Census, Current Population Reports, Series P-23, No. 145, *Population Profile of the United States: 1983–84*, U.S. Government Printing Office, Washington, D.C., 1985

woman would produce three children during her life span). But the ensuing Depression era caused such an accelerated decline that by the late 1930s the rate had fallen to the 2.2 level.

It was the great birth explosion of post-World War II America which completely reversed this pattern. By the latter half of the 1950s, the fertility rate (3.69) was higher than it had been forty years earlier. But by the middle 1980s, the rate (approximately 1.80) was down to half that at the close of the 1950s.

The rate surge of the 1945 to 1960 period virtually restructured, and continues to restructure, all dimensions of American life. For example, baby boom-induced pressures on primary and secondary education ultimately became history; the flip side of the coin later was coping with redundant infrastructure left behind as the baby boom matured.

The boomers' influence on the housing market, however, has always been pervasive—and dominant. And the precipitous decline in fertility in the post-1960 period also set in motion a potent matrix of long-term forces. It is in the balance of the century that their housing-market ramifications will be felt.

While future variations in fertility have the potential to unlease equally profound transformations of American society, and its system of shelter provision, it should be noted that the mid-1980s' fertility-rate thresholds are consistent with a very long-term dynamic. The "birth dearth" of the Depression, the baby-boom eruption, and the baby-bust contraction have been, in retrospect, mere ripples on the historic trend of steady decline. This is a pattern which seems characteristic of advanced economic societies such as Western Europe.

In any case, it should be reiterated that in terms of primary housing consumers, subject to migration, the housing industry is in the fortunate position of knowing the general size of the aggregate potential customer pool of the next twenty years; i.e., they already exist within our statistical counts, if only as children. Within the limitations of the crystal ball, it is our general belief that something approximating the present level of fertility will continue in the near-term future. If women bear on average just under two children, the demand for the very large housing accommodations (defined in terms of the high bedroom counts) of a generation ago probably will not return.

Population Projections: The Balance of the Decade

The art of population projection is still only that, particularly when attempted in a multigenerational format. The vagaries of immigration, particularly, may be substantial. Subject to that uncertainty, however, the forecasting techniques and their results can be viewed with reasonable confidence, particularly as we focus on the adult and near-adult population through the rest of the century (Exhibits 2-5 and 2-6).

The changes from 1984 to 1990 illustrate the tremendous potency of history (Exhibit 2-5). The three factors that dominate represent a continuity from the past. The baby-boom generation by 1990 will have attained the middle years of adulthood. (By the latter date, it will have been four years since the first baby boomers turned 40.) Fully half of the total 1984 to 1990 national population growth increment falls into the 35- to 44-years-of-age sector. The leading and trailing edges of this enormous cohort, i.e., those 45 to 54 years old and those 25 to 34 years old, also demonstrate significant growth through 1990.

In absolute terms, 7.1 million people out of a total population increase of 13 million are in the 35- to 44-years-of-age group, with an

EXHIBIT 2-5

**Population Projections by Age, U.S. Total Population
(Including Armed Forces Abroad): 1990 and 1995
(numbers in thousands)**

Age	1984	1990	Change: 1984-1990		1995	Change: 1990-1995	
			Number	Percent		Number	Percent
Total	236,681	249,657	12,976	5.5%	259,559	9,902	4.0%
Under 5 years	17,816	19,198	1,382	7.8	18,615	(583)	−3.0
5 to 13 years	30,165	32,190	2,025	6.7	34,435	2,245	7.0
14 to 17 years	14,707	12,950	(1,757)	−11.9	14,082	1,132	8.7
18 to 24 years	29,375	25,795	(3,580)	−12.2	23,702	(2,093)	−8.1
25 to 34 years	41,107	43,529	2,422	5.9	40,520	(3,009)	−6.9
35 to 44 years	30,718	37,847	7,129	23.2	41,997	4,150	11.0
45 to 54 years	22,436	25,402	2,966	13.2	31,397	5,995	23.6
55 to 64 years	22,316	21,051	(1,265)	−5.7	20,923	(128)	−0.6
65 years and over	28,040	31,697	3,657	13.0	33,888	2,191	6.9

Note: Census Bureau, Middle Series Projection

Sources: U.S. Bureau of the Census, *Statistical Abstract of the United States: 1986* (106th edition), Washington, D.C., 1985; U.S. Bureau of the Census, Current Population Reports, Series P-25, No. 965, *Estimates of the Population of the United States, by Age, Sex and Race: 1980 to 1984*, U.S. Government Printing Office, Washington, D.C., 1985; U.S. Bureau of the Census, Current Population Reports, Series P-25, No. 952, *Projections of the Population of the United States: 1983 to 2050*, U.S. Government Printing Office, Washington, D.C., 1984

EXHIBIT 2-6

**Population Projections by Age, U.S. Total Population
(Including Armed Forces Abroad): 1995 and 2000
(numbers in thousands)**

			Change: 1995–2000	
Age	1995	2000	Number	Percent
Total	259,559	267,955	8,396	3.2%
Under 5 years	18,615	17,626	(989)	−5.3
5 to 13 years	34,435	34,382	(53)	−0.2
14 to 17 years	14,082	15,382	1,300	9.2
18 to 24 years	23,702	24,601	899	3.8
25 to 34 years	40,520	36,415	(4,105)	−10.1
35 to 44 years	41,997	43,743	1,746	4.2
45 to 54 years	31,397	37,119	5,722	18.2
55 to 64 years	20,923	23,767	2,844	13.6
65 years and over	33,888	34,921	1,033	3.0

Note: Census Bureau, Middle Series Projection

Sources: U.S. Bureau of the Census, *Statistical Abstract of the United States: 1986* (106th edition), Washington, D.C., 1985; U.S. Bureau of the Census, Current Population Reports, Series P-25, No. 965, *Estimates of the Population of the United States, by Age, Sex and Race: 1980 to 1984.* Washington, D.C.: U.S. Government Printing Office, 1985; U.S. Bureau of the Census, Current Population Reports, Series P-25, No. 952, *Projections of the Population of the United States: 1983 to 2050.* Washington, D.C.: U.S. Government Printing Office, 1984

additional 2.4 to 3.0 million persons secured by each of the flanking age brackets. *Virtually all of the positive age-structure shifts are secured in the life-cycle span of peak housing consumption.* And the ramifications of a middle-aged baby boom are accentuated by the "echo." The number of children 13 years old and under will increase by 3.4 million, a major factor further complicating an already complex housing demand equation.

Much more chastening is the baby bust, i.e., the product of the rapid decline in fertility which began in the early 1960s and continued through the middle 1970s. Its coming of age will yield a very substantial loss, both in percentage and absolute terms, of both the 14- to 17- and 18- to 24-year-old segments of our society. And it is the latter group that is a key entrant into modest-level rental housing. *In the brief six-year period from 1984 to 1990, these new housing seekers will shrink in number by fully one in eight—almost 3.6 million individuals.*

A more sanguine demand note will be a very substantial increase—13 percent—in the elderly population. The 3.7-million expansion in the 65-years-of-age and older group will be equal in magnitude to the diminished flow of potential new housing participants, i.e., young adults 18 to 24 years old. *Thus the balance of the 1980s will be a period of general aging of housing consumers, bringing with it attendant shifts in the structure of housing demand.*

The Balance of the Century

The first half of the 1990s will be characterized by trend-line continuation. The oldest members of the baby boom will have entered their late forties while the leading edge of the baby bust will begin to touch thirty. *The youth generation of the 1960s and 1970s, yielding to middle age, will be the dominant market reality.* Housers will have to adjust to these changes: from first-time dwelling units to first-time homeownership is a clear, if difficult, path. The new imperatives are more complex.

The largest market target—42 million persons in size—will be the 35- to 44-years-of-age sector; the fastest growth component will shift to the 45- to 54-year-old bracket. The latter will expand by almost 6-million persons, accounting for over 60 percent of the total national increase; its rate of growth will approach 24 percent, almost six times greater than that projected for the total population (Exhibit 2-5).

With the exception of the elderly—with a 6.9 percent expansion—every other sector of primary housing shoppers will be shrinking. The entire 18- to 34-year age span will decline by more than 5-million individuals. *A maturing baby-bust generation thus presents the probability of diminishing entry-level housing demand to a 25-year low.*

The final years of the century should not introduce any major age–structure surprises (Exhibit 2-6). Shrinkage will still characterize the 25- to 34-year-old sector; the 35- to 44-year-olds continue to bulk large; and the 45- to 54-year-old group remains the dominant growth sector. The age-delineated housing demand profile of America will continue to mature through the 1995 to 2000 era.

The broad sweeps of population and its distribution illustrated here have enormous potency. If we were to appraise the age distributions from the viewpoint of a labor economist, the view would be most positive. Americans of working years remain proportionally high compared to those who, by reasons of age, are outside the labor force, i.e., the young and the old.

Indeed, the low dependency ratio that characterized the post-1980 years will have remained virtually unchanged. As shown in Exhibit 2-7, there will be barely 60 persons in 1995 and 2000 outside the prime working-age group for every 100 people within it. Youth dependency in the 1990s will remain relatively static, as will elderly dependence. Thus there should continue to be high propensities and capacities for shelter consumption, at least as defined by aggregate population numbers.

But a fine screening of age distribution from the viewpoint of savings is far less positive. In the 1980s, the baby-boom generation in early adulthood moved into capital goods accumulation of houses, cars, furniture, etc. And this has been, if anything, a dissaving age group. The traditional premier savers of our society—those in the post-child-rearing stage of the life cycle—were relatively few in number.

Thus the "saver"-age segments in the 1980s were proportionately small; those who needed to invest in capital goods and dissave were relatively substantial in number. The demographic product squeezed America's savings, and with it the pool of capital available to finance housing.

The warning signals of the 1990s are particularly chastening. Developers analyze potential sites which not uncommonly will come into development after only a half-dozen years. Such analyses must be based on the demographics to come, not those of the past. And the

EXHIBIT 2-7

Projected Age–Dependency Ratios, U.S. Total: 1984 to 2000

Year	Total[1]	Youth[2]	Old Age[3]
1984	62.1	42.9	19.2
1990	62.6	41.9	20.7
1995	63.9	42.4	21.5
2000	61.8	40.7	21.1

Notes: 1. Sum of youth and old-age ratios.
         2. Persons under 18 years per 100 persons 18 to 64 years.
         3. Persons 65 years and over per 100 persons 18 to 64 years.

Source: U.S. Bureau of the Census, Current Population Reports, Series P-25, No. 952, *Projections of the Population of the United States: 1983 to 2050.* Washington, D.C.: U.S. Government Printing Office, 1985

dilemmas of consumer preference several years hence must be confronted.

The consumer-age data suggest trade-up if the pattern of previous housing life-styles is continued. While the starter market should be weaker, the imperatives and potentials of specialized housing for the elderly are particularly substantial, both for public and private sponsorship. Thus the demographics to come offer some definition of housing's future. But population data in and of itself can only suggest broad contours and themes. The trends are expressed most directly in terms of households, the basic unit of housing demand.

The Household Revolution

It is the household which is the basic unit of currency determining the vitality of housing demand. The definition of household revolves around an individual or a grouping of individuals occupying or sharing a dwelling unit. It is the manner in which individuals settle into household arrangements that is crucial to the actual demand for shelter. Population changes—in either aggregate or partitioned terms—are translated into specific unit demand through the medium of household configuration. The effects of population shifts can be either magnified or dampened by the realities of specific household patternings.

This chapter will focus on the household revolution which has transformed the demand for shelter in America. Household size shrinkage, the end product of this revolution, will first be examined, followed by a brief analysis of the underlying social forces. Household size and configurational dynamics are then considered; the economic underpinnings of the overall phenomenon, and its fragility, are discussed in the final section.

The Incredible Shrinking Household

Within a fixed population envelope, household size establishes the direct parameters of housing demand. And the dynamic of household size *shifts* can be even more consequential in impacting on the housing market than proportionate *changes* in population as a whole. In New York City, for example, from 1970 to 1980 there was a shrinkage in total population of fully 10 percent; concurrently, the number of households declined by barely two percent. In the State of New Jersey, an even more profound divergence occurred during the same time period. The population increase of 194,000 persons was far outdistanced by the addition of 330,000 households; nearly two households were secured for every additional person gained. Indeed, at the national scale, nearly half of the enormous growth in the nation's housing supply from 1970 to 1980 was absorbed not as a function of population increase, but rather as a consequence of household size decline.

There are a variety of sweeping changes which have taken place in America's households. In order to understand them fully, we must retrace our steps back to the era of the Great Depression. At that time, household size in America had been shrinking for nearly a hundred years. But the unparalleled depth and longevity of the Depression forced abrupt changes. Households had to double up: the wave of early post-World War I suburbanization was reversed; young couples returned to the familial hearth; and, despite the very beginnings of Social Security, the elderly had to be reincorporated with their offspring. This was not a function of a positive reversal of the splintering of family affections in America, but rather a tribute to national economic trauma, a lesson happily forgotten in the years of near-continuous prosperity which followed World War II.

The mobilization of World War II yielded at its peak more than 10-million individuals in the armed services, and enormous levels of displacement as workers were moved to defense production facilities, frequently a long way from their traditional homes. This produced a series of statistical crosscurrents; severe household fragmentation occurred simultaneously with doubling-up caused by wartime housing shortages.

Suffice it to say the 1950 census results indicated, as shown in Exhibit 3-1, an average household size of 3.37 persons, 8 percent below the 3.67 level of 1940. The baby boom offset both the undoubling of households and the enormous additions to the housing stock, so much so that even by 1965—twenty years after the end of World War II—there had been only a relatively small diminution in household size to 3.29 persons.

With the end of the baby boom, and perhaps even more importantly the beginnings of the greatest level of housing production in our history, more abrupt shrinkage began to occur. The average size of household by 1970 was five percent under the 1965 level, and this pattern—a one percent average annual shrinkage—continued through 1981. By that time the average household size in America was down to 2.73 persons, about 20 percent below that of 1950. This is a phenomenon so important that it deserves restating. At its simplest,

EXHIBIT 3-1

Household Size Shifts: 1940 to 1985
(persons per household)

Year	Size
1940	3.67
1950	3.37
1955	3.33
1960	3.33
1965	3.29
1970	3.14
1971	3.11
1972	3.06
1973	3.01
1974	2.97
1975	2.94
1976	2.89
1977	2.86
1978	2.81
1979	2.78
1980	2.76
1981	2.73
1982	2.72
1983	2.73
1984	2.71
1985	2.69

Sources: U.S. Bureau of the Census, *Statistical Abstract of the United States: 1986* (106th edition), Washington, D.C., 1985.

even if the size of household had remained constant from 1950 through 1981 (without considering the issues of adults versus children, i.e., age-structure differentials), we would have required 20 percent fewer housing units. Considering the fact that the total 1981 inventory exceeded 80-million units, the difference is more than 16 million fewer housing units.

But this seemingly inexorable progression stopped in 1982 and 1983. The worst recession since the Depression claimed its toll not only in terms of housing starts, but also in the confidence and economic wherewithal necessary to form a new household. For the first time in a generation, since Depression- and war-induced housing shortages were made up and the baby-boom flood began to ebb, household size in America began to stabilize. But by mid-decade, with a restoration of economic vigor and positive outlook, the pattern of household-size shrinkage resumed.

The size reduction has been widespread and pervasive. As detailed in Exhibit 3-2, it impacted every regional and metropolitan sector of the United States for both owner and rental tenure. And it cut across the profile of household types (Exhibit 3-3). All family households (by definition, two-or-more related individuals) exhibited considerable size declines during the 1970 to 1984 period, led by married-couple configurations. Nonfamily households—persons living alone, or two-or-more unrelated individuals—did, however, experience actual size increases. But since their average size was still only 1.21 persons in 1984, and since this is the fastest-growing household configuration, the end effect was a major contribution to *overall* household size shrinkage, i.e., smaller nonfamily household formats secured greater proportional representation within the total household universe.

EXHIBIT 3-2

Median Household Size, by Region and SMSA Status: 1970 to 1983

	Total		Inside SMSAs						Outside SMSAs	
			Total		In Central Cities		Not in Central Cities			
	1970	1983	1970	1983	1970	1983	1970	1983	1970	1983
Owner Occupied										
United States Total	3.0	2.5	3.1	2.6	2.8	2.4	3.3	2.7	2.7	2.5
Northeast	3.1	2.7	3.2	2.7	2.9	2.5	3.3	2.8	2.9	2.7
North Central	2.9	2.6	3.1	2.7	2.8	2.4	3.4	2.8	2.5	2.4
South	2.8	2.5	3.0	2.5	2.8	2.4	3.1	2.6	2.7	2.5
West	2.9	2.4	3.0	2.5	2.8	2.4	3.2	2.5	2.7	2.4
Renter Occupied										
United States Total	2.3	2.0	2.2	2.0	2.1	1.9	2.4	2.1	2.6	2.2
Northeast	2.2	2.0	2.2	1.9	2.2	1.9	2.3	1.9	2.4	2.0
North Central	2.3	1.9	2.2	1.9	2.1	1.8	2.4	2.0	2.5	2.0
South	2.5	2.2	2.4	2.1	2.3	2.0	2.5	2.2	2.8	2.4
West	2.2	2.1	2.1	2.1	1.9	1.9	2.3	2.2	2.5	2.2

Source: U.S. Department of Commerce, U.S. Bureau of the Census, Current Housing Reports, Series H-150-83, *General Housing Characteristics for the United States and Regions: 1983, Annual Housing Survey: 1983 Part A*, U.S. Department of Housing and Urban Development, sponsor. Washington, D.C.: U.S. Government Printing Office, 1985

EXHIBIT 3-3

Average Household Size by Type of Household, U.S. Total:
1970, 1980 and 1984
(Persons Per Household)

	1970	1980	1984
Total	3.14	2.76	2.71
Family Households	3.61	3.31	3.28
Married-Couple Family	3.66	3.35	3.32
Other Family (Male Householder)	2.99	2.92	2.97
Other Family (Female Householder)	3.28	3.17	3.11
Nonfamily Households	1.12	1.19	1.21
Male Householder	1.19	1.29	1.33
Female Householder	1.09	1.11	1.12

Sources: U.S. Bureau of the Census, Current Population Reports, Series P-20, No. 398, *Household and Family Characteristics: March 1984.* Washington, D.C.: U.S. Government Printing Office, 1985; U.S. Bureau of the Census, Current Population Reports, Series P-23, No. 130, *Population Profile of the United States: 1982.* Washington, D.C.: U.S. Government Printing Office, 1983

Americans used their extant housing stock less intensively; effective unit demand was increased.

The New Social Reality

The changes in household and family configuration in America are the end products of an enormously complex series of inputs. Household size declines are the visible symptoms of the changes which have been taking place within American social patterns. Some of the key dimensions among them are illustrated in Exhibit 3-4, which indicates the changing patterns of marriage and divorce from 1960 through 1984. In 1960, more than three-quarters of all males 18 years of age and over were married; by 1984, the proportion fell to below two-thirds. Comparable declines were experienced by both males and females regardless of race.

Conversely, the percentage of divorced Americans has been soaring, with a doubling and tripling in divorce incidence evident across the sex and race partitions in Exhibit 3-4. Household formation as a func-

EXHIBIT 3-4

**Percent Married and Divorced of the Population, 18 Years Old and Over
1960 to 1984**

Sex and Race	1960	1965	1970	1975	1980	1984
Percent married						
Male	76.4%	76.2%	75.3%	72.8%	68.4%	65.8%
White	77.3	76.9	76.1	73.9	70.0	67.7
Black and other	68.4	70.2	65.4	63.5	54.6	50.6
Female	71.6	70.5	68.5	66.7	63.0	60.8
White	72.2	70.9	69.3	68.0	64.7	62.8
Black and other	66.3	67.6	62.6	57.3	48.7	44.5
Percent divorced						
Male	2.0	2.5	2.5	3.7	5.2	6.1
White	2.0	2.4	2.4	3.6	5.0	6.0
Black and other	2.2	3.4	3.4	4.6	7.0	7.0
Female	2.9	3.3	3.9	5.3	7.1	8.3
White	2.7	3.1	3.8	5.0	6.8	8.0
Black and other	4.8	4.5	4.8	7.1	9.5	11.0

Source: U.S. Bureau of the Census, *Statistical Abstract of the United States: 1985* (105th Edition), Washington, D.C., 1984

tion of marriage, assuming that the two partners in the relationship are moving from single-person households, tends to decrease household count. Divorce, in contrast, tends to produce two households from one; such household "dismemberment" has become an increasingly important component of rental-housing demand, despite the very high remarriage rate of both males and females who are divorced. *Marriage and divorce patterns, in conjunction with reduced fertility and increased numbers of the elderly living alone, underpin the contemporary "reduced-scale" household.*

The New Empire of Singles

Most Americans, judging from the data shown in Exhibit 3-5, ultimately do marry. As a matter of fact, it was more common in 1985 among persons 45 years of age and older than held true 20 years earlier. For example, when we analyze never-married persons 65 years old and over as of 1960, there is an incidence rate of 7.7 percent for men, and 8.5 percent for women. By 1985, the percentage of never-married in this age sector had declined by approximately one-third.

EXHIBIT 3-5

**Single (Never-Married) Persons Aged 18 and Over as a Percent of
Total Population, by Age and Sex: 1960 to 1985**

Age	Male				Female			
	1960	1970	1980	1985	1960	1970	1980	1985
Total	17.3%	18.9%	23.8%	25.2%	11.9%	13.7%	17.1%	18.2%
18 years	94.6	95.1	97.4	98.5	75.6	82.0	88.0	90.7
19 years	87.1	89.9	90.9	95.8	59.7	68.8	77.6	82.7
20 to 24 years	53.1	54.7	68.8	75.6	28.4	35.8	50.2	58.5
25 to 29 years	20.8	19.1	33.1	38.7	10.5	10.5	20.9	26.4
30 to 34 years	11.9	9.4	15.9	20.8	6.9	6.2	9.5	13.5
35 to 39 years	8.8	7.2	7.8	10.1	6.1	5.4	6.2	8.1
40 to 44 years	7.3	6.3	7.1	8.6	6.1	4.9	4.8	5.3
45 to 54 years	7.4	7.5	6.1	6.3	7.0	4.9	4.7	4.6
55 to 64 years	8.0	7.8	5.3	6.1	8.0	6.8	4.5	3.7
65 years and over	7.7	7.5	4.9	5.3	8.5	7.7	5.9	5.1

Sources: U.S. Bureau of the Census, *Statistical Abstract of the United States: 1985*
(105th Edition), Washington, D.C., 1984; and U.S. Bureau of the Census, Current Population Reports, Series P-20, No. 402, *Households, Families, Marital Status, and Living
Arrangements: March 1985* (Advance Report). Washington, D.C.: U.S. Government Printing
Office, 1985

But among more youthful individuals, as we attempt to pierce the
shadows of the future, particularly those cast by the baby-boom generation, a very different pattern emerges. In 1960, barely one in nine
(11.9 percent) men 30 to 34 years of age had never been married; by
1985 it was more than one in five (20.8 percent). Similarly, 53 percent
of the 20- to 24-year-olds had been single (never married) in 1960; but
by 1985, the proportion had increased to over 75 percent.

In earlier eras, Americans clearly defined lifelong relationships
much earlier than in the 1980s. Those who married did so early, and
the remainder had a propensity not to marry at all. As the 1985 benchmarks reveal, there emerged a much longer period of remaining single,
obscuring the ultimate shape of society to come in terms of household
relationships.

And, borne by the crest of change initiated and sustained by the
enormous baby-boom cohort, these patterns reshaped America's housing. *The expansive growth of single-person homebuyers, or patterns of upscale
merchandising, cannot be understood without comprehending the arrival in*

bulk of relatively mature, dependent-free individuals entering their premium earning years. The baby-boom generation brought with it the world of singles and near-singles; the waves set in motion by this demographic eruption may well continue and pattern the post-boom generation as well.

Obscured by the sheer size of the cohort which, even with reduced incidence rates still yields enormous numbers of marriages and substantial numbers of births as well, have been vital changes in social patterning, the impact of which will become more significant to marketers as these individuals are supplanted by the baby-bust generation. For example, the era in which a two-bedroom house generated great wariness on the part of mortgage lenders is over. A whole new marketing perspective emerged as American society segmented not only in income and location, but most strikingly in basic household configuration.

Household Size and Configuration Dynamics

Average household size is only a broad summary measure of central tendency. The full profile of the distribution of sizes provides a more detailed picture of the effect of the social forces at work (Exhibit 3-6).

EXHIBIT 3-6

Persons Per Household (Household Size), U.S. Total: 1970 to 1984
(Numbers in thousands)

	1970		1984		Change: 1970 to 1984	
	Number	*Percent*	*Number*	*Percent*	*Number*	*Percent*
Total	63,401	100.0%	85,407	100.0%	22,006	34.7%
1 Person	10,851	17.1	19,954	23.4	9,103	83.9
2 Persons	18,333	28.9	26,890	31.5	8,557	46.7
3 Persons	10,949	17.3	15,134	17.7	4,185	38.2
4 Persons	9,991	15.8	13,593	15.9	3,602	36.0
5 Persons	6,548	10.3	6,070	7.1	−478	−7.3
6 Persons	3,534	5.6	2,372	2.8	−1,162	−32.9
7 or More Persons	3,195	5.0	1,394	1.6	−1,801	−56.4

Note: Data as of March for the respective years

Source: U.S. Bureau of the Census, Current Population Reports, Series P-60, No. 145, *Money Income and Poverty Status of Families and Persons in the United States: 1983 (Advance Data from the March 1984 Current Population Survey).* Washington, D.C.: U.S. Government Printing Office, 1984

In the 14-year period from 1970 to 1984—which, from a housing point of view may represent only one-half the length of a mortgage and no more than one-sixth of a housing unit's lifetime—the internal structure of America's households literally was revolutionized. *By the mid 1980s, almost one-quarter of the nation's households contained only a single person.* The *median* size of household was well below the two-person level, i.e., more than half (54.9 percent) of all America's housing units were occupied by one or two persons.

Conversely, the popular vision of the underhoused a generation ago centered around large households with inadequately sized accommodations. But the problem began demographically to disappear. As is evident in Exhibit 3-6, the number of households with five or more persons diminished very sharply. Indeed, if we focus on those with seven or more persons, their number declined by more than half (56.4 percent) in just 14 years, and by the mid 1980s accounted for only 1.6 percent of all households.

The classic American family of the 1950s shifted radically from mom and pop, and two or three children, to one- and two-person configurations. In the 1980s, four- and five-person households utilized less than one-quarter of our shelter units.

These phenomena raise persistent questions. Are they transitory—or are they harbingers of things to come? In terms of size, much of America's housing stock, particularly in ownership units, clearly relates to the demographics of the past. Will there be a potential problem of size obsolescence? Of subdivision of existing units? Or will the baby-boom generation, marrying late, still have children to fill the three-, four-, and five-bedroom houses that were so prevalent—and in demand—at their birth?

Certainly, when we view the changes in household composition over the two census periods between 1960 and 1980, as shown in Exhibit 3-7, the progression of change was seemingly remorseless. Married-couple families, for example, accounted for three-quarters (74.3 percent) of all households in 1960; by 1980, they represented barely three out of five (60.8 percent). It was other "atypical" arrangements which secured greater penetration of the family arena, led by female-householder families. Comprising in large part single-parent arrangements, i.e., mother and children, female-householder families increased six-times faster than traditional married couples (58.3 percent versus 9.8 percent) over the 1970 to 1980 period. The divorce-rate

EXHIBIT 3-7

Changes in Household Composition 1960, 1970 and 1980

(Numbers in thousands)

Households	1960		1970		1980		Percent Change	
	Number	Percent	Number	Percent	Number	Percent	1960-1970	1970-1980
Total	52,799	100.0%	63,401	100.0%	80,776	100.0%	20.1%	27.4%
Family households	44,905	85.0	51,456	81.2	59,550	73.7	14.6	15.7
Married-couple family	39,254	74.3	44,728	70.5	49,112	60.8	13.9	9.8
Other family, male householder	1,228	2.3	1,228	1.9	1,733	2.1	0.0	41.1
Other family, female householder	4,422	8.4	5,500	8.7	8,705	10.8	24.4	58.3
Nonfamily households	7,895	15.0	11,945	18.8	21,226	26.3	51.3	77.7
Householder living alone	6,896	13.1	10,851	17.1	18,296	22.7	57.4	68.6
Households of two or more persons	999	1.9	1,094	1.7	2,930	3.6	9.5	167.8

Note: Number and percent may not add due to rounding.

Source: U.S. Bureau of the Census, Current Population Reports, Series P-23, No. 130, *Population Profile of the United States: 1982,* U.S. Government Printing Office, Washington, D.C., 1983

surge (Exhibit 3-4) helped change the very concept of the American family.

Nonfamily households, consisting of householders living alone or of unrelated groups of people, represented more than one-quarter (26.3 percent) of total households by 1980. The fastest-growing segment, as shown in the exhibit, was nonfamily formats of two or more persons, some of them "yuppies" grouped together in order to afford the high rents of fashionable cities or their suburban equivalents. By 1980 there were nearly 3-million nonfamily households of two or more persons, which represents a tripling in a 20-year period. Some of this may well have been a substitute for marriage, or a delayed introduction to that formal bond. In part, however, it undoubtedly reflected reductions in the housing-buying power of some Americans—both young and old alike—inhibiting the singles' life-style. The absolute scale of this phenomenon, however, should not be exaggerated. In the 1970s this group increased by less than two million; married-couple households, on the other hand, increased by nearly 4.5 million.

The largest single increment comprised householders living alone—the new, single-person empire. Not all has been the glamour and grace and upward-mobility potential of youth as we view this sector. Nearly 40 percent of persons living alone were 65 years of age or older, predominantly women. This has presented a challenge—but it has also been an area of great market opportunity in terms of specialized housing demand, when financed and merchandised appropriately.

Housing, by its very definition, is a long-term good with annual additions to the stock rarely representing more than 2.5 percent of the extant total inventory. *There is a possibility, of significant import to investors and builders alike, that social changes have been taking place much more rapidly than adjustments in housing accommodations. The latter may be strained in coping with future demographic imperatives.*

Recessionary Interruptions

The conventional wisdom of housing-start forecasters typically has taken household formation as an independent variable, i.e., an inexorable result of demographics. Augmented with greater or lesser sophistication by appropriate allowances for vacancy rates, conversions, and demolitions, household formation has been the key to forecasts of new

housing requirements. It was only in the early 1980s that we rein-
vented the Depression-era admonition: household formation itself is a
prisoner both of housing availability and the financial competence and
conviction required to invest in it. When an economy falters, when
confidence in the future runs low, there are clear-cut tendencies to
reduce household formation, to further delay marriage, and to avoid
divorce or going off on one's own. Housing availability itself exerts a
powerful influence on demographic realities. When housers look to the
future, therefore, this becomes a very important element of confusion.

The patterns of uncertainty are indicated in Exhibit 3-8, which
shows household trend lines from 1980 through 1985. The first year
of the decade yielded household growth of nearly 1.6 million, roughly
consonant with the experience of the 1970s as well as the general forecasts for the 1980s. The faltering of the economy in 1981–1982, however, severely challenged this rosy vision of unconstrained housing
demand to come.

EXHIBIT 3-8

**1980s' Household Growth Trends: 1980–1985, by Year, and
1960–1985, Annual Average
(Numbers in thousands)**

Year or Period	Total Households	Annual Change	
		Period	Number
1980	80,776	–	–
1981	82,368	1980–81	1,592
1982	83,527	1981–82	1,159
1983	83,918	1982–83	391
1984	85,290	1983–84	1,372
1985	86,789	1984–85	1,499
		Average Annual Change	
1960–70		1.06 million	
1970–80		1.74 million	
1980–83		1.05 million	
1983–85		1.44 million	

Note: Data as of March for the respective years

Source: U.S. Bureau of the Census, Current Population Reports, *Households, Families,
Marital Status and Living Arrangements: March 1985.* Washington, D.C.: U.S. Government
Printing Office, 1985

In the face of the recession which ensued, household growth dropped down below 1.2 million in the 1981 to 1982 period, and then to a level the paucity of which had not been equalled for nearly forty years. In the twelve months ending in March of 1983, there was a net increase of fewer than 400,000 households. Yet, with the economic recovery of 1983–1985, the growth in the numbers of households surged upward to almost 1.5 million annually.

Was this a reassertion of a secular trend of high levels of household formation—and, consequently, housing demand? Or do they both continue to be prisoners of the business cycle? *In an America grown increasingly generously housed, there has been excess internal capacity standing available for more intensive use—and with it, reduced requirements for growth. This does not represent a preferred choice, but it is one which can be attained relatively easily in the face of economic stringency.*

Mid-Decade Status

All of this, however, will be played on a stage set by shifting demographic patterns. The mid-decade dynamics at work are indicated in Exhibit 3-9, where the detailed household composition shifts from 1970 through 1980 can be compared to those of 1980 to 1985. The rules of the game defined in the 1970s required alteration in the first half of the 1980s. The contrast between the two time periods is a preliminary indication of even more shifts to come.

First, and perhaps most consequential, is the shrinkage of the total household target. Household growth, as earlier indicated, increased on average by 1.7 million annually during the 1970s. The equivalent for the first half of the 1980s (1980 to 1985) fell to 1.2 million annually. In the earlier period, family configurations actually accounted for a minority of total household growth—46.6 percent. From 1980 to 1985, however, the revolution slowed; families accounted for more than half—52.5 percent—of total growth. Despite this, virtually all (3.1 million out of 3.2 million, or 97 percent) of the increment in family households from 1980 to 1985 were configurations without children under the age of 18. Indeed, there was an increasing decline in the number of married-couple families with children under the age of 18, while married couples without children under 18 accounted for one-third (33.2 percent) of total household growth. *Thus,*

EXHIBIT 3-9

Detailed Household Compositional Shifts: 1970 to 1985
(Numbers in thousands)

Household Type	1970		1980		1985		Change: 1970-80		Change: 1980-85	
	Number	Percent	Number	Percent	Number	Percent	Number	Percent	Number	Percent
Total	63,401	100.0%	80,776	100.0%	86,789	100.0%	17,375	100.0%	6,013	100.0%
Family Households	51,456	81.2	59,550	73.7	62,706	72.3	8,094	46.6	3,156	52.5
No own children under 18	22,725	35.8	28,528	35.3	31,594	36.4	5,803	33.4	3,066	51.0
With own children under 18	28,731	45.3	31,022	38.4	31,112	35.8	2,291	13.2	90	1.5
Married-couple family	44,728	70.5	49,112	60.8	50,350	58.0	4,384	25.2	1,238	20.6
No own children under 18	19,196	30.3	24,151	29.9	26,140	30.1	4,955	28.5	1,989	33.2
With own children under 18	25,532	40.3	24,961	30.9	24,210	27.9	-591	-3.3	-751	-12.5
Other family, male householder	1,228	1.9	1,773	2.1	2,228	2.6	505	2.9	495	8.2
No own children under 18	887	1.4	1,117	1.4	1,331	1.5	230	1.3	214	3.6
With own children under 18	341	0.5	616	0.8	896	1.0	275	1.6	280	4.7
Other family, female householder	5,500	8.7	8,705	10.8	10,129	11.7	3,205	18.4	1,424	23.7
No own children under 18	2,642	4.2	3,261	4.0	4,123	4.8	619	3.6	862	14.3
With own children under 18	2,858	4.5	5,445	6.7	6,006	6.9	2,587	14.9	561	9.3
Nonfamily Households	11,945	18.8	21,226	26.3	24,082	27.7	9,281	53.4	2,856	47.5
Male householder	4,063	6.4	8,807	10.9	10,114	11.7	4,744	27.3	1,307	21.7
Living alone	3,532	5.6	6,966	8.6	2,922	9.1	3,434	19.8	956	15.9
Female Householder	7,882	12.4	12,419	15.4	13,968	16.1	4,537	26.1	1,549	25.8
Living alone	7,319	11.5	11,330	14.0	12,680	14.6	4,011	23.1	1,350	22.5

Source: U.S. Bureau of the Census, Current Population Reports, Series P-20, No. 402, *Households, Families, Marital Status and Living Arrangements: March 1985* (Advance Report). Washington, D.C.: U.S. Government Printing Office, 1985

*the 1980s have shown an increasing proportion of household expansion
accounted for by families, particularly married couples without children under
age 18.*

A positive change from a societal point of view was the significant
absolute and relative shrinkage in the growth of female-householder
families with children under 18. Their annual growth was over one-
quarter of a million in the 1970s; in the first half of the 1980s, it was
reduced to little more than 100,000 per year. Thus, at mid-decade,
one of the hallmark trends of the 1970s had diminished significantly in
scale.

The shrinkage of nonfamily household growth has been another
striking change of the 1980s. Nonfamilies accounted for 53.4 percent
of the household increase during the 1970 to 1980 period. In the
1980s, the share had declined to 47.5 percent. The absolute annual
nonfamily growth in the 1970s had approached 1 million. For 1980 to
1985, the annual increment was only half that, with both male and
female householders showing the same pattern of decline. And nonfamily householders residing alone also have shown a remarkable slowing
in growth.

The maturing of this single-person market is further illustrated in
Exhibit 3-10. The growth in total number of persons living alone in the
1980s has tailed-off markedly from the explosive pace of the 1970s.
Reflecting particularly the aging of the baby-boom generation was the
abrupt absolute decline of 402,000 in the number of persons under the
age of 25 living alone from 1980 to 1985. But the baby boom still led
the singles parade. The major growth increment in the first five years
of the 1980s took place in the 25- to 44-year-old sector, which
outweighed the substantial growth of singles aged 55 years and over.
Thus, the baby-boom generation continued at work, if in a more
mature format.

At the other end of the age spectrum was a similar phenomenon.
The absolute annual growth of those 65 years of age and older in the
1980s was also less than that of the 1970s. But as the demographic
profile of 1985 for persons living alone is reviewed, the potential burden of support and future shelter requirements is made evident by the
nearly 11-million persons living by themselves who were over the age
of 55. Persons in this age span represented more than half of all "singles" in America. By far, the bulk of them were female—and as will be
noted later—of limited financial resources.

EXHIBIT 3-10

Persons Living Alone, by Sex and Age: 1985, 1980, and 1970

(Numbers in thousands)

Age and Sex	1970 Number	1970 Percent	1980 Number	1980 Percent	1985 Number	1985 Percent	1970–80 Change	1980–85 Change
Total living alone	10,851	100.0%	18,296	100.0%	20,602	100.0%	7,445	2,306
Under 25 years	556	5.1	1,726	9.4	1,324	6.4	1,170	-402
25 to 34 years	893	8.2	3,259	17.8	3,905	19.0	2,366	646
35 to 44 years	711	6.6	1,470	8.0	2,323	11.3	759	853
45 to 54 years	1,303	12.0	1,705	9.3	1,850	9.0	402	145
55 to 64 years	2,319	21.4	2,809	15.4	3,089	15.0	490	280
65 to 74 years	2,815	25.9	3,851	21.0	4,130	20.0	1,036	279
75 years and over	2,256	20.8	3,477	19.0	3,982	19.3	1,221	505
Median age	63.5	–	58.5	–	57.9	–	-5.0	-0.6
Males living alone	3,532	100.0	6,966	100.0	7,922	100.0	3,434	956
Under 25 years	274	7.8	947	13.6	750	9.5	673	-197
25 to 34 years	535	15.1	1,975	28.4	2,307	29.1	1,440	332
35 to 44 years	398	11.3	945	13.6	1,406	17.7	547	461
45 to 54 years	513	14.5	804	11.5	865	10.9	291	61
55 to 64 years	639	18.1	809	11.6	980	12.4	170	171
65 to 74 years	611	17.3	775	11.1	868	11.0	164	93
75 years and over	563	15.9	711	10.2	746	9.4	148	35
Median age	55.7	–	40.9	–	41.4	–	-14.8	0.5
Females living alone	7,319	100.0	11,330	100.0	12,680	100.0	4,011	1,350
Under 25 years	282	3.9	779	6.9	573	4.5	497	-206
25 to 34 years	358	4.9	1,284	11.3	1,598	12.6	926	314
35 to 44 years	313	4.3	525	4.6	916	7.2	212	391
45 to 54 years	790	10.8	901	8.0	986	7.8	111	85
55 to 64 years	1,680	23.0	2,000	17.7	2,109	16.6	320	109
65 to 74 years	2,204	30.1	3,076	27.1	3,262	25.7	872	186
75 years and over	1,693	23.1	2,766	24.4	3,236	25.5	1,073	470
Median age	66.1	–	65.6	–	65.5	–	-0.5	-0.1

Source: U.S. Bureau of the Census, Current Population Reports, Series P-20, No. 402, *Households, Families, Marital Status and Living Arrangements: March 1985* (Advance Report). Washington, D.C.: U.S. Government Printing Office, 1985

Unmarried Couples

One of the principal symbols of the revolution in social mores has been the growth of unmarried-couple households. But their absolute growth from 1980 to 1985 was relatively modest—under 400,000 households (Exhibit 3-11). Practically all of it was still concentrated within the age span encompassing the baby-boom generation—25 to 44 years.

In absolute terms as of 1985, there were nearly two million unmarried-couple households in total, with a median age of 31.5 years. Over half (50.8 percent) of the householders had never been married,

EXHIBIT 3-11

Selected Characteristics of Unmarried-Couple Households: 1985 and 1980
(Numbers in thousands)

Characteristic	1980 Number	1980 Percent	1985 Number	1985 Percent	1980-85 Change	1980-85 Percent Change
Unmarried-couple households	1,589	100.0	1,983	100.0	394	100.0
Sex of householder						
Male	981	61.7	1,224	61.7	243	61.7
Female	608	38.3	758	38.2	150	38.1
Age of householder						
Under 25 years	411	25.9	425	21.4	14	3.6
25 to 34 years	652	41.0	878	44.3	226	57.4
35 to 44 years	185	11.6	325	16.4	140	35.5
45 to 64 years	221	13.9	239	12.1	18	4.6
65 years and over	119	7.5	116	5.8	−3	−0.8
Median age	30.9	−	31.5	−	0.6	−
Marital status of householder						
Never married	778	49.0	1,007	50.8	229	58.1
Married, spouse absent	144	9.1	151	7.6	7	1.8
Separated	121	7.6	131	6.6	10	2.5
Widowed	142	8.9	151	7.6	9	2.3
Divorced	525	33.0	674	34.0	149	37.8
Presence of children						
No children under 15 years	1,159	72.9	1,380	69.6	221	56.1
Some children under 15 years	431	27.1	603	30.4	172	43.7

Source: U.S. Bureau of the Census, Current Population Reports, Series P-20, No. 402, *Households, Families, Marital Status and Living Arrangements: March 1985* (Advance Report). Washington, D.C.: U.S. Government Printing Office, 1985

while about one-third (34 percent) were divorced. And more than two-thirds (69.6 percent) of them had no children under the age of 15. The group as a whole is far from trivial in number; its absolute weight in America's housing needs, however, has been relatively small.

Forecasting the future is always a treacherous proposition. Some of the 1980s' shifts in household configuration growth rates may be transient, still reflecting the doubts and economic trauma of 1981–1982. People who lose faith in the future tend to be conservative in household formation. Underlying these elements, however, has been a more basic and more certain reality: one of demographic maturing and aging, which has a much greater potency in shaping the future.

The increased age at first marriage in the United States also has influenced household formation, housing choice, and fertility rates as well. But it is a much more difficult phenomenon to project. Would it be reversed by a more confident economy with lower unemployment levels? In our opinion, at least for the short-term to intermediate future, i.e., over the next five to ten years, there is little shift in sight.

Positive forecasters saw the great faltering of household formation rates in the early part of the 1980s as providing even greater opportunities in the years to come, i.e., latent demand which would augment the long-line trend. Certainly the snap back of household formation from its low point at the bottom of the early 1980s recession supported their confidence. Their vision of household formation was one of a process which is inexorable, with delays merely intensifying greater demand in the future. Pessimists raised the issue of whether declines in the real income of American households and the very real increases in housing costs as a share of those incomes drastically reduced the rate of household formation. Neither theory has been completely upheld. Within these cosmic considerations, however, there are some clear basics which will structure the future.

4

The Maturing Society and Market Segmentation

The household revolution described in the last chapter has yielded a kettle of eclectic configurations. The principal ingredient was a baby-boom generation coming of age, seasoned by long-term affluence. But by the middle of the 1980s, the boomers began to assume a decidedly middle-aged flavor. Housing consumers have begun to age, a process that will continue for the balance of the century.

The first phase of household maturation and its housing demand ramifications will be explored in this chapter. This sets the stage for the formalized household projections of the next chapter. The major focus here will be on the baby boom-linked aging of America's households, the parameters of stage-in-life-cycle demand segmentation, and the potent dynamic of tenure shifts that has helped partition the overall structure of demand.

The New Middle-Age Focus

By the mid-1980s, the median age of America's population exceeded 30 years. In Mexico, Malaysia, or Brazil, by way of contrast, more than half the population was teenaged or younger. The age gap between mature industrialized nations, such as the United States, and their developing counterparts widened precipitously. America's households reflect this process, rapidly proceeding through the household—and housing—life cycle.

The Maturing Baby Boom Household

The changing age structure of America's population has been detailed in Chapter 2. Its translation into household age quanta is revealed in Exhibit 4-1. By 1984, the dominant number of households—almost one out of four—was still in the 25- to 34-years-of-age sector (as defined by the age of the householder). An additional one out of five was 35 to 44 years old. But it is the latter which had the largest absolute gain (4.1 million) and the highest percentage growth (33 percent) since 1977. The baby-boom household set and its predecessor—the war-induced "goodbye babies"—began to age into this more mature sector.

The critical mass of the baby boom by 1984 had shifted to the 25- to 44-year age span. In the 1977 to 1984 period, this accounted

EXHIBIT 4-1

Households by Age and Family Status, U.S. Change: 1977 to 1984
(Numbers in thousands)

Age	1977	1984	Change: 1977-1984	
			Number	Percent
Total Households	74,142	85,407	11,265	15.2%
Under 25 years	5,991	5,510	(481)	−8.0
25 to 34 years	16,167	19,808	3,641	22.5
35 to 44 years	12,482	16,596	4,114	33.0
45 to 54 years	12,905	12,471	(434)	−3.4
55 to 64 years	11,780	13,121	1,341	11.4
65 years and over	14,816	17,901	3,085	20.8
Family Households	56,472	61,997	5,525	9.8%
Under 25 years	3,880	3,257	(623)	−16.1
25 to 34 years	13,091	14,632	1,541	11.8
35 to 44 years	11,200	14,062	2,862	25.6
45 to 54 years	11,148	10,519	(629)	−5.6
55 to 64 years	9,025	9,843	818	9.1
65 years and over	8,128	9,682	1,554	19.1
Nonfamily Households	17,669	23,410	5,741	32.5%
Under 25 years	2,110	2,253	143	6.8
25 to 34 years	3,076	5,176	2,100	68.3
35 to 44 years	1,283	2,533	1,250	97.4
45 to 54 years	1,757	1,952	195	11.1
55 to 64 years	2,756	3,277	521	18.9
65 years and over	6,688	8,219	1,531	22.9

Source: U.S. Bureau of the Census, Current Population Reports, Series P-20, No. 398, *Household and Family Characteristics: March 1984.* Washington, D.C.: U.S. Government Printing Office, 1985

for more than two-thirds (7.8 million) of the slightly more than 11 million total increase in households. The only group that approached it in importance were households headed by individuals 65 years of age and older, which increased by 3.1 million. The 55- to 65-year-old sector demonstrated only very small growth (1.3 million households).

The total 1977 to 1984 household change was nearly evenly divided between family and nonfamily segments. Each of them reflects the new middle-aged reality of America. The largest single growth increment comprised 2.9 million *family* households, 35 to 44 years of age. When, however, rates of growth are examined, the household revolution of America is again emphasized. For example, *nonfamily* households with heads 35 to 44 years old nearly doubled (from an admittedly miniscule base)—and this at an age where the family is the dominant mode. While 25- to 34-year-old family households grew by 11.8 percent, their non-family counterparts increased by 68.3 percent.

There is, therefore, a very powerful crest-of-the-wave phenomenon. When we examine the full household inventory, the total is heavily weighted toward the family sector. When we look at the 1977 to 1984 changes to yield insight into configurations to come, the dynamic is different: one which implies alternative housing-consumption patterns. A perspective on this issue can be secured by an examination of headship rates.

Headship Rates: A Basic Barometer

Underlying the age-specified household formation patterns are dynamic changes in headship rates, i.e., the proportion of any population group that are household heads (or householders). A headship rate of 1.0 defines a situation where every member of a population subgroup is a household head. A headship rate of .5 reveals that exactly one-half are household heads. (In the former case, the number of households is equal to the total subgroup population; in the latter, the number of households is equal to one-half of the total subgroup population. Exhibit 4-2 details age-specific headship rates partitioned by family status for 1970, 1980, and 1984.

For the total household set, headship rates have generally demonstrated increases over the 1970 to 1984 period, i.e., more households generated by a fixed level of population. This was accounted for by an

EXHIBIT 4-2

Headship Rates, U.S. Total, by Age and Family Status: 1970, 1980 and 1984

	1970	*1980*	*1984*
Total Households			
Under 25 years	13.1%	15.6%	13.7%
25 to 34 years	46.9	49.8	48.5
35 to 44 years	51.2	54.5	54.1
45 to 54 years	53.3	55.2	55.8
55 to 64 years	58.1	58.4	59.1
65 years and over	61.4	63.1	64.0
Family Households			
Under 25 years	10.0	9.0	8.1
25 to 34 years	42.0	37.9	35.8
35 to 44 years	47.2	47.4	45.8
45 to 54 years	46.8	46.8	47.1
55 to 64 years	44.8	44.5	44.3
65 years and over	35.3	34.5	34.6
Nonfamily Households			
Under 25 years	3.1	6.6	5.6
25 to 34 years	4.9	11.9	12.7
35 to 44 years	4.1	7.1	8.3
45 to 54 years	6.5	8.4	8.7
55 to 64 years	13.3	13.9	14.8
65 years and over	26.1	28.9	29.4

Source: Center for Urban Policy Research calculations

increase of headship rates within all age groups. However, the process slowed considerably in the 1980s.

Different patterns emerge when family status is taken into account. Family headship rates have tended to remain stable over time, with the exception of the younger age brackets, where they have actually declined. And the highest rates in the distribution fall into the middle-aged sectors—35 to 54 years of age. In contrast, nonfamily headship rates have experienced very rapid increases over time, particularly in the younger age segments. And they are lowest in the middle-aged sectors. *Thus there is a clear-cut stage in life cycle tendency: family status dominates the middle-age span, while nonfamily status is of maximum impact at the younger and older portions of the household age spectrum.*

Headship rates are a key parameter in the household projection process, as the following chapter will attest. They also serve as a basic barometer of the scale of the household-formation process. Their historic trends reveal the shifts that have taken place in contemporary America and strongly suggest the format of baby-boom households to come as they proceed through successive stages of the family life cycle. *If headship rates stabilize at their 1984 plateau, the aging of the massive baby-boom cohort into the 35- to 54-year-old span implies a revitalization of the family household, i.e., family headship rates peak in that age sector, as nonfamily headship rates dip.* But will the baby boomers age into the same household configurations as their predecessors? In our opinion they will.

The Stage in Life Cycle

The historical potency of stage-in-life tendencies cannot be underestimated in anticipating future demand. Middle-age or near-middle-age is the period of peak family activity. The total 1984 profiles of America's households by age and family standing, shown in Exhibit 4-3, reemphasize this reality. If we focus on the bottom of the exhibit, it is evident that nonfamily households tend to be most prominent at the tail ends of the age distribution, i.e., householders under 25 years of age and those 65 years-of-age and over. Only at these stages does family status fall to 60 percent or below for the respective age segments. In the bracket encompassing householders 35 to 54 years of age, however, family configurations account for almost 85 percent of the total. Indeed, as shown in the central portion of Exhibit 4-3, the share of *all* nonfamily households accounted for by the 35- to 54-year-old span falls to less than 20 percent. *The baby boom is inevitably progressing to a stage in their life cycle where family households predominate.*

The aging of households is also distinctly linked to the types of dwelling units which they can either afford or prefer. Homeownership, as shown in Exhibit 4-4, peaks at between 55 and 64 years of age—with four out of five (79.4 percent) householders in that sector achieving homeownership. This reflects a long-term continuous buildup as the household life cycle progresses. From an 18-percent ownership rate among householders 20 to 24 years old, for example, the 50-percent level is reached by age 30, only to ascend to nearly three-quarters by

EXHIBIT 4-3

Householders by Age and Family Status, U.S. Total: 1984
(Numbers in thousands)

	Total Households	*Family Households*	*Nonfamily Households*
Total households	85,407	61,997	23,410
Under 25 years	5,510	3,257	2,253
25 to 34 years	19,808	14,632	5,176
35 to 44 years	16,596	14,062	2,533
45 to 54 years	12,471	10,519	1,952
55 to 64 years	13,121	9,843	3,277
65 years and over	17,901	9,682	8,219
	Percent Distribution		
Total Households	100.0%	100.0%	100.0%
Under 25 years	6.5	5.3	9.6
25 to 34 years	23.2	23.6	22.1
35 to 44 years	19.4	22.7	10.8
45 to 54 years	14.6	17.0	8.3
55 to 64 years	15.4	15.9	14.0
65 years and over	21.0	15.6	35.1
	Percent Distribution		
Total Households	100.0%	72.6%	27.4%
Under 25 years	100.0	59.1	40.9
25 to 34 years	100.0	73.9	26.1
35 to 44 years	100.0	84.7	15.3
45 to 54 years	100.0	84.3	15.7
55 to 64 years	100.0	75.0	25.0
65 years and over	100.0	54.1	45.9

Source: Calculated from Exhibit 4-2

age 40, and to the peak, as we have seen, at nearly 80 percent by age 55. Decline then sets in. But so strong is America's preference for homeownership that in households whose head is 75 years and over the ownership rate remains above 70 percent. *Thus, if all other factors are held constant, an aging population should be one dominated by homeownership and much less inclined toward rental facilities.*

The classic conceptualization of life-cycle-segmented shelter requirements can be envisioned as static, discrete sets of housing facilities with each set occupied by households of similar demographic

EXHIBIT 4-4

Homeownership, by Age of Householder, U.S. Total: 1984
(Numbers in thousands)

	Total Households	*Percent Owners*
All households	85,407	64.6%
15 to 19 years	375	12.8
20 to 24 years	5,135	18.0
25 to 29 years	9,848	38.4
30 to 34 years	9,960	54.4
35 to 39 years	9,059	66.4
40 to 44 years	7,537	72.0
45 to 54 years	12,471	77.4
55 to 64 years	13,121	79.4
65 to 74 years	10,700	77.3
75 years and over	7,201	72.3

Source: U.S. Bureau of the Census, Current Housing Reports, Series P-20, No. 398, *Household and Family Characteristics: March 1984.* Washington, D.C.: U.S. Government Printing Office, 1985

characteristics—but not the same households—over time. The names of the occupants shift, but not their attributes.

In Exhibit 4-5, the conventional progression of household life cycle stages is sketched out; at each of the stages, there is a tendency

EXHIBIT 4-5

Life Cycle Segmentation

Contemporary "Conventional" Progression

1. Single "First Timers"
2. Advancing Singles
3. Young Marrieds
4. Compact Family
5. Expanding Family
6. Established Family & Pre-Empty Nesterhood
7. Empty Nesterhood
8. Active Retired and Retired

Alternative "Standings"

1. Permanent Singles or Resingled
2. Mingles
3. Never Nesters
4. Single Parent Families

to gravitate toward specific dwelling unit accommodations. Young singles, particularly "first-time" singles, may dominate garden-apartment facilities, with a subset (advanced singles) of more affluence—and in a higher tax bracket—advancing into the more modest condominium-occupancy formats. Young marrieds historically have led a relatively brief tenure in garden apartments, and have moved increasingly into condominium alternatives. The compact family may take advantage of this latter format, but as it expands will have a strong tendency to move into traditional freestanding, single-family dwellings.

Attaining affluence, American homebuyers have been relatively mobile, unlike their western European peers. A further shift into prestige housing for those who can afford it, sometimes just at the point when their offspring are on the very verge of vacating the facility (pre-empty nesterhood). With the nest emptied, the appeal of less maintenance-prone condominium facilities, sometimes in an adults-only format, becomes evident. This appeal gains intensity as active-retired and fully-retired status are reached; the proliferation of specialized retirement communities stands as visible testimony. The terminal stages of life are reflected in the vast boom in nursing homes and the renewed interest in terminal-care facilities of all kinds.

Certainly this is not a pattern which has been enjoyed by all Americans. In numerous Center for Urban Policy Research (CUPR) studies, for example, we have observed classic suburban tract developments built at the time of the Korean War, i.e., approximately 1950, in which 30 to 40 percent of all of the original purchasers were still the occupants more than 30 years later. It is, however, a progression which has lent a very virile dynamic to America's housing industry, both in terms of new construction and, perhaps even more strikingly, in terms of resale patterns.

To these classic stages now must be added alternative "standings" which are far from unique, but whose very scale commands increasing attention (Exhibit 4-5). This would include the permanent singles, or those re-singled; the mingles, i.e., unrelated adults (often of the opposite sex) sharing facilities; the rise of what might be termed the "never-nesters," i.e., married couples who have foregone child rearing; and a group whose incidence rate is most important as noted in the previous chapter—the surge of single-parent families.

It is the mix of these demand sectors which is crucial in determining the long-term vigor of the housing market. As we view the future from the perspective of the middle 1980s, it is evident that, just as a function of age, America is moving from the era of the young-married and compact families into the years of expanding families. And, by the latter 1990s, we move into an era that comes close to being dominated by pre-empty nesters. Much less significant are the younger life-cycle segments of first-time singles as well as young marrieds as a group.

Life-cycle riding—following the remorseless consumption spree of the baby boom at each of its life-cycle stages—has been a dominant business-oriented marketing strategy. By the mid 1980s, Yuppies (young upscale professionals) and Puppies (pregnant upscale professionals) marked the merchandising mecca of the moment. But this too is giving way, with Grumpies (grown-up mature persons) or some other yet-to-be-devised acronym destined to present the "new" marketing phase. A revised calculus of housing demand will emerge, reflecting the relentless progression of age.

All of these elements, however, must be viewed within the changing patterns of behavior and household configurations that Americans seem to be adopting. Thus the crest-of-the-wave phenomena earlier discussed, and the question of their continuance, assume critical importance as we attempt to gauge housing demand and consumption.

America's Golden Housing Era: Tenure Shifts

The demographics of the 1970s, in terms of both age and household characteristics, were enormously positive for housing. The baby boom moved into the mainstream of housing consumption, buoyed at least at the beginning of the decade by the economic confidence based on a generation of rising incomes during the 1950s and 1960s. When confidence ebbed under the onslaught of energy crisis and inflation, housing still benefited, assuming the roles of investment, tax shelter and inflation hedge. The end result was an enormously ebullient housing market.

And the latter were merely enabling elements: much more basic were the underlying demand factors reflecting America's desires and aspirations. To put the matter as simply as possible, those who could afford ownership secured it in awe-inspiring scale. Left behind were those typically of less affluence who, while they may have shared the aspiration levels of the more fortunate, simply could not afford them—

and remained relegated to rental housing. Thus, as shown in the first part (1970 to 1979) of Exhibit 4-6, ownership gained market penetration in every household configuration. While the absolute growth was dominated by married-couple families, which tended to have the highest income levels, the rate of growth was even more striking among less orthodox household formats. For example, one-person *owner* households grew by nearly 70 percent between 1970 and 1979.

EXHIBIT 4-6

Owner Household Composition by Age, U.S. Total: 1970, 1979 and 1983
(Numbers in thousands)

Household Type	1970	1979	1983	Change: 1970 to 1979 Number	Percent	Change: 1979 to 1983 Number	Percent
Total Households	39,886	51,411	54,724	11,525	28.9%	3,313	6.4%
2-or-more-Person	35,124	43,424	45,895	8,300	23.6	2,471	5.7
Married Couple	30,806	37,058	39,073	6,252	20.3	2,015	5.4
Under 25 years	800	1,018	743	218	27.3	(275)	−27.0
25 to 29 years	2,252	3,106	2,772	854	37.9	(334)	−10.8
30 to 34 years	2,938	4,409	4,540	1,471	50.1	131	3.0
35 to 44 years	7,097	8,066	9,041	969	13.7	975	12.1
45 to 64 years	13,230	14,540	15,051	1,310	9.9	511	3.5
65 years and over	4,490	5,919	6,926	1,429	31.8	1,007	17.0
Other Male	1,298	1,932	2,325	634	48.8	393	20.3
Under 65 years	974	1,581	1,919	607	62.3	338	21.4
65 years and over	324	351	406	27	8.3	55	15.7
Other Female	3,019	4,435	4,497	1,416	46.9	62	1.4
Under 65 years	2,159	3,398	3,470	1,239	57.4	72	2.1
65 years and over	860	1,037	1,027	177	20.6	(10)	−1.0
1-Person	4,762	7,987	8,829	3,225	67.7	842	10.5
Male	1,329	2,516	3,071	1,187	89.3	555	22.1
Under 65 years	708	1,674	2,008	966	136.4	334	20.0
65 years and over	621	842	1,063	221	35.6	221	26.2
Female	3,433	5,471	5,758	2,038	59.4	287	5.2
Under 65 years	1,367	2,012	2,114	645	47.2	102	5.1
65 years and over	2,066	3,460	3,645	1,394	67.5	185	5.3

Source: U.S. Department of Commerce, U.S. Bureau of the Census, Current Housing Reports, Series H-150-83, *General Housing Characteristics for the United States and Regions: 1983, Annual Housing Survey: 1983, Part A,* U.S. Department of Housing and Urban Development, sponsor. Washington, D.C.: U.S. Government Printing Office, 1985

The contrast with rental housing is made painfully evident in Exhibit 4-7. The total rate of growth in the number of renter households (15.3 percent) was barely half that of homeowners (29 percent). Strikingly evident were the absolute reduction in the number of married-couple renter families; rental housing lost more than a fifth of its married-couple tenants. *Essentially all growth in rental-housing consumption was centered on atypical household formats.*

EXHIBIT 4-7

Renter Household Composition by Age, U.S. Total: 1970, 1979 and 1983
(Numbers in thousands)

Household Type	1970	1979	1983	Change: 1970 to 1979 Number	Percent	Change: 1979 to 1983 Number	Percent
Total Households	23,560	27,160	29,914	3,600	15.3%	2,754	10.1%
2-or-more-Person	17,171	17,412	19,757	241	1.4	2,345	13.5
Married Couple	12,759	10,063	11,448	(2,696)	−21.1	1,385	13.8
Under 25 years	2,282	1,702	1,651	(580)	−25.4	(51)	−3.0
25 to 29 years	2,408	2,166	2,462	(242)	−10.0	296	13.7
30 to 34 years	1,531	1,461	1,927	(70)	−4.6	466	31.9
35 to 44 years	2,154	1,628	2,097	(526)	−24.4	469	28.8
45 to 64 years	3,148	2,019	2,197	(1,129)	−35.9	178	8.8
65 years and over	1,236	1,087	1,115	(149)	−12.1	28	2.6
Other Male	1,143	2,090	2,515	947	82.9	425	20.3
Under 65 years	1,010	1,995	2,390	985	97.5	395	19.8
65 years and over	132	95	124	(37)	−28.0	29	30.5
Other Female	3,270	5,259	5,794	1,989	60.8	535	10.2
Under 65 years	2,899	4,868	5,390	1,969	67.9	522	10.7
65 years and over	370	391	403	21	5.7	12	3.1
1-Person	6,389	9,748	10,157	3,359	52.6	409	4.2
Male	2,604	4,055	4,584	1,451	55.7	529	13.0
Under 65 years	1,998	3,353	3,850	1,355	67.8	497	14.8
65 years and over	606	703	734	97	16.0	31	4.4
Female	3,785	5,694	5,573	1,909	50.4	(121)	−2.1
Under 65 years	2,111	3,364	3,241	1,253	59.4	(123)	−3.7
65 years and over	1,674	2,329	2,332	655	39.1	3	0.1

Source: U.S. Department of Commerce, U.S. Bureau of the Census, Current Housing Reports, Series H-150-83, *General Housing Characteristics for the United States and Regions: 1983, Annual Housing Survey: 1983, Part A,* U.S. Department of Housing and Urban Development, sponsor. Washington, D.C.: U.S. Government Printing Office, 1985

The Maturing Society and Market Segmentation

The years immediately following 1979 were chaotic for America's economy—and its housing system as well. The second energy crisis, and the devastation of very high interest rates emanating from the nation's attempt to cope with unparalleled levels of inflation, had few precedents to serve as guides. The result was the harsh downturns of 1980 and 1981–1982 which yielded levels of housing starts that reached a 40-year low. The housing buying power of the American household suffered severely as real incomes diminished. Thus as the period from 1979 to 1983 is viewed in Exhibits 4-6, 4-7 and 4-8, the housing results are evident—rental housing secured a much greater

EXHIBIT 4-8

**Owner and Renter Household Income, by Household Configuration,
U.S. Total: 1983**

Household Type	Owner Households	Renter Households	Renter/Owner Income Ratio
Total Households	$24,400	$12,400	0.51
2-or-more-Person	27,400	14,200	0.52
Married Couple	29,100	17,900	0.62
Under 25 years	19,900	14,300	0.72
25 to 29 years	27,100	19,400	0.72
30 to 34 years	30,300	19,700	0.65
35 to 44 years	33,700	20,200	0.60
45 to 64 years	32,300	19,100	0.59
65 years and over	16,100	12,400	0.77
Other Male	24,300	14,000	0.58
Under 65 years	26,200	14,400	0.55
65 years and over	15,600	8,500	0.54
Other Female	15,900	8,500	0.53
Under 65 years	16,700	8,300	0.50
65 years and over	13,400	9,700	0.72
1-Person	10,400	9,900	0.95

Source: U.S. Department of Commerce, U.S. Bureau of the Census, Current Housing Reports, Series H-150-83, *Financial Characteristics of the Housing Inventory of the United States and Regions: 1983, Annual Housing Survey: 1983, Part C*, U.S. Department of Housing and Urban Development, sponsor. Washington, D.C.: U.S. Government Printing Office, 1985

share of market, particularly among the young, as the triumphant
march of homeownership of the previous decade was abruptly hum-
bled.

Since 1983, there has been some measure of resurgence. By mid-
decade, buoyed up by much more modest interest rates, an increase in
housing-buying power and, most consequentially, a much greater level
of confidence in, and real performance by, the economy, the swing in
housing direction once again moved toward ownership. But even by
mid-decade, there was a clear-cut decline in the proportion of
America's younger households, i.e., those under the age of 30 years,
who were purchasing homes rather than renting them. There were
many factors that have entered into this patterning. One of the more
pertinent was the relative availability and cheapness of rental housing
spurred on by very generous tax depreciation allowances. Yet another
was the removal of the fear of inflation, which motivated many 1970s'
homebuyers. But certainly the crucial factor was housing-buying power
and economic capacity to secure ownership.

When trends in renter–owner income ratios are examined over
time, the finances of renters are re-emphasized, as shown in Exhibit 4-
9. *There is a clear-cut degeneration over time in the ratio of renter incomes to
those of owners. Rental housing has been skimmed of its more affluent tenantry; led by married couples and the more economically well-endowed of the
atypical formats, a substantial migration to homeownership took place.*

This generalization cuts across all the real divisions of our society.
Thus, as shown in Exhibit 4-10, whether we examine central cities or
suburban areas, or rural ones as well, the imbalance between owner
and renter income growth is evident. And this holds true by region of
the country as well (Exhibit 4-11).

Renters, in general, have become poorer. Their absolute income
gains in the 13-year period, marked by strong inflationary tendencies,
averaged well under half those of owners. And, as we will explore in
Chapter 14, this has led to escalating rent–income ratios—and has
sadly limited the capacity to raise rents in accordance with expenses. It
is not that *individual* renters have seen their incomes decline neces-
sarily, but rather a vast cream-skimming has taken the most affluent of
renter groups and moved them into homeownership. And by the end
of the 1970s, the ravages of inflation had made ownership more and
more imperative to serve as a refuge, not only from the elements, but
from the then-declining potency of the dollar.

EXHIBIT 4-9

Trends in Renter/Owner Income Ratios: 1973 to 1983

Household Type	1973	1979	1981	1983
Total Households	0.63	0.54	0.52	0.51
2-or-more-Person	0.68	0.57	0.54	0.52
Married Couple	0.73	0.66	0.63	0.62
Under 25 years	0.85	0.79	0.74	0.72
25 to 29 years	0.83	0.74	0.73	0.72
30 to 34 years	0.77	0.70	0.65	0.65
35 to 44 years	0.72	0.67	0.61	0.60
45 to 64 years	0.74	0.63	0.59	0.59
65 years and over	0.80	0.79	0.73	0.77
Other Male	0.69	0.61	0.56	0.58
Under 65 years	0.66	0.57	0.52	0.55
65 years and over	0.65	0.59	0.56	0.54
Other Female	0.73	0.56	0.56	0.53
Under 65 years	0.68	0.53	0.52	0.50
65 years and over	0.75	0.68	0.75	0.72
1-Person	1.13	1.04	1.01	0.95

Sources: U.S. Department of Commerce, U.S. Bureau of the Census, Current Housing Reports, Series H-150-83, *Financial Characteristics of the Housing Inventory for the United States and Regions: 1983, Annual Housing Survey: 1983, Part C*, U.S. Department of Housing and Urban Development, sponsor. Washington, D.C.: U.S. Government Printing Office, 1985; and previous annual editions of this volume for the respective years

The decade of the 1970s saw the positive demographics of enormous levels of household formation combining with homeownership to yield an unparalleled decade of housing affluence. It also produced a level of demand and market segmentation that could not have been envisioned a generation ago. While within the decade there were enormous swings between boom-and-bust production years, the sum of housing delivery and consumption had no parallel in our history.

The baby boomers were a motive force during this evolution; they wanted everything their parents had, but sooner, and in their own unique fashion. Singles and mingles, ownership and condominiums, restructured the American shelter arena. As they enter their middle years, however, two dynamics appear in conflict. Stage in life-cycle forces, potent historically, would portend a dominance of family-oriented households. In contrast, the extension of unique baby-boom life-styles could well alter the historic

EXHIBIT 4-10

Owner and Renter Household Income by Geographic Area, U.S. Total: 1970 to 1983

	1970	1979	Change: 1970-1979		1979	1983	Change: 1979-1983	
			Number	Percent			Number	Percent
Owner Total	$ 9,700	$18,300	$8,600	88.7%	$18,300	$24,400	$6,100	33.3%
Inside SMSAs	11,000	20,300	9,300	84.5	20,300	27,600	7,300	36.0
In Central Cities	10,100	18,000	7,900	78.2	18,000	24,700	6,700	37.2
Not in Central Cities	11,600	21,400	9,800	84.5	21,400	29,100	7,700	36.0
Outside SMSAs	7,500	15,200	7,700	102.7	15,200	19,500	4,300	28.3
Renter Total	6,300	10,000	3,700	58.7	10,000	12,400	2,400	24.0
Inside SMSAs	6,700	10,300	3,600	53.7	10,300	13,100	2,800	27.2
In Central Cities	6,100	9,100	3,000	49.2	9,100	11,500	2,400	26.4
Not in Central Cities	7,700	11,800	4,100	53.2	11,800	15,700	3,900	33.1
Outside SMSAs	5,300	9,000	3,700	69.8	9,000	10,900	1,900	21.1

Source: U.S. Department of Commerce, U.S. Bureau of the Census, Current Housing Reports, Series H-150-83, General Housing Characteristics for the United States and Regions: 1983, Annual Housing Survey: 1983, Part A, U.S. Department of Housing and Urban Development, sponsor. Washington, D.C.: U.S. Government Printing Office, 1985

EXHIBIT 4-11

Renter and Owner Household Income by Region, U.S. Total: 1970 to 1983

	1970	1979	Change: 1970-1979		1979	1983	Change: 1979-1983	
			Number	Percent			Number	Percent
Owner Total	$ 9,700	$18,300	$8,600	88.7%	$18,300	$24,400	$6,100	33.3%
Northeast	10,900	19,100	8,200	75.2	19,100	26,300	7,200	37.7
Midwest	10,000	18,900	8,900	89.0	18,900	24,300	5,400	28.6
South	8,200	16,200	8,000	97.6	16,200	21,700	5,500	34.0
West	10,700	20,500	9,800	91.6	20,500	28,000	7,500	36.6
Renter Total	$ 6,300	10,000	3,700	58.7	10,000	12,400	2,400	24.0
Northeast	6,900	9,800	2,900	42.0	9,800	12,400	2,600	26.5
Midwest	6,700	10,000	3,300	49.3	10,000	11,800	1,800	18.0
South	5,400	9,700	4,300	79.6	9,700	12,400	2,700	27.8
West	6,500	10,700	4,200	64.6	10,700	13,500	2,800	26.2

Source: U.S. Department of Commerce, U.S. Bureau of the Census, Current Housing Reports, Series H-150-83, *General Housing Characteristics for the United States and Regions: 1983, Annual Housing Survey: 1983, Part A*, U.S. Department of Housing and Urban Development, sponsor. Washington, D.C.: U.S. Government Printing Office, 1985

precedents. Both of these scenarios must be viewed within the reality of America's economy.

The 1970s signaled an increasing demand for homeownership that seemed overwhelming. Affluence led to homeownership; its role as the principal symbol of the good life was unsurpassed. The economic shocks of the turn-of-the-decade years raised questions about the future that remain unresolved even in the mid-1980s. Our own analysis suggests a return to ownership dominance for the balance of the century. The next chapter will explore one alternative extrapolation into the future, projecting the household potentials of the 1990s.

5

Future Households: Scale and Shape

In this chapter, we present the results of projecting the housing and household choices of 1984 into future household profiles. The process used here assumes that headship rates, i.e., the propensity to form households of specific types by given age groups, will remain at 1984 levels. We further define housing *tenure choice* by the market penetration of owner/renter formats within the various household age-configurational segments as of 1984. By applying what is known about past household dynamics to future population parameters, an initial reading of one of housing's more probable future courses is secured.

The past often must serve as a blueprint for the future. Only the most omniscient seer can hazard the task of visualizing the shape of things to come without reference to history. Undoubtedly, new household and housing patterns will emerge; but many of the key relationships and forces of the past will extend into the future.

The remorseless process of aging, for example, will—fortunately or unfortunately—persist. Housing consumers 35 to 44 years of age in 1985 will inevitably become the 45- to 54-year-old consumers of 1995 (at least the great bulk of them will). And as such consumers mature, the changes discussed in the last several chapters will emerge. Nonetheless, while certain directions can be foreseen and quantitatively delineated, forecasting their exact scale and variation is, to say the least, an uncertain art form.

The issues of future housing demand and supply requirements are crucial not only to national economic forecasting, but also to all those—public or private, directly or indirectly—involved with the housing cycle. Primary in providing some definition to housing's broad future is the issue of projected household growth. How many households will be formed within a finite period of time in the future? What will their age profile look like? What shape or configuration are they likely to assume? Will these future consumers be disposed to choose— or be forced to choose—rental tenure or ownership? Will their age and configurational attributes yield further insight as to other proclivities: are they going to be first-time homebuyers, or is there a strong potential for the upscale, trade-up market? And, at the other end of the spectrum, given our present knowledge and linkages between age, household configuration, and income, will there be a renewed demand for "social housing"?

The questions are many; the answers are difficult. There are two areas of relative certainty, however (and here again, stress must be added to *relative*). The first of these is the stability of projections of the adult population to come—certainly for the balance of the century. The number of children may fluctuate, but the prime housing consumers— adults at the householder ages—are relatively finite; they already exist. Secondly, once again, unless there are massive societal changes, the linkages between age and the household and shelter life cycles have been established so thoroughly in the past as to warrant at least initial extension into the future.

The reader must be warned once again that many elements—not least of them the economy, to say nothing of changing tastes—may wreak havoc with the scenario. Business-cycle vagaries will always yield short-term fluctuations; the pervasive tendency to read long-term trends into current events is an ever-present pitfall that has left bankruptcies in its wake. Fortunately, housing is an enormously potent good—its consumption ramifications subject to more inertia, to more in the way of conservative "doing tomorrow what we did yesterday," than any other consumer good. The internal structure has a tremendous capacity to persist, whatever the shape of the fashionable "externals" of the moment.

The Basic Course

The market demographics of the decade to come pose sharp contrasts, and with them opportunities. The principal definition of these elements is presented in Exhibits 5-1 and 5-2, which indicate projected household growth *increments* by age, configuration, and housing tenure from

EXHIBIT 5-1

**Projected Household Growth Increments, by Age, Type and Tenure,
U.S. Total: 1984 to 1995
(Numbers in thousands)**

Age	Total	Family				Nonfamily	
			Other Family				
		Married Couple	Male House-holder	Female House-holder		Male House-holder	Female House-holder
			Owner Households				
Under 25 years	(152)	(97)	(6)	(11)		(24)	(15)
25 to 34 years	(120)	(93)	(2)	(8)		(11)	(5)
35 to 44 years	4,200	3,317	102	420		222	140
45 to 54 years	3,895	3,063	90	375		172	195
55 to 64 years	(591)	(424)	(12)	(47)		(29)	(80)
65 years and over	2,899	1,497	52	235		218	896
Total	10,132	7,263	224	964		549	1,132
			Renter Households				
Under 25 years	(711)	(259)	(21)	(117)		(171)	(143)
25 to 34 years	(138)	(58)	(4)	(24)		(30)	(21)
35 to 44 years	1,892	781	72	471		364	204
45 to 54 years	1,140	431	43	245		219	202
55 to 64 years	(153)	(52)	(4)	(20)		(33)	(45)
65 years and over	952	211	14	73		146	508
Total	2,982	1,054	101	628		494	705

1984 to 1995, and 1995 to 2000. (The projection apparatus details are presented at the end of this chapter.)

Total household growth during the first 11 years is projected to be slightly over 13 million, i.e., an average annual household gain of 1.2 million—a drastic reduction from the 1.7 million of the 1970s (Exhibit 5-1). Thus, the coming of age of the baby-bust generation during the next decade begins to take its shelter toll. In the same time period, the maturing baby-boom generation yields a general propensity to form *family* households, particularly in the *homeownership* sector. The latter phenomenon is indicated by the approximately three-quarters share (10

EXHIBIT 5-2

Projected Household Growth Increments, by Age, Type and Tenure, U.S. Total: 1995 to 2000
(Numbers in thousands)

Age	Total	Family			Nonfamily	
			Other Family			
		Married Couple	Male House-holder	Female House-holder	Male House-holder	Female House-holder
		Owner Households				
Under 25 years	49	31	2	3	8	5
25 to 34 years	(918)	(716)	(19)	(62)	(85)	(36)
35 to 44 years	652	515	16	65	35	22
45 to 54 years	2,478	1,949	57	239	109	124
55 to 64 years	1,321	947	26	105	64	178
65 years and over	441	228	8	36	33	136
Total	4,024	2,954	90	386	164	429
		Renter Households				
Under 25 years	227	83	7	37	55	46
25 to 34 years	(1,058)	(448)	(27)	(187)	(231)	(164)
35 to 44 years	294	121	11	73	57	32
45 to 54 years	725	274	27	156	139	128
55 to 64 years	342	117	8	44	73	100
65 years and over	145	32	2	11	22	77
Total	675	179	29	134	114	219

million out of 13 million) of net household growth which is captured by ownership through 1995. If we review past trends, this would indicate a strengthened demand for ownership, with the reduction in total new housing requirements (as a function solely of household growth) primarily centered on the rental sector. *In essence, holding other factors constant, the demographics call for a stronger ownership sector-weaker rental growth.*

Underlined in Exhibit 5-1 are the demand sectors which register increases above one-half million households. Married-couple configurations dominate the growth increments through 1995 which, again, are the result of an aging baby-boom generation. This is further reflected in the center of the growth market—owner couples 35 to 54 years of age. Much less significant than in the 1970s are more youthful groups, and nonfamily household configurations. *Renter household growth is buoyed up not by youth (there is a decline of more than 700,000 in the under 25-year-old renter sector), but rather by absolute expansion in the more mature groups, particularly the 35- to 44-year-olds.*

The potency of a maturing demography is further revealed by the years immediately prior to the century's end (1995–2000). All of the dynamics projected for the 1984 to 1995 period will be present in the latter period. Household growth, for example, will continue its shrinkage to below 950,000 annually. The net gain of renter households will be most diminished, however, to only 135,000 a year as compared to 800,000 additional owner households. The terminal five years of the century thus will be characterized by relatively small household increments and a more modest level of housing activity even further concentrated in the ownership sector. The aging of the baby-boom generation will be mirrored by the new dominance of households 45 to 54 years of age. This will be the leading growth sector of the 1995 to 2000 period. By way of contrast, the shrinkage generated by the baby-bust generation will impact the 25- to 34-year-old householder group, which will contract by nearly two million in a brief five-year period.

The future of housing demand will be quite different from the two generations following World War II. It is a scenario of a slowing of household growth being mirrored by a decline in the numerical level of housing starts. But as a function of age and household type, the demand increment will be skewed to the upscale.

This is of particular relevance for builders of rental units. Given the traditional linkages of married couples to higher incomes, the 35- to 54-year-old bulge—of 1.6 million married-couple *renter* households between 1984 and 2000—provides some allure. Rental demolition rates normally are much higher than they are for individually owned homes; the replacement requirements equally commensurate. When this is combined with the changing consumer pattern of renters, it portends significant opportunities. Given the relatively positive income attributes of the new growth sectors among renters, the potential of hybrid formats—of rental units with purchase options or lease/purchase agreements—is particularly noteworthy.

The other side of the coin is a far less salubrious growth in female renter householders. These are groups, as will be shown subsequently, which have the lowest housing buying power. But by the 1990s, their growth will diminish substantially.

The rise of the elderly remains a potent housing reality through 1995, but their expansion in absolute terms is more limited than in past decades. More than three million owner households 65 years old and over, and more than one million renter equivalents, account for approximately three in ten of total household growth. In the years following 1995, however, their share of growth declines even further. Nonetheless, the rise of the "elderly" elderly (those over 75 years of age) suggests the potential expansion of new alternate housing opportunities.

The 1970s may have been the era of singles and mingles; the 1990s represent a return to a much more conventional pattern, with the vast historical middle (at least within the mythology of the American family!) reasserting itself. It is a picture of perhaps more modest housing production in number of units, but at higher levels of amenity—and cost.

From a demographic point of view, the period as a whole suggests a modestly proportioned base for the housing industry. Lurking in the shadows, as we come to the end of the century, is the drastic negative impact of the baby-bust generation, signaled initially by the shrinkage in the total number of households under 25 years of age, and then the 25- to 34-year-old sector by the year 2000. The first-time homebuyer and the builder of rental units may well have to worry about replacement buyers/tenantry as the century draws to a close.

As shown in Exhibits 5-3 through 5-6, it is the years to 1990 which are the most positive. The share of growth of both owners and renters is concentrated there, while from 1990 to 2000 there is an abrupt shrinkage. This is principally focused among renters, with a halving of the average annual growth increment as we move from the late 1980s to the early 1990s, and another halving by the late 1990s. Thus the decline in total household growth accelerates perceptibly through the 16-year period, particularly among rental shelter seekers.

From a market perspective, the growth potency of the now-aging baby-boom generation is evident. The paucity in scale of its baby-bust successor will try the ingenuity of the housing industry in equally profound fashion. A biblical parable is suggested: early years of fruitfulness, followed by years of relative want.

All of this is subject to changes in the housing consumption patterns of Americans, and the income realities which subtly, and not so subtly, influence them. *But holding this latter element constant leaves a*

EXHIBIT 5-3

Projection Summary: Total and Age Distribution, 1984 to 1990
(Numbers in thousands)

			Total				
	1984		1990		Change: 1984-1990		Average Annual Change
Tenure	Number	Percent	Number	Percent	Number	Percent	
Total	85,407	100.0%	93,268	100.0%	7,861	100.0%	1,310
Owner	55,157	64.6	60,875	65.3	5,718	72.7	953
Renter	30,250	35.4	32,393	34.7	2,143	27.3	357

		Age Distribution						
	Owner				Renter			
			Change 1984-1990				Change: 1984-1990	
Age	1984	1990	Number	Percent	1984	1990	Number	Percent
Total	55,157	60,875	5,718	10.4%	30,250	32,393	2,143	7.1%
Under 25 years	972	855	(117)	−12.1	4,539	3,991	(548)	−12.1
25 to 34 years	9,201	9,761	560	6.1	10,607	11,253	646	6.1
35 to 44 years	11,441	14,093	2,652	23.2	5,155	6,350	1,195	23.2
45 to 54 years	9,648	10,959	1,311	13.6	2,823	3,207	384	13.6
55 to 64 years	10,421	9,895	(526)	−5.0	2,700	2,564	(136)	−5.0
65 years and over	13,475	15,311	1,836	13.6	4,426	5,029	603	13.6

vision of the wind-up years of the century starting out in a sturdy fashion, but tiring badly as we hit the last decade.

Detailed Parameters

The household ramifications arising just from an aging America deserve to be restated. While times and events certainly will alter the course depicted here, it still represents the future central housing path.

1. Between 1970 and 1980, the numbers of households in the United States increased by 1.7 million per year. A massive retrenchment took place in the early 1980s, as worldwide recession placed an economic damper on household formation. Between 1980 and 1983, the average annual gain in

EXHIBIT 5-4

Projection Summary: Total and Age Distribution, 1990 to 1995
(Numbers in thousands)

Tenure	1990		1995		Change: 1990-1995		Average Annual Change
	Number	Percent	Number	Percent	Number	Percent	
Total	93,268	100.0%	98,522	100.0%	5,253	100.0%	1,051
Owner	60,875	65.3	65,290	66.3	4,415	84.0	883
Renter	32,393	34.7	33,232	33.7	839	16.0	168

Age Distribution

Age	Owner		Change: 1990-1995		Renter		Change: 1990-1995	
	1990	1995	Number	Percent	1990	1995	Number	Percent
Total	60,875	65,290	4,415	7.3%	32,393	33,232	839	2.6%
Under 25 years	855	820	(35)	−4.1	3,991	3,828	(163)	−4.1
25 to 34 years	9,761	9,081	(680)	−7.0	11,253	10,469	(784)	−7.0
35 to 44 years	14,093	15,641	1,548	11.0	6,350	7,047	697	11.0
45 to 54 years	10,959	13,543	2,584	23.6	3,207	3,963	756	23.6
55 to 64 years	9,895	9,830	(65)	−0.7	2,564	2,547	(17)	−0.7
65 years and over	15,311	16,374	1,063	6.9	5,029	5,378	349	6.9

households barely exceeded one million, virtually equivalent to the 1960s' experience.

2. The 1984 to 1990 projections show annual average household increases shifting to the 1.3-million level. This scale of growth falls somewhat in between the furious pace of the 1970s and the more sedate patterns of the 1960s and early 1980s.

3. A further diminishment in the 1990s is also projected. Between 1990 and 1995, the annual average gain in the number of households should retreat toward one million, i.e., the equivalent of the disaster years of the early 1980s. A much more mature America of nearly 100-million households will be dominated by those "settled in" to their middle years. By the last five years of the century, the shrinkage will

EXHIBIT 5-5

Projection Summary: Total and Age Distribution, 1995 to 2000
(Numbers in thousands)

Tenure	1995 Number	1995 Percent	Total 2000 Number	2000 Percent	Change: 1995-2000 Number	Change: 1995-2000 Percent	Average Annual Change
Total	98,522	100.0%	103,221	100.0%	4,699	100.0%	940
Owner	65,290	66.3	69,313	67.2	4,024	85.6	805
Renter	33,232	33.7	33,907	32.8	675	14.4	135

	Age Distribution Owner				Renter			
Age	1995	2000	Change: 1995-2000 Number	Change: 1995-2000 Percent	1995	2000	Change: 1995-2000 Number	Change: 1995-2000 Percent
Total	65,290	69,313	4,024	6.2%	33,232	33,907	675	2.0%
Under 25 years	820	868	49	5.9	3,828	4,055	227	5.9
25 to 34 years	9,081	8,164	(918)	−10.1	10,469	9,411	(1,058)	−10.1
35 to 44 years	15,641	16,293	652	4.2	7,047	7,341	294	4.2
45 to 54 years	13,543	16,022	2,478	18.3	3,963	4,688	725	18.3
55 to 64 years	9,830	11,152	1,321	13.4	2,547	2,889	342	13.4
65 years and over	16,374	16,815	441	2.7	5,378	5,523	145	2.7

become a stampede, with household growth averaging only 900,000 annually.

4. This pattern is confirmed by related demographic and economic anticipations in the United States. Labor force projections of the Bureau of Labor Statistics, for example, suggest an average annual labor force growth of 1.8-million persons during the 1980s, but only 1.2 million in the 1990 to 1995 period. These projections represent a severe slippage from the 1970s, when the labor-force bulge yielded an unparalleled gain of 2.4 million participants annually. The impending transition reflects the reduction in newcomers (the baby busters).

5. Homeownership will expand its share of shelter. During the 1970s, 70 percent of the household gain comprised owner households. Between 1984 and 1990, ownership is projected

EXHIBIT 5-6

Projection Summary by Household Configuration: 1984 to 2000
(Numbers in thousands)

	Owner				Renter			
			Change: 1984–1990				Change: 1984–1990	
	1984	1990	Number	Percent	1984	1990	Number	Percent
Total	55,157	60,875	5,718	10.4%	30,250	32,393	2,143	7.1%
Family								
Married Couple	38,845	42,906	4,061	10.5	11,244	12,043	799	7.1
Male Householder	1,183	1,306	123	10.4	847	913	66	7.8
Female Householder	4,677	5,206	529	11.3	5,201	5,634	433	8.3
Nonfamily								
Male Householder	3,558	3,903	345	9.7	6,194	6,569	375	6.1
Female Householder	6,894	7,556	662	9.6	6,764	7,234	470	7.0

	Owner				Renter			
			Change: 1990–1995				Change: 1990–1995	
	1990	1995	Number	Percent	1990	1995	Number	Percent
Total	60,875	65,290	4,415	7.3%	32,393	33,232	839	2.6%
Family								
Married Couple	42,906	46,110	3,204	7.5	12,043	12,297	254	2.1
Male Householder	1,306	1,406	100	7.6	913	948	35	3.8
Female Householder	5,206	5,642	436	8.4	5,634	5,829	195	3.5
Nonfamily								
Male Householder	3,903	4,108	204	5.2	6,569	6,687	119	1.8
Female Householder	7,556	8,027	471	6.2	7,234	7,470	236	3.3

EXHIBIT 5-6 (continued)

Projection Summary by Household Configuration: 1984 to 2000
(Numbers in thousands)

	Owner				Renter			
			Change: 1995–2000				Change: 1995–2000	
	1995	2000	Number	Percent	1995	2000	Number	Percent
Total	65,290	69,313	4,024	6.2%	33,232	33,907	675	2.0%
Family								
Married Couple	46,110	49,064	2,954	6.4	12,297	12,475	179	1.5
Male Householder	1,406	1,496	90	6.4	948	977	29	3.0
Female Householder	5,642	6,028	386	6.8	5,829	5,964	134	2.3
Nonfamily								
Male Householder	4,108	4,272	164	4.0	6,687	6,802	114	1.7
Female Householder	8,027	8,456	429	5.3	7,470	7,689	219	2.9

to account for over 72 percent of household growth, with a further surge to 85 percent in the 1990 to 2000 decade.

6. However, with overall household growth increments contracting, this sharp marginal increase in proportion will boost the total share of homeownership by the year 2000 to only 67.2 percent, as compared to 64.4 percent in 1980, and 62.9 percent in 1970. Nonetheless, the long-term homeownership ethic, in the absence of radical shifts in tax policy or major socioeconomic disruptions, will reach a historic pinnacle by 2000.

7. Housing producers will have to be wary of the potentially modest scale of housing requirements. For example, even though ownership will account for over 83 percent of the tenure selections of the 1990–1995 household increment, this translates in absolute terms to 883,000 owner households annually, fully one-quarter lower than the 1.2-million yearly average of the 1970s.

8. And suppliers of new rental accommodations face even more drastic adjustments. Renter households in the 1970s grew by more than one-half million annually. Their projected yearly increment in the 1990 to 1995 period will fall below 170,000. The demographically induced decline of new labor-force entrants will be paralleled by the shrinkage of new recruits into the ranks of renter households. But more married couples may choose rental housing, reversing withdrawal from this shelter choice which characterized the 1970s.

9. The future age partitions of America's households accentuate the probability of these dynamics. Through the balance of the 1980s, households 35 to 44 years of age dominate the growth profile, but in the 1990s, they will be supplanted by (i.e., they will progress into) the 45- to 54-year-old sector. Yuppies will be transformed into Grumpies—grown-up mature persons. Jogging, health foods, and exercise clubs cannot deflect aging. Mature adulthood, however, brings with it increasing rates of homeownership, as detailed in the previous chapter. Householders at their fiftieth birthday approach an 80-percent homeownership rate.

10. Rentership rates, in contrast, are highest in the younger age brackets, and the latter will decline. Contraction is the rule in

the under-25-years-of-age sector during the balance of the 1980s and will be reflected in the number of 25- to 34-year-old householders in the 1990s. The latter will decrease by almost two million in the five years between 1995 and 2000 (renters and owners combined); but this age sector will still remain the largest rental target, accounting for nine million out of 34 million renter households.

11. And in the 1990s, the seemingly relentless growth of the elderly will begin to abate. The demographic cohort produced by the "birth dearth" of the 1920s and 1930s (which, in turn, as it helped form the "nesting generation" of the 1950s, spawned the baby-boom eruption) will have begun to settle into their retirement years. Households over 65 years of age will secure their smallest growth contingents in more than half a century. But because of the reduced scale of overall growth, they will maintain their market share. The potency of housing for the elderly will be more a tribute to their increased housing buying power than their growth in number.

12. Coinciding with the overall aging tendencies will be changes in the configuration of America's households. Although not sufficient to resurrect the American family norm of the 1950s—a norm which seemed to collapse in a single generation—married-couple families will make a decided comeback. Between 1970 and 1984, married couples increased by about 5.5 million, barely 25 percent of the total household increase. The 1984 to 1995 projections, however, indicate married couples increasing by almost 8.3 million, representing 63 percent of the 13.1 million total household increment. This penetration increased from 1995 to 2000 with married couples responsible for two-thirds (3.1 million) of the market total growth of 4.7 million.

13. In contrast, the explosive growth of both family- and nonfamily-female householders should abate. For example, female householder families increased by more than 3.2 million between 1970 and 1980; between 1984 and 1995, they will increase by less than 1.6 million. Since this is a lower-incomed household configuration (as will be elaborated upon in the next chapter), one of the nation's more potent shelter dilemmas may be mitigated.

14. The diverging growth paths of married-couple and female-householder families underscore our vision of the tilt toward a more upscale market climate. In particular, the bulk of the growth in married-couple families will be married-couple *owners* between the ages of 35 and 54 years. Again, as we will detail in the next chapter, these comprise the most affluent household sector.

15. Will the generation that promised never to trust anyone over 30 reach the point where they will cast a hostile glance at anyone under 40? Will it reinvent the housing and family folkways of the 1950s as the stabilizing effects of mature adulthood take hold? The revolution of alternate life-styles of the 1960s was never as widespread as its critics feared. The Woodstock generation clings to housing in a fashion reminiscent of its predecessors. But in the housing demand arena, developers must complement the shelter formats of the past with targeted approaches. The marketing ingenuity that adapted to the vagaries of the 1970s and 1980s will have to be equally nimble to deal with the imperatives of the 1990s.

It is income, translated into housing-buying power, that will provide the locomotive of the future housing-demand train. While "the demographics of affluence" may not typify the balance of the century, the maturing of America should yield household income possibilities far in excess of those of the 1970s. It is this potential that will be addressed in the following chapter.

Projection Methodology

The basic household-projection methodology is the product of two separate age-segmented projections—headship rates and population. Of the two, it is the former which can exhibit more substantial future volatility. Population, in contrast (assuming migration does not shift markedly), is much less sensitive. Within the United States, the pool of all future householders (household heads) through the next 15 years is presently alive. The scale of household formation emanating from this pool, however, will be dependent on historical and emerging social and economic forces. The latter will yield the level and shape of future headship rates.

Exhibit 5-7 is the historic (1984) base of our analytical procedures. Households are segmented by age of householder and type of configuration, and further partitioned by owner and rental tenure. Headship rates for 1984 were derived by dividing each column of Exhibit 5-7 by the population vector of Exhibit 5-8. The result, as detailed in Exhibit 5-9, is two 30-cell headship rate matrices, one for owner tenure and one for rental. Thus, headship rates are specified by age, household configurations, and tenure.

EXHIBIT 5-7

Owner and Renter Households by Age and Type, U.S. Total: 1984
(Numbers in thousands)

		Family			*Nonfamily*	
			Other Family			
Age	*Total*	*Married Couple*	*Male House-holder*	*Female House-holder*	*Male House-holder*	*Female House-holder*
		Owner Households				
Total	55,157	38,845	1,183	4,677	3,558	6,894
Under 25 years	972	617	37	69	153	96
25 to 34 years	9,201	7,177	192	619	852	362
35 to 44 years	11,441	9,035	277	1,143	606	381
45 to 54 years	9,648	7,586	223	929	426	484
55 to 64 years	10,421	7,473	209	826	508	1,406
65 years and over	13,475	6,959	244	1,092	1,014	4,166
		Renter Households				
Total	30,250	11,244	847	5,201	6,194	6,764
Under 25 years	4,539	1,652	137	745	1,093	911
25 to 34 years	10,607	4,493	274	1,878	2,316	1,646
35 to 44 years	5,155	2,127	197	1,284	991	556
45 to 54 years	2,823	1,067	107	607	542	500
55 to 64 years	2,700	921	66	348	574	790
65 years and over	4,426	983	66	339	677	2,362

Source: U.S. Bureau of the Census, Current Population Reports, Series P-20, No. 398, *Household and Family Characteristics: March 1984.* Washington, D.C.: U.S. Government Printing Office, 1985

EXHIBIT 5-8

Resident Population of the United States by Age: 1984
(Numbers in thousands)

Age	Population
Under 25 years	40,092
25 to 34 years	40,840
35 to 44 years	30,670
45 to 54 years	22,349
55 to 64 years	22,210
65 years and over	27,985
Total: 15 years and over	184,147

Source: U.S. Bureau of the Census, Current Population Reports, Series P-25, No. 952, *Projections of the Population of the United States, by Age, Sex, and Race: 1983 to 2080.* Washington, D.C.: U.S. Government Printing Office, 1984

EXHIBIT 5-9

Headship Rates by Age, Type and Tenure of Households, U.S. Total: 1984

		Family			Nonfamily	
			Other Family			
Age	Total	Married Couple	Male House-holder	Female House-holder	Male House-holder	Female House-holder
			Owner Households			
Under 25 years	2.42	1.54	0.09	0.17	0.38	0.24
25 to 34 years	22.53	17.57	0.47	1.52	2.09	0.89
35 to 44 years	37.30	29.46	0.90	3.73	1.98	1.24
45 to 54 years	43.17	33.94	1.00	4.16	1.91	2.17
55 to 64 years	46.92	33.65	0.94	3.72	2.29	6.33
65 years and over	48.15	24.87	0.87	3.90	3.62	14.89
			Renter Households			
Under 25 years	11.32	4.12	0.34	1.86	2.73	2.27
25 to 34 years	25.97	11.00	0.67	4.60	5.67	4.03
35 to 44 years	16.81	6.94	0.64	4.19	3.23	1.81
45 to 54 years	12.63	4.77	0.48	2.72	2.43	2.24
55 to 64 years	12.16	4.15	0.30	1.57	2.58	3.56
65 years and over	15.82	3.51	0.24	1.21	2.42	8.44

For example, of those individuals 35 to 44 years of age in 1984, 37.3 percent were heads of household who owned their own home, and 16.8 percent were heads of household who rented. Further segmenting the 35- to 44-year-old owner group, 29.5 percent were married couple owners, 0.9 percent "other family" male owners, 3.7 percent "other family" female owners, 2.0 percent "nonfamily" male owners, and 1.2 percent "nonfamily" female owners. The sum of these configurational-specified rates equals the 37.3 percent total.

We have assumed that future headship rates will remain at their 1984 levels. It is this assumption that is most critical to the entire procedure. As was detailed in Chapter 4, headship rates increased substantially during the 1970s, particularly for nonfamily households. This was the principal dynamic underlying the configurational revolution of that era. Whether it can continue is open to very real questions, particularly given the sobering evidence provided by the 1980–1982 recession. The exercise presented here does not assume the "revolution" will be undone, but rather that it will not advance beyond the threshold reached in 1984.

The headship rates of Exhibit 5-9 are then applied to the Census Bureau age-specified population projections for 1990, 1995, and 2000. The population projections, presented in Exhibits 5-10, 5-11, and 5-12, encompass total population (including armed forces overseas).

EXHIBIT 5-10

Resident Population of the United States by Age: 1990
(Numbers in thousands)

Age	Population
Under 25 years	35,252
25 to 34 years	43,326
35 to 44 years	37,780
45 to 54 years	25,386
55 to 64 years	21,090
65 years and over	31,799
Total: 15 years and over	194,632

Source: U.S. Bureau of the Census, Current Population Reports, Series P-25, No. 952, *Projections of the Population of the United States, by Age, Sex, and Race: 1983 to 2080.* Washington, D.C.: U.S. Government Printing Office, 1984

EXHIBIT 5-11

Resident Population of the United States by Age: 1995
(Numbers in thousands)

Age	Population
Under 25 years	33,808
25 to 34 years	40,309
35 to 44 years	41,929
45 to 54 years	31,372
55 to 64 years	20,951
65 years and over	34,006
Total: 15 years and over	202,375

Source: U.S. Bureau of the Census, Current Population Reports, Series P-25, No. 952, *Projections of the Population of the United States, by Age, Sex, and Race: 1983 to 2080.* Washington, D.C.: U.S. Government Printing Office, 1984

These are converted to resident population equivalents, since the latter formed the base for the original headship rates. This is done by deleting the overseas armed forces estimates.

The products of the application of the headship rates to the population projections are the household projections detailed in Exhibit 5-13 (1990), Exhibit 5-14 (1995), and Exhibit 5-15 (2000). The resulting

EXHIBIT 5-12

Resident Population of the United States by Age: 2000
(Numbers in thousands)

Age	Population
Under 25 years	35,816
25 to 34 years	36,235
35 to 44 years	43,678
45 to 54 years	37,113
55 to 64 years	23,767
65 years and over	34,921
Total: 15 years and over	211,530

Source: U.S. Bureau of the Census, Current Population Reports, Series P-25, No. 952, *Projections of the Population of the United States, by Age, Sex, and Race: 1983 to 2080.* Washington, D.C.: U.S. Government Printing Office, 1984

EXHIBIT 5-13

Household Projections by Age, Type and Tenure: 1990
(Numbers in thousands)

Age	Total	Family			Nonfamily	
			Other Family			
		Married Couple	Male House-holder	Female House-holder	Male House-holder	Female House-holder
		Owner Households				
Under 25 years	855	543	33	61	135	84
25 to 34 years	9,761	7,614	204	657	904	384
35 to 44 years	14,093	11,130	341	1,408	746	469
45 to 54 years	10,959	8,617	253	1,055	484	550
55 to 64 years	9,895	7,096	198	784	482	1,335
65 years and over	15,311	7,907	277	1,241	1,152	4,734
Total	60,875	42,906	1,306	5,206	3,903	7,556
		Renter Households				
Under 25 years	3,991	1,453	120	655	961	801
25 to 34 years	11,253	4,766	291	1,992	2,457	1,746
35 to 44 years	6,350	2,620	243	1,582	1,221	685
45 to 54 years	3,207	1,212	122	689	616	568
55 to 64 years	2,564	875	63	330	545	750
65 years and over	5,029	1,117	75	385	769	2,684
Total	32,393	12,043	913	5,634	6,569	7,234

age, configuration, and tenure matrices are identical in form to Exhibit 5-7, our 1984 starting point. The summary exhibits of intraperiod changes have already been presented at the beginning of this chapter.

Alternative household projections sets can be generated with different headship-rate assumptions. For example, under the premise that the headship rate eruption of the 1970s represents an inexorable force that will continue through the balance of the century, then future headship rates can be forecast via any linear or nonlinear projection model, using the 1970 to 1980 period, for example, as a historical baseline. The end result would be a forecast of more households in total, and for greater numbers of "atypical" households.

EXHIBIT 5-14

Household Projections by Age, Type and Tenure: 1995
(Numbers in thousands)

| | | | Family | | Nonfamily | |
| | | | Other Family | | | |
Age	Total	Married Couple	Male House-holder	Female House-holder	Male House-holder	Female House-holder
			Owner Households			
Under 25 years	820	520	31	58	129	81
25 to 34 years	9,081	7,084	190	611	841	357
35 to 44 years	15,641	12,352	379	1,563	828	521
45 to 54 years	13,543	10,649	313	1,304	598	679
55 to 64 years	9,830	7,049	197	779	479	1,326
65 years and over	16,374	8,456	296	1,327	1,232	5,062
Total	65,290	46,110	1,406	5,642	4,108	8,027
			Renter Households			
Under 25 years	3,828	1,393	116	628	922	768
25 to 34 years	10,469	4,435	270	1,854	2,286	1,625
35 to 44 years	7,047	2,908	269	1,755	1,355	760
45 to 54 years	3,963	1,498	150	852	761	702
55 to 64 years	2,547	869	62	328	541	745
65 years and over	5,378	1,194	80	412	823	2,870
Total	33,232	12,297	948	5,829	6,687	7,470

Similarly, the recession-reduced headship rates of the 1980–1984 period, if extrapolated into the future, would yield more negative numbers. The 1984 figure used here represents a measure of compromise. In addition, the projections can be "refined" by sharpening the major partitions of our headship rate matrices. The age brackets can be narrowed, more detail can be added to the configurational profile, e.g., the presence of children under 18 years of age, etc., and racial partitions can be employed.

Variations on all of these refinements have been major ongoing tasks on the CUPR research agenda.

EXHIBIT 5-15

Household Projections by Age, Type and Tenure: 2000
(Numbers in thousands)

Age	Total	Family			Nonfamily	
			Other Family			
		Married Couple	*Male House-holder*	*Female House-holder*	*Male House-holder*	*Female House-holder*
			Owner Households			
Under 25 years	868	551	33	62	137	86
25 to 34 years	8,164	6,368	170	549	756	321
35 to 44 years	16,293	12,867	394	1,628	863	543
45 to 54 years	16,022	12,597	370	1,543	707	804
55 to 64 years	11,152	7,997	224	884	544	1,505
65 years and over	16,815	8,684	304	1,363	1,265	5,199
Total	69,313	49,064	1,496	6,028	4,272	8,456
			Renter Households			
Under 25 years	4,055	1,476	122	666	976	814
25 to 34 years	9,411	3,986	243	1,666	2,055	1,460
35 to 44 years	7,341	3,029	281	1,829	1,411	792
45 to 54 years	4,688	1,772	178	1,008	900	830
55 to 64 years	2,889	986	71	372	614	845
65 years and over	5,523	1,227	82	423	845	2,947
Total	33,907	12,475	977	5,964	6,802	7,689

6

Income: Accelerator and Brake

Household and housing demand expectations rest on the motor power of income—and the fiscal capacity to purchase shelter in the future. The housing train can be switched to the fast track via robust incomes, or be detained by faltering ones. Generally, two theses can be espoused regarding income realities to come.

The first, predicated on the erratic performance of the economy during the post-1973 years—jagged falls alternating with surges, but the latter of limited potency—envisions constrained income-growth potentials. The declines in real household and family income experienced during the post-1973 years are seen as evidence of an America past its economic prime—not simply a case of classic business-cycle setbacks. Thus, the productive pie will fail to expand sufficiently to allow meaningful household income advances. A related proposition is the notion of a "disappearing middle class," with new resource growth captured mainly by an elite upper-class stratum.

Shedding the concern of economic uncertainty, the second thesis proclaims an era where the "demographics of affluence" hold sway. Premised on historical patterns—economic wherewithal is linked to age and marriage—the inevitable maturing and "nesting" of Americans will lead to more economically well-endowed households, and more potent shelter demand. The maturing of the baby boom yields a more seasoned labor force, and with it increased productivity.

Both perspectives beleaguer the forecaster. The purpose of this chapter is to briefly review the constructs of each position in the context of the household projections already presented. The vision of an emerging period of new demographic "winners" will be considered first.

The Demographics of Affluence

Historical experience indicates that as people mature, so do their incomes. Inexperienced, entry-level workers earn far less than their more seasoned peers, and young households and families have lower incomes, other factors being equal, than older ones. These relationships underpin the assertions of a coming period of demographically inspired prosperity.

Exhibit 6-1 details median household and family income by householder age for 1984. Median incomes rise from the very modest levels of the youngest households (under 25 years old) to a peak at middle age (45 to 54 years old). Thereafter, incomes start to fall as retirement begins to take hold. Thus an age-related income cycle is apparent—one which becomes accentuated over time.

A baby boom near its income peak (35 to 54 years old) will characterize the 1990s; this is a far cry from the 1970s when the nation was stressed by a bulge of young households. America will be propelled into an era of affluence via the sheer force of a maturing demography.

The mix of household configurations will also contribute to this future. As shown in Exhibit 6-2, family income is more than twice that of nonfamilies. Two-worker, married-couple families are situated at the highest rungs of the income ladder; householders living alone at the

EXHIBIT 6-1

Median Household and Family Income, by Age of Householder, U.S. Total: 1984
(In Current Dollars)

Age of Householder	All Households	Family Households
Total	$22,415	$26,433
Under 25 years	14,028	13,791
25 to 34 years	23,735	25,157
35 to 44 years	29,784	31,154
45 to 54 years	31,516	34,482
55 to 64 years	24,094	29,303
65 years and over	12,799	18,215

Source: U.S. Bureau of the Census, Current Population Reports, Series P-60, No. 151, *Money Income of Families and Persons in the United States: 1984.* Washington, D.C.: U.S. Government Printing Office, 1986

EXHIBIT 6-2

Median Household Income, by Type of Household: 1984
(1984 Dollars)

Type of Household	Median Income
Total Households	$22,415
Family Households	26,433
Married-Couple Families	29,612
Wife Employed Full-Time, Householder Year-Round, Full-Time Worker	40,632
Male Householder, No Wife Present	23,325
Female Householder, No Husband Present	12,803
Nonfamily Households	12,987
Householder Living Alone	11,512

Source: U.S. Bureau of the Census, Current Population Reports, Series P-60, No. 151, *Money Income of Households, Families and Persons in the United States: 1984.* Washington, D.C.: U.S. Government Printing Office, 1986

lowest. While the 1970s' household growth was dominated by singles and mingles, families—particularly married-couple families—will be the stalwarts of the 1990s. Configurational shifts, therefore, also portend a more prosperous income future.

The family-income matrix presented in Exhibit 6-3 brings together both the age and configurational dimensions. Married couples 35 to 55 years of age have the highest incomes, a demographic "certainty" that has proven resolute over time. And it is this sector which, as shown in the previous chapter, will be *the* household growth component during the balance of the century.

Demographically focused crystal balls, then, perceive an evolving environment of affluence. This period will be led by a maturing baby-boom generation, more fertile with income than offspring, edging marketing strategies further upscale.

While one can look askance at such proclamations, it is hard to deny that future demographic realities *are* favorable and represent, at a minimum, potentials not evident for more than a generation. But will the number of high-velocity careers necessary to replicate past age-related income patterns materialize in the future? How many house-

EXHIBIT 6-3

Median Family Income, by Family Type and Age of Householder: 1984
(1984 Dollars)

Age of Householder	Total	Family Household Type		
			Other Family	
		Married Couple	Male Householder	Female Householder
Total	$26,433	$29,612	$23,325	$12,803
15 to 24 years	13,791	17,396	13,736	5,337
25 to 34 years	25,157	28,251	23,875	8,999
35 to 44 years	31,154	35,436	26,132	14,402
45 to 54 years	34,482	38,081	29,770	18,317
55 to 64 years	29,303	31,330	22,546	17,659
65 years and over	18,215	18,567	19,497	15,880

Source: U.S. Bureau of the Census, Current Population Reports, Series P-60, No. 151, *Money Income of Households, Families and Persons in the United States: 1984.* Washington, D.C.: U.S. Government Printing Office, 1986

holds can actually ride the steep earnings curves? Or will earnings and income curves flatten under the burdens of onerous demographic numbers?

An Economic Lid

A more ominous picture has also been drawn from the statistics of the 1970s and early 1980s. During that erratic inflation-prone period, the post-World War II trek to ever-increasing affluence came to an abrupt halt. As shown in Exhibit 6-4, median family incomes, in constant dollars, virtually doubled between 1950 and 1973. But under the stress of multiple economic shocks, income malaise characterized the years which followed. Between 1973 and 1982, *real* median family income in America declined by 10 percent; in constant dollars, it fell to the level of the late 1960s. By 1985, despite the advent of economic expansion, the median American family had not yet matched the income peak achieved twelve years earlier, nor the housing buying power.

The intervening years, however, were not marked by steady decline, but by fluctuations paralleling the business cycle. Median family income declined precipitiously (- 6 percent) between 1973 and

EXHIBIT 6-4

United States Median Family Income: 1950 to 1985
(In Actual and Constant 1985 Dollars)

| | Median Family Income | |
Year	Actual Dollars	Constant 1984 Dollars
1950	$ 3,319	$14,832
1960	5,620	20,414
1970	9,867	27,336
1973	12,051	29,172 P
1974	12,902	28,145 *
1975	13,719	27,421 *
1976	14,958	28,267
1977	16,009	28,419
1978	17,640	29,087 P
1979	19,661	29,029
1980	21,023	27,446 *
1981	22,388	26,481 *
1982	23,433	26,116 *
1983	24,549	26,642
1984	26,433	27,376
1985	27,735	27,735

Gains in Real Income
(Constant 1985 Dollars)

Period	Number	Percent	Average Annual Gain
1950–1960	$5,582	37.6%	$558
1960–1970	6,922	33.9	692
1970–1973	1,836	6.7	612
1973–1975	(1,751)	–6.0	876
1975–1979	1,608	5.9	402
1979–1982	(2,913)	–10.0	(971)
1982–1985	1,619	6.2	540

Note: P indicates peak income year
            * indicates recession year

Source: U.S. Bureau of the Census, Current Population Reports, Series P-60, No. 154, *Money Income and Poverty Status of Families and Persons in the United States: 1985 (Advance Data from the March 1986 Current Population Survey)*. Washington, D.C.: U.S. Government Printing Office, 1986

1975, as the nation endured the first oil shock and a major economic recession. Between 1975 and 1979, income growth resumed (+ 5.9 percent) as economic recovery and expansion took place. By 1979, the income peak of 1973 was almost replicated, but the second energy shock and the "rolling" recession of 1980–1982 brought with it three straight years of income contraction (- 10 percent). Income then resumed its upward pace (+ 6.2 percent) between 1982 and 1985 as economic recovery ensued. Still, the economic trauma of the post-1973 years has yet to be fully purged.

It can be persuasively argued that median family income is not the most appropriate tool to measure typical economic well-being. Per capita personal income, for example, increased by over 1 percent annually during the 1973 to 1985 period. Nevertheless, its rate of growth was still below that experienced during the 1960s, despite record workforce and job expansion during the 1970s. The issue rising from alternative income data series is not whether the post-1973 period lagged the 1960s (it clearly had), but rather, whether we slipped into absolute decline.

The 1970s and early 1980s were sobering years; not only was the business cycle "rediscovered," but also its impact on income was strongly underscored. In the absence of sustained high-level national economic expansion, the limited growth thesis suggests that America's capacity for future income gains appears questionable.

But demographic elements again have been brought forth as an explanatory balm, both for faltering incomes and the performance of the economy. The latter, for example, had to absorb the huge baby-boom cohort during the 1970s. Inundated with a surplus of young and inexperienced workers, capital investment was delayed, productivity lagged, and overall economic performance suffered. The sheer weight of new, relatively low-paid workers—and the lower-income households and families they formed—served to dampen growth in median incomes.

Such rationalizations have some measure of validity. Virtually all of the family growth of the 1970s was accounted for by householders who were 65 years old and over, and between 25 and 34 years old— age groups whose incomes lagged the overall medians. Thus the rise of many young family formations, distant in time from their peak-earning years; the steady expansion in the number of elderly families, long past their prime-income years; and a decline in the size of the 45- to 54-year-old sector, a group in their premium-earning period, all served to mute the patterns of family-income growth in America.

The effects of the lid of the post-1973 economy still remain chastening despite the recovery and expansion of the mid-1980s. But it is our conclusion that, barring unforeseen calamities, the major factors are in place potentially to return the American economy to a state of positive "normalcy" not seen since the mid-1960s. If this potential is realized, sustained income growth again can resume. The possibilities of the huge maturing baby-boom cohort replicating the configuration- and age-related income experience of Exhibit 6-3 are alluring, as is an economy—comparatively free of external shocks, at least of energy-crunch magnitude—bulwarked by an experienced and increasingly productive work force. Potent housing purchasing-power increases would then be available to bolster a shelter industry facing an inevitable shrinkage in clientele.

A Disappearing Middle Class?

But there are other clouds on the demographic–housing horizon besides the spectre of a lackluster economy. Not all Americans will glory in the affluent 1990s, even if the latter is realized. A number of demographic subsectors may find an economically perilous future; many of these are included in concerns about a "disappearing middle class."

The fragmentation of the mass middle market of post-World War II America has been a well-recognized phenomenon; market segmentation strategies began to dominate the 1970s. But only during the recession of the early 1980s did the concern of the possibility of a shrinking middle class come to the fore.

While precise partitions are lacking, the income span between $20,000 and $50,000 can be considered a very broadly defined middle class. The distribution of family incomes (in constant 1985 dollars) provides some insight into the question of middle-class fragmentation. In 1973, 52.8 percent of America's families fell into this broad middle swath. By 1982, during the depths of recession, the share had fallen to 48.8 percent. Concurrently, the under-$20,000 category increased from 30.7 percent to 36.4 percent of all families, while the $50,000-and-over segment declined from 16.5 percent to 14.8 percent.

	1973	1982
less than $20,000	30.7%	36.4%
$20,000 to $49,999	52.8	48.8
$50,000 and over	16.5	14.8

Thus the lower part of the income distribution exhibited growth while the basic center and upper levels experienced shrinkage. This pattern strongly suggested that a number of families had fallen out of the middle class, depleting the once-monolithic mass middle market. While the growth of a more prosperous segment has been claimed, when defined by incomes of $50,000 and over it is not readily apparent.

This comparison, however, is affected by the choice of baselines, starting from a peak (1973) in the business cycle and ending in a recession year (1982). When viewed from recession to recession (1975 to 1982), or recovery year to recovery year (1976 to 1983) as detailed below, a slightly different pattern emerges: the expansion of the lower-income strata (under $20,000) is less pronounced, while the upper-income ($50,000 and over) sector demonstrates growth.

	1976	1983
less than $20,000	32.7%	36.2%
$20,000 to $49,999	52.4	48.2
$50,000 and over	14.9	15.6

As was shown earlier in this chapter, income growth parallels the business cycle, making baseline selection critical in analyses of this type. Generally, recessionary phases of the business cycle—1973 to 1975, for example, and 1979 to 1982—are accompanied by expansion in the lower-income sector and contraction in the upper bracket. In recovery phases, such as 1975 to 1978 and 1982 to 1985, the exact opposite occurs: the lower-income group (under $20,000) loses share while the upper-income sector ($50,000 and over) gains. Thus income distributions tend to fluctuate in line with major economic swings.

	1973	1975	1979	1982
less than $20,000	30.7%	33.8%	31.9%	36.4%
$20,000 to $49,000	52.8	52.3	51.3	48.8
$50,000 and over	16.5	13.9	16.8	14.8

	1975	1978	1982	1985
less than $20,000	33.8%	31.6%	36.4%	34.0%
$20,000 to $49,000	52.3	51.3	48.8	47.7
$50,000 and over	13.9	17.1	14.8	18.3

But superimposed on these cycles is evidence of the extremes of the distribution expanding at the expense of the broad middle throughout the post-1973 period. Again, demographic forces were one of the contributing elements. Substantial increases in "dual"-income, married-couple families on the one hand, and female-householder families on the other, served to bulk up, respectively, the upper- and lower-income household segments. (See Exhibits 6-5 through 6-8).

And other factors were at work, including structural changes in the economy which caused harsh dislocations. The severity of the 1974–1975 and 1980–1982 recessions—successively the worst downturns since the Great Depression—exacted a major toll in this regard.

A longer perspective provides a more positive note. In comparing the 1971 distribution to that of 1985—both recovery years—the major change has been the thickening-up of the upscale market, a much more significant shift than "lower-class" expansion. What this suggests is not so much the pulling apart of the middle class, but the increasing prominence of upscale America.

	1971	1985
less than $20,000	33.2%	34.0%
$20,000 to $49,999	53.7	47.7
$50,000 and over	13.1	18.3

EXHIBIT 6-5

Families by Type and Median Family Income: 1975 and 1984
(Families as of March of the following year)
(Numbers in thousands)

Family Configuration	Number of Families		Change: 1975–1984	
	1975	1984	Number	Percent
Total Families	56,245	62,706	6,461	11.5%
Married-Couple Families	47,318	50,350	3,032	6.4
Wife in paid labor force	20,833	26,938	6,105	29.3
Wife employed	19,334	25,401	6,067	31.4
Full-time	13,512	18,109	4,597	34.0
Part-time	5,821	7,292	1,471	25.3
Wife unemployed	1,449	1,537	88	6.1
Wife not in paid labor force	26,486	23,412	(3,074)	–11.6
Male Householder (spouse absent)	1,444	2,228	784	54.3
Female Householder (spouse absent)	7,482	10,129	2,647	35.4

Family Configuration	Median Family Income		Change: 1975–1984	
	1975	1984	Number	Percent
Total Families	$13,917	$26,433	$12,516	89.9%
Married-Couple Families	14,867	29,612	14,745	99.2
Wife in paid labor force	17,237	34,668	17,431	101.1
Wife employed	17,584	35,352	17,768	101.0
Full-Time	18,262	37,025	18,763	102.7
Part-Time	16,223	31,350	15,127	93.2
Wife unemployed	13,260	23,114	9,854	74.3
Wife not in paid labor force	12,752	23,582	10,830	84.9
Male Householder (spouse absent)	12,995	23,325	10,330	79.5
Female Householder (spouse absent)	6,844	12,803	5,959	87.1

Source: U.S. Bureau of the Census, Current Population Reports, Series P-60, No. 151, *Money Income of Households, Families and Persons in the United States: 1984.* Washington, D.C.: U.S. Government Printing Office, 1986

The data of Exhibit 6-5 highlight the underlying demographics. Between 1976 and 1985 the largest family configuration growth sectors were married-couple families with wives employed full-time (4.6 million), and female-householder families (2.6 million). The 1984 median

EXHIBIT 6-6

All Married-Couple (Husband–Wife) Families and Subgroup with Husband and Wife Both Year-Round, Full-Time Workers: 1975 to 1984
(Family totals as of March of the following year)

Year	All Married-Couple (Husband–Wife) Families	Husband and Wife Year-Round, Full-Time Workers	
		Number	Percent
1975	47,318	7,385	15.6%
1976	47,497	7,730	16.3
1977	47,385	8,130	17.2
1978	47,692	8,959	18.8
1979	48,180	9,308	19.3
1980	49,294	9,360	19.0
1981	49,630	9,627	19.4
1982	49,908	9,297	18.6
1983	50,090	10,254	20.5
1984	50,350	10,936	21.7

Sources: U.S. Bureau of the Census, Current Population Reports, P-60, No. 151, *Money Income and Poverty Status of Households, Families, and Persons in the United States: 1984.* Washington, D.C.: U.S. Government Printing Office, 1986; and previous annual editions for the respective years

EXHIBIT 6-7

All Married-Couple (Husband–Wife) Families and Subgroup with Wife Employed Full-Time/Householder Year-Round, Full-Time Worker:
1975 to 1984 – Median Income
(Family totals as of March of the following year)

Year	All Married-Couple (Husband–Wife) Families	Wife Employed Full-Time/ Householder Year-Round, Full-Time Worker
1975	$14,867	$20,185
1976	16,203	21,387
1977	17,616	23,045
1978	19,340	25,377
1979	21,503	28,189
1980	23,141	31,099
1981	25,065	33,956
1982	26,019	36,391
1983	27,286	37,999
1984	29,612	40,632

Sources: U.S. Bureau of the Census, Current Population Reports, P-60, No. 151, *Money Income and Poverty Status of Households, Families, and Persons in the United States: 1984.* Washington, D.C.: U.S. Government Printing Office, 1986; and previous annual editions for the respective years

EXHIBIT 6-8

Median Family Income: 1984
Householder Year-Round, Full-Time Worker/Wife Employed Full-Time, by
Age of Householder

Householder Age	Income
Total	$40,632
18 to 24 years	25,610
25 to 34 years	35,751
35 to 44 years	42,566
45 to 54 years	47,476
55 to 64 years	45,168

Source: U.S. Bureau of the Census, Current Population Reports, Series P-60, No. 151, *Money Income of Families and Persons in the United States: 1984.* Washington, D.C.: U.S. Government Printing Office, 1986

income of the former was $37,025; the median income of the latter was only $12,803. Thus the higher-incomed demographic sector outpaced the absolute growth of the lower-incomed group.

Providing further momentum to this dynamic has been the growing presence of married-couple families with both spouses working year-round, full-time (Exhibit 6-6). Their absolute growth between 1976 and 1985 (3.6 million) was also in excess of that of the female householder sector. The dual year-round, full-time-worker configuration represents an even more select income-elite (Exhibit 6-7), particularly in its more mature formats (Exhibit 6-8).

If the economy of the 1990s proves resilient, and the projected demographics approximate reality to come, middle-class shrinkage may turn out to be far more positive than negative. Fears of the demise of the middle class may have been misleading; the emergence of a new "super class" in both income—and scale—may be the primary housing-market focus of the decade to come.

Within the context of an uncertain, and perhaps perilous, economic environment, the future of housing demand will largely be the future of the baby-boom generation. By 1995, it will have been 49 years since the birth (1946) of its first member; 31 years since its last (1964). Virtually the entire generation will have moved en masse into the 35- to 54-years-of-age span, the classic peak-earning years. The majority will have "paired and nested," many of whom will be privileged "super couples" of two working professionals. And the resources that they command will be fully brought to bear on housing.

The baby boom continually redefined consumer marketing frontiers as it matured. The baby boom has been, literally, a spending boom, initially supported by its parents' pocketbooks. Its own expenditure streams gathered momentum in the 1970s, secured increasing authority during the 1980s, and will reach virtual hegemony in the 1990s. And housing may well represent the final consumption frontier. The remorseless spree which started at the bottom—diapers—will have completely targeted the shelter market.

But the baby boom has never been, nor will it ever be, a monolithic whole. The leading edge of the generation, which rode the housing inflationary cycle of the 1970s, will have far more housing purchasing power than its rear-guard contingents. In addition, the participants in the "new" post-industrial/information economy will have far higher income potentials than those imprisoned in the old. And there will be demographic sectors of less-than-affluent financial capacity—single-parent families key among them. Not everyone will be able to secure adequate accommodations on an "express"-housing train.

III

Housing Supply

7

Housing Supply:
The Potent Baseline

Housing production in America is one of the nation's premier businesses. Its scale and impact on the economy are barely hinted at when we reflect on an inventory that, by the mid 1980s, approached 100-million units with a market value easily in excess of $3 trillion; a dynamism only partially revealed by average annual removals from the total stock twice as large as the standing inventory of Cleveland; and annual additions whose value, in mid-1980s' terms, approached $150 billion. Its quality and quantity are reflections of the wealth of America. But it also serves as a vital economic stimulus: private residential investment alone usually accounts for over four percent of Gross National Product.

But even these data fail to provide insight into its full significance within American society as a whole. Housing typically has been rated by most Americans as the single, most dominant input into their life-style: homeownership has a priority without equal among our aspirations. America's success at providing housing for the vast ranks of its middle class has been the envy of the balance of the world.

The enormous changes which have taken place in America's institutional provisions for housing, land use, finance, and construction technology have raised challenge and opportunity in a fashion without parallel since the beginning of the New Deal. The enabling mechanisms and institutions engendered at that time seemingly have run their life cycle. In the early 1980s, we saw sustained shrinkage in the number of thrift institutions, the homogenization of the nation's financial markets, the end of sheltered housing credit, and the emergence of new mortgage instrumentalities. *The sum product of these elements is far from determined. They will try our ingenuity in the future.*

The Big Picture

The drastic changes in housing markets which have taken place in the 1980s—the worst housing downturn since World War II, followed by a mid-decade boom—were built on a ten-year base of unparalleled success—a standard for the future. The 1970 to 1980 period still remains the benchmark—the reference point—for evaluating the 1980s and beyond.

Despite being characterized as the era of unprecedented economic "shocks," in retrospect the 1970s turned out to be America's housing decade. The nation's housing inventory expanded by an increment virtually twice that of any preceding intercensal decade. Powered initially by the last phase of the then-unquestioned post-World War II prosperity, housing production subsequently was underpinned by the post-shelter society; in the face of accelerating inflation, a scared America sought a safe port in the economic storm. Housing became much more important as a form of investment, of forced savings (and tax savings), and as a refuge from inflation than as shelter from the elements. Housing seemingly was capable of surmounting any obstacle in its path. The results depicted in Exhibit 7-1 illustrate the phenomenon.

During the 1960s, now viewed with nostalgia as a period of stable growth, the nation's total housing inventory expanded by 10.3 million units. But this gain was easily eclipsed by the 19.7-million-unit increment of the following decade. It was the 1970s that also confirmed the increased dominance of homeownership, with an increase of nearly 12-million owner-occupied units. And while this dwarfed the addition of rental facilities, the growth of the latter, in turn, had an absolute scale (5.0 million) nearly 60 percent higher than in the previous decade (3.3 million).

In the 20 years from 1960 to 1980, America's total housing stock increased by more than 50 percent—its owner-occupied facilities, by nearly 60 percent. By 1980, 64.4 percent of America's households were homeowners. Yet within a year of the termination of this golden period, housing starts would plummet to a level not seen since World War II.

Regional Variations

While the accomplishments of America's housing supply system were shared by every area of the United States, there were marked regional variations. The census-defined South and West regions, partic-

EXHIBIT 7-1

Changes in the Housing Inventory, U.S. Total: 1960 to 1983
(Numbers in thousands)

	1960	1970	1980	1983	Change: 1960-1970		Change: 1970-1980		Change 1980-1983	
					Number	Percent	Number	Percent	Number	Percent
All Housing Units	58,326	68,672	88,397	93,519	10,346	17.7%	19,725	28.7%	5,122	5.8%
Year-Round Units	56,584	67,699	86,678	91,675	11,115	19.6	18,979	28.0	4,997	5.8
Occupied Units	53,024	63,445	80,378	84,638	10,421	19.7	16,933	26.7	4,260	5.3
Owner Occupied	32,797	39,886	51,787	54,724	7,089	21.6	11,901	29.8	2,937	5.7
Percent of Total	61.9%	62.9	64.4	64.7						
Renter Occupied	20,227	23,560	28,591	29,914	3,333	16.5	5,031	21.4	1,323	4.6
Percent of Total	38.1%	37.1	35.6	35.3						

Source: U.S. Department of Commerce, U.S. Bureau of the Census, Census of Population and Housing 1960, 1970 and 1980; U.S. Department of Commerce, U.S. Bureau of the Census, Current Housing Reports, Series H-150-83, *General Housing Characteristics for the United States and Regions: 1983, Annual Housing Survey: 1983, Part A*, U.S. Department of Housing and Urban Development, sponsor. Washington, D.C.: U.S. Government Printing Office, 1985

ularly the Sunbelt, secured the largest inventory gains during the 23-year period isolated in Exhibit 7-2. In contrast, the Northeast and North Central regions, representing the Frostbelt, tended to lag, although they still had substantial levels of absolute growth. Indeed, their increase in housing supply, as will be elaborated upon in subsequent chapters, was far in excess of absolute levels of population growth in the post-1970 period.

America's housing geography changed markedly between 1960 and 1983. In the former year, the Northeast and North Central states accounted for 31.6 million, or 54 percent, of the nation's 58.3 million housing units. By 1983, however, despite an absolute growth to 43.9 million units, their share of the nation's total inventory (93.5 million units) declined to 47 percent. Housing's critical mass had shifted from the older Frostbelt territories to the burgeoning Sunbelt, paralleling America's economic and demographic transformation.

In this context, housing's role was not merely as a passive respondent to the latter parameters, consequential as they were. Rather, it was also a substantial motive force in and of itself, with construction employment and related housing expenditures representing potent feedbacks into the overall pulling power of regions. And this is to say nothing of the potential of abundant and relatively inexpensive housing as a force of instigating and sustaining demographic and economic shifts. Despite the successful mid-decade counter-revolution against energy prices and the resurrection of the Northeast, the basic mass of America shifted.

SMSA Status

This circular effect is also present in the second partition employed in Exhibit 7-2—SMSA–central-city–suburban status. In 1960, central cities accounted for 35 percent (20.4 million units) of the nation's total housing inventory. Although they secured net gains of nearly 7-million units during the ensuing 23 years, by 1983 their share had contracted to 29.5 percent.

The suburbs secured inventory gains of 17-million units nationally between 1960 and 1983, increasing their proportionate share from 31.2 percent to 37.9 percent; they replaced central cities as the dominant locus of America's housing stock in every region of the country. And after 1970, the new exurbanization of America was marked by the rapid

EXHIBIT 7-2

All Housing Units by Region and SMSA Status: 1960 to 1983

Year and Location	Total					Percent Distribution				
	U.S.	North-east	Mid-west	South	West	U.S.	North-east	Mid-west	South	West
1960, Total	58,326	14,798	16,798	17,173	9,558	100.0%	100.0%	100.0%	100.0%	100.0%
Inside SMSAs	38,633	11,834	10,514	9,052	7,233	66.2	80.0	62.6	52.7	75.7
Central Cities	20,440	6,005	5,695	5,208	3,531	35.0	40.6	33.9	30.3	36.9
Not in Central Cities	18,193	5,695	5,208	3,844	3,701	31.2	39.4	28.7	22.4	38.7
Outside SMSAs	19,693	2,964	6,284	8,121	2,325	33.8	20.0	37.4	47.3	24.3
1970, Total	68,672	16,642	18,971	21,030	12,029	100.0	100.0	100.0	100.0	100.0
Inside SMSAs	46,289	13,036	12,206	11,651	9,395	67.4	78.3	64.3	55.4	78.1
Central Cities	22,608	6,212	5,978	6,166	4,252	32.9	37.3	31.5	29.3	35.3
Not in Central Cities	23,681	6,824	6,228	5,486	5,143	34.5	41.0	32.8	26.1	42.8
Outside SMSAs	22,383	3,606	6,765	9,379	2,634	32.6	21.7	35.7	44.6	21.9
1983, Total	93,519	20,053	23,874	31,150	18,443	100.0	100.0	100.0	100.0	100.0
Inside SMSAs	62,293	15,266	15,187	17,550	14,290	67.3	76.1	63.6	56.3	77.5
Central Cities	27,257	6,695	6,582	8,129	5,851	29.5	33.4	27.6	26.1	31.7
Not in Central Cities	35,036	8,571	8,604	9,422	8,439	37.9	42.7	36.0	30.2	45.8
Outside SMSAs	31,226	4,786	8,687	13,600	4,153	33.8	23.9	36.4	43.7	22.5

Source: U.S. Department of Commerce, U.S. Bureau of the Census, Current Housing Reports, Series H-150-83, *General Housing Characteristics for the United States and Regions: 1983, Annual Housing Survey: 1983, Part A*, U.S. Department of Housing and Urban Development, sponsor. Washington, D.C.: U.S. Government Printing Office, 1985

expansion and increasing share of housing captured by territories located outside SMSAs.

Thus by 1983, America's in-place housing stock had strongly tilted toward the new growth zones of the nation. Sunbelt, suburbs, and exurbia represented the dominant zones of housing concentration. This was the base upon which the housing experience of the balance of the 1980s evolved.

Tenure and Location

Rental housing, in political debate, often has been viewed as essentially the domain of the central city, with measures to aid it seen as limited in appeal. Whatever the historical merits of this statement, its validity has long been eroded by rental growth in non-central city locations. The data in Exhibit 7-3, which segments the nation's occupied housing units by tenure and geographic location for 1970, 1976, and 1983, suggests the reality. In each of these years, approximately three-fourths of the total rental-housing stock was located inside SMSAs. But the central city share was reduced from 47.1 percent in 1970 to 42.7 percent in 1983. By the latter year, over 57 percent of the total national rental housing stock was located outside of central cities; approximately 9.8-million suburban units comprised 32.9 percent of the total, and an additional 7.3 million nonmetropolitan units accounted for 24.3 percent.

While the number of rental housing units in the United States increased more slowly than owner-occupied dwelling units, it did so in a much more dispersed fashion than historically had been the case. Thus rental housing programs have a far wider significance than to central cities alone.

The areal pattern of owner-occupied housing is even more accentuated than that of the rental sector. In central cities, for example, the number of owner-occupied units from 1970 to 1983 increased by slightly over 2.0 million. During the same period the net gain in suburbia was nearly four times that amount (7 million), with a 5.8-million-unit increase experienced outside of SMSAs.

The sum of these two processes, i.e., the total number of occupied units by area, regardless of tenure, is shown at the top of Exhibit 7-3. Overall, the number of occupied housing units in central cities in the 13 years from 1970 to 1983 increased by 3.8 million; in contrast, the growth in suburbia was 10.2-million units, while the gains outside of SMSAs approached 7.3-million units. For every unit-increase in cen-

EXHIBIT 7-3

Occupied Housing Units, Tenure by SMSA Status: 1970, 1976 and 1983
(Numbers in thousands)

| | | | Inside SMSAs | | |
	Total	Total	In Central Cities	Not in Central Cities	Out-side SMSAs
Occupied Units					
1970: Number	63,445	43,859	21,395	22,464	19,586
Percent	100.0	69.1	33.7	35.4	30.9
1976: Number	74,005	50,452	22,930	27,522	23,553
Percent	100.0	68.2	31.0	37.2	31.8
1983: Number	84,638	57,798	25,161	32,637	26,840
Percent	100.0	68.3	29.7	38.6	31.7
Owner Occupied					
1970: Number	39,886	26,090	10,300	15,790	13,796
Percent	100.0	65.4	25.8	39.6	34.6
1976: Number	47,904	30,895	11,349	19,546	17,009
Percent	100.0	64.5	23.7	40.8	35.5
1983: Number	54,724	35,166	12,372	22,794	19,558
Percent	100.0	64.3	22.6	41.7	35.7
Renter Occupied					
1970: Number	23,560	17,769	11,095	6,674	5,790
Percent	100.0	75.4	47.1	28.3	24.6
1976: Number	26,101	19,557	11,581	7,976	6,544
Percent	100.0	74.9	44.4	30.6	25.1
1983: Number	29,914	22,632	12,788	9,844	7,282
Percent	100.0	75.7	42.7	32.9	24.3

Source: U.S. Department of Commerce, U.S. Bureau of the Census, Current Housing Reports, Series H-150-83, *General Housing Characteristics for the United States and Regions: 1983, Annual Housing Survey: 1983, Part A,* U.S. Department of Housing and Urban Development, sponsor. Washington, D.C.: U.S. Government Printing Office, 1985

tral cities, there were three in suburbia, and two in areas outside of metropolitan areas.

By 1983, *less than one-third (29.7 percent) of the nation's occupied housing stock was in central cities. Indeed, the number of housing units outside SMSAs exceeded the number within central cities. To the degree that housing programs, therefore, are specifically geared for central cities, they may have difficulty securing as broad a constituency and support level as was once the case.*

Housing Tenure Trends and Race

In reviewing the changes in housing tenure over time, it is worthwhile to secure a longer perspective. The data in Exhibit 7-4, therefore, covers the decades from 1920 to 1980, and for individual years to 1983. The United States was long a nation predominantly of renters. In 1920, 54.4 percent of all occupied housing units were rental while 45.6 percent were owner-occupied. The proportion of homeownership accelerated in the relative prosperity of the 1920s. By 1930 the proportion of homeowners had moved up to 47.8 percent. The disastrous impact of the Great Depression was reflected in a retreat to 43.6 percent at the end of the decade (1940).

It was the enormous expansion of homeownership through increased sophistication of mortgage mechanisms as well as the forced savings accumulated during war-induced prosperity that moved American housing ownership past the halfway mark. By 1950, the 55.0 percent level was achieved, with continued increments experienced through 1980 to 64.4 percent.

In the lower part of Exhibit 7-4, the data are partitioned by race. In 1920 less than one-quarter—23.9 percent—of non-white households resided in owner-occupied units, a proportion less than half that of whites (48.2 percent). While non-whites still lag, even allowing for changes in racial coverage, their increased homeownership is indicated by the statistics for 1983: the ratio of homeownership of whites to non-whites was approximately three to two—67.7 percent versus 46.2 percent.

While the pattern of change is pervasive, there are substantial regional variations in homeownership by race. These are indicated in Exhibit 7-5. More than half (51.1 percent) of all black households in the South as of 1983 owned their own homes. The Northeast, in contrast, was characterized by only a 32.7 percent black-ownership rate, far lower than any other region.

The incidence of homeownership for blacks, regardless of whether central cities, suburban areas, or areas outside SMSAs are considered,

EXHIBIT 7-4

Occupied Housing Units—Tenure by Race of Household Head: 1920 to 1980
(Numbers in thousands)

Year, Race, and Residence	Total Occupied	Owner Occupied		Renter Occupied	
		Number	*Percent*	*Number*	*Percent*
Total					
1920	24,352	11,114	45.6%	13,238	54.4%
1930	29,905	14,280	47.8	15,624	52.2
1940	34,855	15,196	43.6	19,659	56.4
1950	42,826	23,560	55.0	19,266	45.0
1960	53,024	32,797	61.9	20,227	38.1
1970	63,445	39,886	62.9	23,560	37.1
1980	80,390	51,795	64.4	28,595	35.6
1983	84,638	54,724	64.7	29,914	35.4
Race					
White					
1920	21,826	10,511	48.2%	11,315	51.8%
1930	26,983	13,544	50.2	13,439	49.8
1940	31,561	14,418	45.7	17,143	54.3
1950	39,044	22,241	57.0	16,803	43.0
1960	47,880	30,823	64.4	17,057	35.6
1970	56,606	37,005	65.4	19,601	34.6
1980	68,810	46,671	67.8	22,139	32.2
1983	72,562	49,144	67.7	23,418	32.3
Black and "Other"					
1920	2,526	603	23.9%	1,923	76.1%
1930	2,922	737	25.2	2,185	74.8
1940	3,293	778	23.6	2,516	76.4
1950	3,783	1,319	34.9	2,464	65.1
1960	5,144	1,974	38.4	3,171	61.6
1970	6,839	2,881	42.1	3,959	57.9
1980	11,580	5,124	44.2	6,456	55.8
1983	12,076	5,580	46.2	6,496	53.8

Note: As of April 1, except 1983 (October). Statistics on the number of occupied units are essentially comparable although identified by various terms: the term "family" applies to figures for 1920 and 1930; "occupied dwelling unit," 1940 and 1950; and "occupied housing units," 1960 to 1983. For 1920, includes the small number of quasi-families; for 1930, represents private families only. Prior to 1960, excludes Hawaii and Alaska. Tenure allocated for housing units which did not report.

Source: U.S. Bureau of the Census, *Statistical Abstract of the United States: 1985* (105th Edition), Washington, D.C., 1984

EXHIBIT 7-5

Occupied Housing Units – Percent of Home Ownership, by Race of Household Head, Inside and Outside SMSAs, by Region: 1960 to 1983

(Refers to 243 standard metropolitan statistical areas (SMSAs) as defined in 1970 Census Publication)

		Total		Inside SMSAs Total		In Central Cities		Not in Central Cities		Outside SMSAs	
		White	Black	White	Black	White	Black	White	Black	White	Black
1960:	United States	64.4	38.4	62.1	35.7	51.1	31.7	73.4	51.6	69.0	44.8
	Northeast	58.1	27.0	55.5	26.4	37.5	22.3	72.6	46.7	70.0	42.0
	Midwest	69.1	35.8	67.3	34.2	56.0	31.4	79.2	56.5	72.0	54.3
	South	66.4	41.6	65.9	39.7	60.5	35.9	72.3	51.3	67.1	43.6
	West	62.5	44.6	61.6	42.5	55.0	38.4	67.7	54.0	65.5	54.6
1970:	United States	65.4	41.6	62.3	38.5	51.3	34.8	71.1	54.1	72.1	51.7
	Northeast	60.4	28.6	57.4	28.1	38.8	24.2	71.7	47.3	72.1	42.6
	Midwest	70.2	42.0	67.8	41.3	56.5	38.9	76.5	58.8	74.4	56.3
	South	68.2	46.9	65.3	43.4	59.5	39.1	70.7	57.3	71.9	52.0
	West	60.2	40.1	58.6	40.0	52.0	36.6	63.6	49.6	66.1	42.1
1983:	United States	67.7	45.0	64.4	40.9	53.1	36.9	71.4	51.9	73.5	59.3
	Northeast	63.9	32.7	60.7	32.3	41.7	27.9	72.5	48.5	74.2	40.9
	Midwest	71.8	43.4	69.8	42.9	60.2	40.2	75.4	55.1	75.1	50.8
	South	71.4	51.1	67.7	45.0	58.3	39.5	73.9	57.3	75.9	61.0
	West	61.0	39.6	59.0	39.0	52.6	39.1	63.1	38.9	68.0	52.3

Note: For 1960 represents "Black and 'Other'."

Source: U.S. Department of Commerce, U.S. Bureau of the Census, Current Housing Reports, Series H-150-83, *General Housing Characteristics for the United States and Regions: 1983, Annual Housing Survey: 1983, Part A*, U.S. Department of Housing and Urban Development, sponsor. Washington, D.C.: U.S. Government Printing Office, 1985

is consistently lower than holds true for whites. The ratios as of 1983 are relatively constant, at the three-to-two level. On the whole, however, the data indicate an increased proportion of minority homeownership and certainly one which is not confined to any region or areal subset within the country.

The only exception is those areas of heavy black inmigration and general population growth. In the suburban areas, for example, black-ownership rates tended to decline between 1970 and 1983. This pattern is mainly a function of very large influxes of blacks responding to suburban rental opportunities. This tends to obscure the expansion in the absolute number of black suburban homeowners.

The march of the United States toward homeownership regardless of race—which for the moment we can synonymize with improvement in housing quality—dominated post-World War II America. Whether it can be sustained throughout the century concerns planners, developers, and policymakers alike.

8

Housing Production Cycles

The enviable track record compiled by America's "shelterers" has not been the result of a sustained smooth process. The housing industry rides a perilous roller coaster; extreme variations in construction rates beget a level of risk and uncertainty with few competitors within the American economic system.

The key monitor of the residential construction process is the level of housing starts. (As defined by the Census Bureau, the start of construction of a privately owned housing unit is when excavation begins for the footings or foundations of a building intended primarily as a housekeeping residential structure and designed for nontransient occupancy. All housing units in a multifamily building are defined as being started when excavation for the building has begun.) Exhibit 8-1 provides annual housing-start averages for the decades between 1890 and 1980 and the equivalent for 1980 through 1985. For the first 30 years of this period, from 1890 through 1919, average annual starts hovered in the 300,000 range; it was the 1920s which emerged as the first of America's golden housing decades. A sudden housing eruption in post-World War I America generated an average of over 700,000 starts annually. But this pace was quickly relegated to history.

The drastic toll of the Great Crash and the economic depression which followed is evidenced by a decline that has no parallel in modern times, a drop of fully 60 percent. It should be noted that in the worst of those years—1933—the level of starts actually was under 100,000 units, barely 10 percent of the 1925 high. Beginning with World War II-generated worker housing, the 1940s marked a reversal, but only to the level of two decades before.

Wartime shortages eventually disappeared, as the age of the great tract developers came to full bloom. Aided by the GI and VA mortgage apparatus, housing became a true locomotive of the American economy. There were more than 1.5 million average new starts in the

EXHIBIT 8-1

New Housing Units Started, Public and Private, U.S. Total: 1890 to 1985
(numbers rounded to thousands)

Period	Annual Average Housing Starts
1890–1899	294,000
1900–1909	361,000
1910–1919	359,000
1920–1929	703,000
1930–1939	273,000
1940–1949	744,000
1950–1959	1,507,000
1960–1969	1,442,000
1970–1979	1,548,000
1980–1985	1,449,000

Note: Prior to 1960, excludes farm housing

Sources: U.S. Department of Commerce, Bureau of the Census, *Historical Statistics of the United States, Colonial Times to 1970, Bicentennial Edition, Part I* (Washington, D.C.: U.S. Government Printing Office, 1975); U.S. Bureau of the Census, *Construction Reports*, Series C-20, "Housing Starts," Monthly

1950s, nearly equal in magnitude to the combined annual levels of the preceding thirty years. And this is the proximate level which has continued through the 1980s.

The Annual Roller Coaster

Decade-long averages smooth variation and mask the true underlying turbulence within the market. Housing has been subject to a continuous boom–bust cycle, scarcely matched even by the most volatile of other economic sectors. This is illustrated in Exhibit 8-2, which provides annual housing starts from 1964 through 1985. The early portions of the period detailed in the exhibit (pre-1970) cover part of the record expansion of the business cycle which took place from 1961 to 1969—an expansion lasting an unparalleled 105 months. Yet starts still fluctuated during this period, with the variation from high- to low-start years exceeding 20 percent.

After this extraordinary record of relative stability became history, the vagaries of the business cycle reappeared, and with them a basic reality: residential investment bears the brunt of national economic cyclicity.

As detailed in Exhibit 8-2, housing starts began in the 1970s at the 1.4-million level. During the next three years (1971 through 1973), they averaged fully 50 percent higher, only to turn down with equal precipitousness during 1974–1975; housing starts in 1975 (1.2 million) were less than half those of 1972 (2.4 million). The patient recovered with incredible vigor: by 1977–1978, the 2-million-start level once more was achieved. However, the roller coaster was soon to return to the ravine; housing starts were virtually halved by 1981–1982. The

EXHIBIT 8-2

New Privately Owned Housing Units Started, by Structure Size, United States Total: 1970 to 1985[1]

			In Structures With					
	Total		1 Unit		2 to 4 Units		5 Units or More	
Year	Number	Percent	Number	Percent	Number	Percent	Number	Percent
1964	1,529	100.0%	971	63.5%	108	7.1%	450	29.4%
1965	1,473	100.0	964	65.4	87	5.9	422	28.6
1966	1,165	100.0	779	66.9	61	5.2	325	27.9
1967	1,292	100.0	844	65.3	72	5.6	376	29.1
1968	1,508	100.0	899	59.6	82	5.4	527	34.9
1969	1,467	100.0	811	55.3	85	5.8	571	38.9
1970	1,434	100.0	813	56.7	85	5.9	536	37.4
1971	2,052	100.0	1,151	56.1	120	5.8	781	38.1
1972	2,356	100.0	1,309	55.6	141	6.0	906	38.5
1973	2,045	100.0	1,132	55.4	118	5.8	795	38.9
1974	1,338	100.0	888	66.4	68	5.1	382	28.6
1975	1,160	100.0	892	76.9	64	5.5	204	17.6
1976	1,538	100.0	1,162	75.5	87	5.7	289	18.8
1977	1,987	100.0	1,451	73.0	122	6.1	414	20.8
1978	2,020	100.0	1,433	70.9	125	6.2	462	22.9
1979	1,745	100.0	1,194	68.4	122	7.0	429	24.6
1980	1,292	100.0	852	65.9	109	8.4	331	25.6
1981	1,084	100.0	705	65.0	91	8.4	288	26.6
1982	1,062	100.0	663	62.4	80	7.5	320	30.1
1983	1,703	100.0	1,068	62.7	114	6.7	522	30.7
1984	1,750	100.0	1,084	61.9	121	6.9	544	31.1
1985	1,742	100.0	1,072	61.5	93	5.3	576	33.1

Note: 1. Numbers and percents may not add due to rounding.

Source: U.S. Bureau of the Census, *Construction Reports*, Series C-20, "Housing Starts," Monthly

70-percent resurgence of 1983 was equally sudden and was not fore-seen by economic forecasters. While starts in subsequent years contin-ued in a strongly positive pattern, the crystal balls of the professional seers rarely had been so uncertain.

There is no rigid immutability to housing cycles. As the data in Exhibit 8-2 are reviewed, however, they suggest that the typical down-turn in housing has been two to three years in length, the typical upturn rarely longer than three or, at most, four years.

Indeed, a thesis can be advanced that <u>an upsurge actually depends upon a base of frustrated demand generated by recessionary downswings;</u> once saturated, the underlying positive dynamics begin to falter in their turn. Thus the very precipitousness of the housing downturn of the early 1980s provided the launching platform for the high plateau of housing production in the mid-decade years. The latter boom, in turn, was certainly as vigorous as in any comparable period in the nation's history—particularly when the impact of direct government-subsidy programs (which characterized the early 1970s' surge) is discounted.

Variation by Configuration

From the viewpoint of both consumers and producers, the abrupt changes in total production are even more variable when the focus is on configuration. Single-family (1-unit) units accounted for more than three-quarters of total starts in 1976, but amounted to little more than half of 1973's total. (It should be noted in this context that in addition to single-family detached houses, the Census Bureau defines as one-unit structures, attached units which are separated from adjoining units by a ground-to-roof wall, no common attic or basement, and having separate utilities which are not shared with any of the other units.)

It is multi-unit structures, i.e., those with five units or more, in which the turbulence of the market—to say nothing of builders' mistakes—is most accentuated. Thus, the great wave of federal sup-port for low-income, multifamily housing, in combination with a first generation condominium boom, particularly in Florida, nearly tripled multifamily starts from 325,000 units in 1966 to over 900,000 units in 1972.

But the impact of a shift in federal housing policy—and the deflation of the condominium boom of the early 1970s—burst the multi-unit balloon. Only 204,000 starts were achieved in structures with five units or more in 1975, barely one-fifth of the 1972 peak. By 1983, a more vigorous housing market—in combination with a generous investment tax policy—increased that total by two and one-half times, to well over one-half-million starts. Even at this level, multifamily starts accounted for only 30 percent of total, far lower than their share (nearly 40 percent) at the beginning of the decade.

The Gross National Product and Housing

The patterns of variation discussed above—both absolute and in configuration—do not take place in an economic vacuum, but are highly dependent on the business cycle (which is measured by Gross National Product [GNP]). *In this context, however, housing is not solely a passive responder to the national economy, but also a key contributor to it. Housing historically has been viewed as a powerful countercyclical tool, either as a stimulus leading the way out of recession, and pulling the balance of American economy with it—or as a damper banking the flames of an overheated business cycle.*

The basic interrelationships are indicated in Exhibit 8-3, which provides data on GNP (in constant 1982 dollars) from 1964 through 1985, together with total private housing starts. In general, the data mirror the spectrum of economic elation and trauma besetting America since 1970: business-cycle peaks in 1973 and 1978–1979, the energy crises of 1973–1974 and 1979–1980 which underlay subsequent recessions (noted in the exhibit), and the economic recovery which dominated the mid-1980s. The correspondence between the two data series is evident, as every residential builder will testify.

Accentuating this picture is a clear multiplier effect—relatively small dips in GNP are reflected in enormous downturns in housing. A less-than-2-percent downturn in GNP from 1973 to 1975 had as its parallel a near-halving of private housing starts. Conversely, during business-cycle peaks, as in 1972–1973, 1978, and 1983–1985, the recovery rate in starts is equally accentuated.

Housing starts vary enormously even within the calendar year, regardless of the business cycle (Exhibit 8-4). Thus, in a reasonably solid housing year, 1979, the level of starts in January was less than half those of the early summer. Similarly, 1985—another year of rela-

EXHIBIT 8-3

**Privately Owned Housing Unit Starts and Gross National Product,
U.S. Total: 1964 to 1985**

Year	Gross National Product (in Constant 1982 Dollars) (in billions of dollars)	Privately Owned Housing Unit Starts (numbers in thousands)
1964	$1,973	1,529
1965	2,088	1,473
1966	2,208	1,165
1967	2,271	1,292
1968	2,366	1,508
1969	2,423	1,467
1970	2,416 *	1,434 *
1971	2,485	2,052
1972	2,609	2,356
1973	2,744	2,045
1974	2,729 *	1,338 *
1975	2,695 *	1,160 *
1976	2,827	1,538
1977	2,959	1,987
1978	3,115	2,020
1979	3,192	1,745
1980	3,187 *	1,292 *
1981	3,249 *	1,084 *
1982	3,166 *	1,062 *
1983	3,278	1,703
1984	3,492	1,750
1985	3,571	1,742

Note: * indicates recession year

Sources: U.S. Department of Commerce, Bureau of Economic Analysis, *Survey of Current Business*, Monthly; U.S. Bureau of the Census, *Construction Reports*, Series C-20, "Housing Starts," Monthly

tively steady production—was highlighted by a nearly equivalent seasonal ratio. The requirement of seasonal adjustment in order to annualize housing starts, therefore, is a highly dangerous one. The multipliers that are utilized in the typically low-production months of January, February, March, and December are quite high—the possibility of adjustment error most substantial.

Similarly, housing—by its very nature—requires a long pipeline of preparation. Not uncommonly, major housing developments may have as much as a five-year (and more) period of gestation in order to secure land, zoning agreements, as well as the other elements that make it possible. Despite this, as shown in Exhibit 8-4, there is clear statistical evidence of a capacity to reverse field more abruptly than the normal vision of the housing-production cycle would suggest. Thus, even before the terminal point of the 1981–1982 recession (November), the mid-year pickup in housing—well above normal seasonal vagaries—is evident.

Thus, two basic phenomena are revealed in Exhibit 8-4. First, a seasonality dimension—with starts demonstrating monthly fluctuations during a calendar year—represents a constant, regardless of business-cycle phase. Spring upturns and winter slowdowns are a basic pattern of America's shelter industry.

Second, the monthly data highlight in detail the entrance into, and the emergence out of, the worst recession since the Great Depression. For example, the starts in June of 1982 (91,100) were less than half those of both June 1979 (191,800) and June 1984 (184,000), pre- and post-recession years, respectively. Thus short-term observation periods reveal even further volatility within the production system.

EXHIBIT 8-4

Monthly Privately Owned Housing Units Started,
U.S. Total: 1979–1985
(numbers in thousands)

	1979	1980	1981	1982	1983	1984	1985
January	88.2	73.1	84.5	47.2	91.3	109.1	105.4
February	84.5	79.9	71.9	51.3	96.3	130.0	95.4
March	152.9	85.1	107.8	78.2	134.6	137.5	145.0
April	161.0	96.2	123.0	84.1	135.8	172.7	175.8
May	189.1	91.7	109.9	98.8	174.9	180.7	170.2
June	191.8	116.4	105.8	91.1	173.2	184.0	163.2
July	164.2	120.1	99.9	106.8	161.6	162.1	160.7
August	170.3	129.9	86.3	96.0	176.8	147.4	160.7
September	163.7	138.3	84.1	106.4	154.9	148.5	147.7
October	169.0	152.7	87.2	110.5	159.3	152.3	173.0
November	118.7	112.9	64.6	108.9	136.0	126.2	124.1
December	91.6	95.9	59.1	82.9	108.3	98.9	120.5

Note: Not seasonally adjusted

Source: U.S. Bureau of the Census, *Construction Reports*, Series C-20, "Housing Starts," Monthly

Alternative Investment Parameters

While housing-start compilations serve as the conventional gauge of housing activity—and have become a virtual staple of the popular media's increased economic reporting in the 1980s—broader measures of residential construction confirm all of the preceding phenomena. The data in Exhibits 8-5 and 8-6, secured from the National Income and Product Accounts, detail private nonfarm residential investment, both in absolute (constant 1982 dollars) terms and as a share of GNP.

EXHIBIT 8-5

Gross National Product and Gross Private Domestic Residential Investment: 1964 to 1985

Year	Gross National Product (in constant 1982 dollars) (in billions of dollars)	Private Residential Investment (in constant 1982 dollars) (in billions of dollars)	
		Total	Percent
1964	$1,973	$115	5.8%
1965	2,088	114	5.5
1966	2,208	103	4.7
1967	2,271	101	4.4
1968	2,366	116	4.9
1969	2,423	115	4.7
1970	2,416 *	109 *	4.5
1971	2,485	141	5.7
1972	2,609	167	6.4
1973	2,744	163	5.9
1974	2,729 *	130 *	4.8
1975	2,695 *	115 *	4.3
1976	2,827	141	5.0
1977	2,959	168	5.7
1978	3,115	178	5.7
1979	3,192	171	5.4
1980	3,187 *	137 *	4.3
1981	3,249 *	127 *	3.9
1982	3,166 *	105 *	3.3
1983	3,278	149	4.5
1984	3,492	168	4.8
1985	3,571	171	4.8

Note: * indicates recession year

Source: U.S. Department of Commerce, Bureau of Economic Analysis, *Survey of Current Business*, Monthly

EXHIBIT 8-6

Quarterly Gross National Product and Gross Private Domestic Residential Investment: 1980 to 1985

Year and Quarter	Gross National Product *(in constant 1982 dollars) (in billions of dollars)*	Private Residential Investment *(in constant 1982 dollars) (in billions of dollars)*	
		Total	*Percent*
1980 I	$3,233	$155	4.8%
II	3,157	124	3.9
III	3,159	127	4.0
IV	3,199	142	4.4
1981 I	$3,261	$139	4.3%
II	3,250	134	4.1
III	3,265	122	3.7
IV	3,219	110	3.4
1982 I	$3,170	$101	3.2%
II	3,180	103	3.2
III	3,155	100	3.2
IV	3,159	116	3.7
1983 I	$3,191	$127	4.0%
II	3,259	146	4.5
III	3,303	162	4.9
IV	3,357	160	4.8
1984 I	$3,449	$167	4.8%
II	3,493	170	4.9
III	3,510	171	4.9
IV	3,516	166	4.7
1985 I	$3,548	$167	4.7%
II	3,557	170	4.8
III	3,584	173	4.8
IV	3,595	176	4.9

Source: U.S. Department of Commerce, Bureau of Economic Analysis, *Survey of Current Business*, Monthly

As shown in Exhibit 8-5, peak residential investment years correspond to broad economic upswings (1971–1973, 1977–1979, and 1983–1985) while investment troughs are linked to recessionary lows (1970, 1975 and 1982). Thus non-farm residential investment clearly mirrors with vigor the swings of the business cycle. The impression of vulnerability was further reinforced when the sharp recession of 1981–82 yielded a level of residential investment (in 1982) at the low point for the more than 20-year period which is illustrated.

It is striking to note that while some critics of housing investment have viewed it as competitive to, and impacting on, the reindustrialization of America, the actual percentage of GNP invested in shelter during the 1980s does not show any convincing pattern of increase; rather, it has been well toward the lower end of its historic pattern.

This conclusion is further illustrated in Exhibit 8-6, which provides quarterly data from 1980 through 1985 for both GNP and residential investment. The pattern gives further definition to the tight linkage between total private nonfarm residential investment and the nation's economy as a whole, and documents the impact on housing in monetary terms upon entering into and exiting from the recessionary lows of the business cycle.

An alternative base of comparison, and an additional amplification of housing's volatility, is the Census Bureau data series tracking the value of new construction put in place. As detailed in Exhibit 8-7 (in constant 1977 dollars), *residential construction demonstrates far more severe cyclical swings than total new construction* (which includes both non-residential and residential components). During the business-cycle peaks of the post-1970 period, new housing units accounted for over 36 percent of total new construction; when the economy stumbled—in 1981 and 1982, for example—the share dropped to 25 percent and below.

Single-family dwellings (1-unit) exhibit even greater variation. In 1977, for example, the $55 billion of new, single-family construction accounted for 31.7 percent of the value of total new construction put in place. But in 1982, its share tumbled to 15 percent as its construction value fell to $22.5 billion, barely 40 percent of the 1977 peak. In contrast, units constructed in buildings with two or more units have demonstrated more stability post 1974 (after the pipeline of federal housing funding emptied out, and the early condominium boom collapsed).

Changing Shelter Formats

Shifts in housing production also occur in the shape and format of inventory additions, often occasioned by shifting market forces. As the

EXHIBIT 8-7

Value of New Construction Put in Place in Constant 1977 Dollars: 1970 to 1985

Year	Total New Construction	Total Residential Buildings		Residential Components								
				Total		New Housing Units				Additions, Alterations		Non-Housekeeping	
						1 Unit		2 or More Units					
		Total	Percent	Total	Percent	Total	Percent	Total	Percent	Total	Percent	Total	Percent
1970	167,618	57,581	34.4%	43,873	26.2%	26,656	15.9%	17,217	10.3%	11,252	6.7%	2,456	1.5%
1973	198,850	87,033	43.8	72,984	36.7	44,632	22.4	28,352	14.3	10,597	5.3	3,451	1.7
1974	170,289	66,393	39.0	53,596	31.5	34,593	20.3	19,003	11.2	10,563	6.2	2,233	1.3
1975	152,198	56,074	36.8	41,506	27.3	33,051	21.7	8,455	5.6	13,190	8.7	1,378	0.9
1976	163,457	67,737	41.4	52,884	32.4	44,797	27.4	8,087	4.9	13,805	8.4	1,049	0.6
1977	173,395	80,689	46.5	67,472	37.8	55,016	31.7	10,456	6.0	14,218	8.2	1,000	0.6
1978	181,987	81,226	44.6	65,891	36.2	54,223	29.8	11,668	6.4	14,231	7.8	1,104	0.6
1979	178,951	75,958	42.4	60,268	33.7	46,630	26.1	13,638	7.6	14,003	7.8	1,687	0.9
1980	161,098	60,911	37.8	44,080	27.4	31,858	19.8	12,223	7.6	14,739	9.1	2,092	1.3
1981	157,387	55,893	35.5	40,484	25.7	28,686	18.2	11,798	7.5	12,911	8.2	2,497	1.6
1982	153,636	50,900	33.1	36,443	23.7	26,188	17.0	10,255	6.7	11,793	7.7	2,664	1.7
1983	170,869	74,973	43.9	59,122	34.6	44,608	26.1	14,514	8.5	12,533	7.3	3,318	1.9
1984	191,225	85,681	44.8	67,689	35.4	50,247	26.3	17,442	9.1	N/A	–	4,139	2.2
1985	203,860	86,790	42.6	66,420	32.6	49,078	24.1	17,343	8.5	N/A	–	4,450	2.2

Source: U.S. Bureau of the Census, *Construction Reports*, Series C-30, "Value of New Construction Put in Place," Monthly

housing buying power of Americans stumbled in the late 1970s and 1980s (examined in detail in Chapter 6), the traditional detached single-family dwelling lost market share. In its stead, attached single-family units (townhouses) secured increasing penetration.

Exhibit 8-8 documents this basic reality. In 1975, townhouses accounted for only 4.3 percent of total single-family-unit starts. This share steadily increased over the next eight years, surging to 16 percent by 1983. Production of this configuration more than doubled in absolute terms between 1982 and 1984—from 86,000 to 210,000 units—and quintupled between 1975 and 1984.

A parallel market shift is evident in terms of condominium ownership formats. While not constrained to townhouse configurations (they are also applicable to multifamily dwellings), condominium shares of total housing starts closely replicate the townhouse pattern described above. As shown in Exhibit 8-9, condominiums accounted for only 5.6

EXHIBIT 8-8

**Townhouse Starts and Share of Single-Family Units,
U.S. Total: 1973 to 1985
(numbers in thousands)**

Year	Single Family Total		Detached		Townhouses	
	Number	*Percent*	*Number*	*Percent*	*Number*	*Percent*
1973	1,132	100.0%	970	91.6%	89	8.4%
1974	888	100.0	822	92.6	66	7.4
1975	892	100.0	854	95.7	38	4.3
1976	1,162	100.0	1,107	95.3	55	4.7
1977	1,451	100.0	1,377	94.9	74	5.1
1978	1,433	100.0	1,347	94.0	86	6.0
1979	1,194	100.0	1,096	91.8	98	8.2
1980	852	100.0	774	90.8	78	9.2
1981	705	100.0	628	89.1	77	10.9
1982	663	100.0	577	87.0	86	13.0
1983	1,068	100.0	896	83.9	171	16.0
1984	1,084	100.0	875	80.7	210	19.4
1985	1,072	100.0	905	84.4	167	15.6

Note: Percentages in 1973 based on total reported; 73,000 units not specified

Source: U.S. Bureau of the Census, *Construction Reports*, Series C-20, "Housing Starts," Monthly

EXHIBIT 8-9

Condominium Starts, U.S. Total, 1973 to 1985
(numbers in thousands)

| | Total Condominiums | | Structure Type | |
| | | | | |
Year	Number	Percent of Total Private Starts	Single-Family Units	Multifamily Units
1973	241	11.8%	69	172
1974	176	13.2	46	130
1975	65	5.6	20	45
1976	94	6.1	30	64
1977	132	6.6	41	91
1978	155	7.7	42	113
1979	199	11.4	43	156
1980	185	14.3	35	150
1981	181	16.7	36	145
1982	170	16.0	40	130
1983	276	16.2	77	199
1984	291	16.6	96	194
1985	225	12.9	79	146

Source: U.S. Bureau of the Census, *Construction Reports*, Series C-20, "Housing Starts," Monthly

percent of total starts in 1975. (The higher market shares in 1973 and 1974 marked the early, and ultimately abortive, condominium boom centered in Florida in the early 1970s.) By the 1980s, condominiums increased their market presence to over 16 percent. And the great majority of these starts were set in multifamily configurations. Thus, while not mutually exclusive, the surging growth in townhouse configurations and condominium formats was striking in the first half of the 1980s.

One other, and often overlooked, dimension of the nation's housing production system is mobile homes. (As defined by the Census Bureau, a mobile home is a moveable dwelling 8 feet or more wide and 40 feet or more long, designed to be towed on its own chassis, with transportation gear integral to the unit when it leaves the factory, and without need of a permanent foundation. These mobile homes include multiwides, which are counted as single units, and expandable mobile homes. Excluded are travel trailers, motor homes, and modular housing.) Exhibit 8-10 provides the basic statistics on mobile home ship-ments in the United States from 1965 to 1984.

With the exception of the pre-oil-embargo boom (1968–1973), manufacturers' shipments of mobile homes have added approximately one-quarter of a million new additions annually to America's housing stock. Thus they represent a far-from-trivial component of the shelter system; while the mobile-home shipment stream is also afflicted by cyclical variability (the nadir of 1975 stands out prominently), the impact is much more muted. The general economic recovery of 1983 saw mobile-home production increase by slightly more than 20 per-cent, from 240,000 units in 1982 to 296,000 units in 1983. Conven-

EXHIBIT 8-10

**Manufacturers' Shipments of Mobile Homes and Privately Owned
Housing Units Started, U.S. Total: 1965 to 1985
(Numbers in Thousands)**

Year	Manufacturers' Shipments of Mobile Homes	Single-Family Structures Started Plus Mobile Home Shipments	Total Private Housing Units Started Plus Mobile Home Shipments
1965	217	1,180	1,689
1966	217	996	1,382
1967	240	1,084	1,532
1968	318	1,217	1,826
1969	413	1,223	1,879
1970	401	1,214	1,835
1971	497	1,648	2,549
1972	576	1,885	2,933
1973	567	1,699	2,612
1974	329	1,217	1,667
1975	213	1,105	1,373
1976	246	1,409	1,784
1977	277	1,728	2,264
1978	276	1,709	2,296
1979	277	1,471	2,023
1980	222	1,074	1,514
1981	241	946	1,325
1982	240	902	1,302
1983	296	1,363	1,999
1984	296	1,380	2,045
1985	284	1,356	2,025

Source: U.S. Bureau of the Census, *Construction Reports*, Series C-20, "Housing Starts," Monthly

tional housing starts, in contrast, soared by almost 70 percent during the same period.

Booms and busts intersect the long-term dynamics of America's shelter industry. Housing is both caboose and locomotive to the economy, both a reflection of, and a potent input into, its cycles. Housing's year-to-year vagaries make short-term projections particularly hazardous—a reality accentuated when we turn to regional variations.

9

Regional Shifts Revisited

Superimposed on the swings of the economic cycle are the evolving vigor and pulling power of America's regions. The "Rise of the Sunbelt" and the "Decline of the North" (the Northeast and Midwest states) were not as immutable as the vision of the early 1980s suggested. They nevertheless encompassed very real dynamics strongly impacting the provision of shelter; the pattern of housing production and activity on a regional basis reflected this reality. In the sections which follow, we attempt to provide insight into these changing patterns, as well as to overview the available data series which capsulize and monitor housing development.

Regional Variations in Total Starts

Total privately owned housing unit starts, partitioned by region, are presented in Exhibit 9-1. The data confirm the pattern highlighted earlier: the South and West had been the major gainers from 1970 until the mid-1980s. Housing starts in the Northeast and Midwest faltered, while Sunbelt activity in the aggregate soared. From a baseline in 1970 of approximately 15 percent of the nation's housing starts, the Northeast's share declined to the 10-percent level by the late 1970s, and remained there until the mid-1980s' upswing. By 1985, the Northeast had returned to its market share level of 1970. The early pattern was paralleled by the Midwest as both smokestack areas struggled to adjust to a new industrial reality. The latter region, however, was in greater difficulty, experiencing a marked contraction in starts continuing into the mid-1980s. A 26-percent market share in 1976 diminished to less than 14 percent by 1985. Thus while the economy of the Northeast met the post-industrial imperatives, the Midwest still

HOUSING SUPPLY

EXHIBIT 9-1

New Privately Owned Housing Units Started by Region: 1970 to 1985
(Numbers in thousands)

Year	United States Total	Region			
		Northeast	Midwest	South	West
1970	1,434	218	294	612	311
1971	2,052	264	434	869	486
1972	2,357	329	443	1,057	527
1973	2,045	277	440	899	429
1974	1,338	183	317	553	285
1975	1,160	149	294	442	275
1976	1,538	169	400	569	400
1977	1,987	202	465	783	538
1978	2,020	200	451	824	545
1979	1,745	178	349	748	470
1980	1,292	125	218	643	306
1981	1,084	117	165	562	240
1982	1,062	117	149	591	205
1983	1,703	168	218	935	382
1984	1,750	204	243	866	436
1985	1,733	251	238	778	466

Percent Distribution

Year	United States Total	Northeast	Midwest	South	West
1970	100.0%	15.2%	20.5%	42.7%	21.7%
1971	100.0	12.9	21.2	42.3	23.7
1972	100.0	14.0	18.8	44.8	22.4
1973	100.0	13.5	21.5	44.0	21.0
1974	100.0	13.7	23.7	41.3	21.3
1975	100.0	12.8	25.3	38.1	23.7
1976	100.0	11.0	26.0	37.0	26.0
1977	100.0	10.2	23.4	39.4	27.1
1978	100.0	9.9	22.3	40.8	27.0
1979	100.0	10.2	20.0	42.9	26.9
1980	100.0	9.7	16.9	49.8	23.7
1981	100.0	10.8	15.2	51.8	22.1
1982	100.0	11.0	14.0	55.6	19.3
1983	100.0	9.9	12.8	54.9	22.4
1984	100.0	11.7	13.9	49.5	24.9
1985	100.0	14.5	13.7	44.9	26.9

Source: U.S. Bureau of the Census, *Construction Reports*, Series C-20, "Housing Starts," Monthly

suffered the pangs of industrial withdrawal, and its housing pulling power reflected this.

The situation was far different in the South. At the beginning of the 1970s, it secured roughly 42 percent of the nation's total starts; ten years later, the South's share was well over 50 percent, but then retreated to its earlier posture. The western pattern is much more complex. Its peak share of market was 27 percent in 1977 and 1978. While one tends to equate the West with California, the region also includes the Mountain states. The boom–bust experience of the energy and natural resources developments in the latter territories has undoubtedly contributed to the West's housing dynamics. By the bottom of the 1981–1982 recession, its share fell below 20 percent. The subsequent recovery for the region as a whole masked the trauma that befell the energy patch. Nonetheless, by mid-decade the pattern of momentum in housing starts showed the Sunbelt (the South and West) with a 72-percent share, the older Frostbelt with 28 percent.

But housing starts, by their very definition, are not coterminous with completions. As shown in Exhibit 9-2, the lag time which is involved—compounded by financial vagaries—alters the pattern; the basic parameters of comparative regional vigor, however, are quite similar.

As defined by the Census Bureau, one-unit structures are considered completed when all finish flooring has been installed (or carpeting, if used in place of finish flooring). If the building is occupied before all construction is finished, it is classified as completed at the time of occupancy. In buildings with two or more housing units, all the units in the building are counted as completed when 50 percent or more of the units are occupied or available for occupancy.

In both Exhibits 9-1 and 9-2, the enormous variations in housing activity as a function of the economic cycle in the nation as a whole—as well as in each of its regions—are evident. When these are further compounded by the rifle-shot recession of the early 1980s, which particularly impacted the aging industrial heartland, the results are dramatic indeed. In 1977 there were 465,000 privately owned housing starts in the Midwest region; by 1982, five years later, the figure was well under one-third of that total—149,000 units.

The South represents a much more benign picture, with its increasing share of population essentially buffering its housing industry (at least by northern standards) from national economic downturns.

Mobile Homes

The mobile-home sector of the housing industry has demonstrated even greater regional biases. Exhibit 9-3, which provides data on

EXHIBIT 9-2

New Privately Owned Housing Units Completed by Region:[1]   1970 to 1985
(Numbers in thousands)

Year	United States Total	Region			
		Northeast	Midwest	South	West
1970	1,401	N.A.	N.A.	N.A.	N.A.
1971	1,706	226	348	727	405
1972	1,971	280	405	828	458
1973	2,014	286	429	846	453
1974	1,692	226	369	738	359
1975	1,297	182	308	522	285
1976	1,362	169	353	506	335
1977	1,657	177	400	636	444
1978	1,868	182	417	752	517
1979	1,871	188	415	762	506
1980	1,502	146	274	696	386
1981	1,266	127	218	626	294
1982	1,005	120	143	539	203
1983	1,390	139	201	746	305
1984	1,652	168	221	867	396
1985	1,703	214	230	812	447
		Percent Distribution			
1970	100.0%	N.A.	N.A.	N.A.	N.A.
1971	100.0	13.2%	20.4%	42.6%	23.7%
1972	100.0	14.2	20.5	42.0	23.2
1973	100.0	14.2	21.3	42.0	22.5
1974	100.0	13.4	21.8	43.6	21.2
1975	100.0	14.0	23.7	40.2	22.0
1976	100.0	12.4	25.9	37.2	24.6
1977	100.0	10.7	24.1	38.4	26.8
1978	100.0	9.7	22.3	40.3	27.7
1979	100.0	10.0	22.2	40.7	27.0
1980	100.0	9.7	18.2	46.3	25.7
1981	100.0	10.0	17.2	49.4	23.2
1982	100.0	12.0	14.2	53.6	20.2
1983	100.0	10.0	14.5	53.7	21.9
1984	100.0	10.2	13.4	52.5	24.0
1985	100.0	12.6	13.5	47.7	26.2

Note: 1. Components may not add due to rounding.

Source: U.S. Bureau of the Census, *Construction Reports*, Series C-25, "Characteristics of New Housing" (Washington, D.C.: U.S. Government Printing Office, Annual)

EXHIBIT 9-3

New Mobile Homes Placed for Residential Use by Region: 1974 to 1985
(Numbers in thousands)

Year	United States Total	Region			
		Northeast	*Midwest*	*South*	*West*
1974	332.0	23.3	67.5	170.8	70.4
1975	229.3	14.7	48.5	110.8	55.2
1976	249.6	16.8	51.5	114.8	66.5
1977	257.5	16.7	50.7	112.5	77.7
1978	279.9	17.4	49.5	135.3	77.7
1979	279.9	16.9	47.3	145.2	70.5
1980	233.7	12.3	32.3	140.3	48.7
1981	229.2	12.0	30.1	143.5	43.6
1982	234.1	12.4	25.6	161.1	35.0
1983	278.1	16.3	34.3	186.0	41.4
1984	287.9	19.8	35.2	193.4	39.4
1985	283.4	20.2	38.6	187.6	36.9
		Percent Distribution			
1974	100.0%	7.0%	20.3%	51.4%	21.2%
1975	100.0	6.4	21.1	48.3	24.1
1976	100.0	6.7	20.6	46.0	26.6
1977	100.0	6.5	19.7	43.7	30.2
1978	100.0	6.2	17.7	48.3	27.8
1979	100.0	6.0	16.9	51.9	25.2
1980	100.0	5.3	13.8	60.0	20.8
1981	100.0	5.2	13.1	62.6	19.0
1982	100.0	5.2	11.1	68.9	14.9
1983	100.0	5.9	12.3	66.9	14.9
1984	100.0	6.9	12.2	67.2	13.7
1985	100.0	7.1	13.6	66.2	13.0

Note: Components may not add due to rounding.

Source: U.S. Bureau of the Census, *Construction Reports*, Series C-20, "Housing Starts," Monthly

mobile homes placed for residential use by region from 1974 to 1975, highlights a growing disparity: during the first half of the 1980s, the South and West combined secured over 80 percent of all mobile-home placements. Indeed, the South's share alone exceeded the two-thirds level, while the West's absolute increment, until 1983, had exceeded the combined placements of the Northeast and Midwest states.

The lack of receptivity to this shelter configuration in the Northeast, whether as a function of consumer demand or local governmental inhibitions (or both), is revealed by a market share of less than 7 percent, virtually half its share of total conventional housing starts (12 percent). Mobile-home placements in the South alone exceeded the absolute level of total housing starts in the Northeast in the early-1980s. Thus, the widespread use of this residential configuration in the southern tier of the United States provided reinforcement to the region's national housing dominance.

The Census definition of mobile homes, cited earlier, considerably underestimates the importance of "manufactured housing" as a whole. While once nearly completely subsumed under the mobile-home label, increasingly—both in configuration and in statistical count, if not in its actual construction—it tends to be lodged under the conventional housing rubric. *The blurring of definitions as a function of technology certainly is not unique to housing; but the observer should be warned that the statistical partitions are breaking down as developers increasingly mix stick-built, component, modular, and sometimes, manufactured and "mobile" units within a single development.*

Townhouses

Townhouse development, i.e., attached single-family dwellings, experienced a record surge in both market share and absolute level in the 1980s. Did this herald a new housing reality in America? Certainly, comparable configurations were a feature of urban life well before the turn of the century. The masonry row housing of Baltimore or Philadelphia had its equivalent in Boston and Brooklyn—and on a much more modest level, typically using wood-frame construction, in southern cities as well. The burst of housing exuberance after World War II largely focused on detached, one-family housing as the preferred market good. But, by the mid-1980s there was an increased level of interest, and of development, in attached housing which meets the townhouse definition. It became an increasingly familiar configuration in suburbia.

The regional allocation of this type of configuration is widespread. The Northeast, significantly, had a much more substantial share of market than its overall pattern of private housing starts would suggest, while townhouse starts in the South and West were roughly comparable to their total housing activity (see Exhibit 9-4). Only in the depressed Midwest was there significant lag.

EXHIBIT 9-4

Townhouse Starts by Region: 1973 to 1985
(Numbers in thousands)

Year	United States Total	Region			
		Northeast	*Midwest*	*South*	*West*
1973	89	13	14	27	35
1974	66	8	11	25	22
1975	40	6	7	12	16
1976	55	8	11	17	19
1977	74	12	11	26	25
1978	86	11	14	33	28
1979	98	17	11	38	31
1980	78	10	10	40	19
1981	77	13	11	37	17
1982	86	14	11	41	20
1983	171	27	16	90	38
1984	210	48	23	103	36
1985	167	50	14	74	28
		Percent Distribution			
1973	100.0%	14.6%	15.7%	30.3%	39.3%
1974	100.0	12.1	16.7	37.9	33.3
1975	100.0	14.6	17.1	29.3	39.0
1976	100.0	14.5	20.0	30.9	34.5
1977	100.0	16.2	14.9	35.1	33.8
1978	100.0	12.8	16.3	38.4	32.6
1979	100.0	17.5	11.3	39.2	32.0
1980	100.0	12.7	12.7	50.6	24.1
1981	100.0	16.7	14.1	47.4	21.8
1982	100.0	16.3	12.8	47.7	23.3
1983	100.0	15.8	9.4	52.6	22.2
1984	100.0	22.9	11.0	49.0	17.1
1985	100.0	30.1	8.4	44.6	16.8

Source: U.S. Bureau of the Census, *Construction Reports*, Series C-20, "Housing Starts," Monthly

This growing penetration had many causes: changing demographic patterns, including the rise of childless households; the availability of more generous zoning provisions for such accommodations; new financial and cost structures (particularly that of land); and perhaps the greater market acceptance of the condominium format, which is often adapted to townhouse configurations.

Condominiums

The rise in importance of condominiums in the United States lags the equivalent in Western Europe. But as shown in Exhibit 9-5, by the mid-1980s it had taken hold across the nation, particularly in the South and West. The latter two regions secured 72 percent of all condominium starts in 1984; but even the Northeast's share in 1984 (18.2 percent) was greater than its proportional representation in total housing starts.

EXHIBIT 9-5

Condominium Starts by Region: 1973 to 1985
(Numbers in thousands)

Year	United States Total	Region			
		Northeast	Midwest	South	West
1973	241	29	26	119	67
1974	175	21	17	78	59
1975	65	12	14	18	21
1976	95	16	15	26	38
1977	132	16	20	48	48
1978	156	12	23	60	62
1979	198	10	26	95	68
1980	186	17	19	91	58
1981	181	17	15	101	48
1982	170	21	14	103	32
1983	276	34	21	153	68
1984	291	53	29	137	72
1985	225	75	21	76	53
		Percent Distribution			
1973	100.0%	12.0%	10.8%	49.4%	27.8%
1974	100.0	12.0	9.7	44.6	33.7
1975	100.0	18.5	21.5	27.7	32.3
1976	100.0	16.8	15.8	27.4	40.0
1977	100.0	12.1	15.2	36.4	36.4
1978	100.0	7.6	14.6	38.2	39.5
1979	100.0	5.0	13.1	47.7	34.2
1980	100.0	9.2	10.3	49.2	31.4
1981	100.0	9.4	8.3	55.8	26.5
1982	100.0	12.4	8.2	60.6	18.8
1983	100.0	12.3	7.6	55.4	24.6
1984	100.0	18.2	10.0	47.1	24.7
1985	100.0	33.3	9.3	33.8	23.6

Source: U.S. Bureau of the Census, *Construction Reports*, Series C-20, "Housing Starts," Monthly

The regional flow of the condominium format will parallel changes in the number of its principal areas of market penetration: young childless couples and the elderly. The household profiles discussed earlier are particularly relevant here.

10

Housing Cost Structures

It was housing supply—and its absolute provision—which was the major issue of public debate and concern of policymakers in the half-century after the Great Depression. Subsequently, however, the crucial focus has been shared with housing costs, not only for the poor but increasingly for the middle-class as well. *America's unparalleled exposure to inflation and income lags changed the calculus of shelter.*

The Consumer Price Index

Lost in the midst of short-term imperatives are the broad questions of defining just what has happened to the price of housing, how it best can be measured, and indeed, what the appropriate measures are with which to appraise the changing burdens on the family's exchequer. In Exhibit 10-1, the Consumer Price Index (CPI), and several of its components, are presented for the 1960 to 1985 period. None of the parameters, it should be noted, are beyond controversy as benchmarks of the general inflation experience.

The broad pattern of inflation is indicated by the behavior of the all-items price index shown at the left-hand side of the exhibit. Overall, from 1960 to 1970, the index increased by 31.1 percent; but the decade-long interval masks the acceleration in the deflowering of the dollar that was taking place. In the first half of the decade, for example, there was (by 1980s' standards, at least) essentially price stability—with an increase of only 6.5 percent, or barely one percent a year. From 1965 to 1970, perhaps indicating one of the costs of a Vietnam-era fiscal policy of "guns and butter," the pace nearly quadrupled, as it rose by 23.1 percent.

This established the starting point of the most horrendous decade of inflation in America's history. From 1970 to 1975, the all-items

EXHIBIT 10-1

Consumer Price Index, United States, Selected Items: 1960 to 1985[1]

Year	All Items	Home Ownership	Rent	Fuel Oil and Coal	Gas and Electricity
1960	88.7	86.3	91.7	89.2	98.6
1965	94.5	92.7	96.9	94.6	99.4
1970	116.3	128.5	110.1	110.1	107.3
1971	121.3	133.7	115.2	117.5	114.7
1972	125.3	140.1	119.2	118.5	120.5
1973	133.1	146.7	124.3	136.0	126.4
1974	147.7	163.2	130.6	214.6	145.8
1975	161.2	181.7	137.3	235.3	169.6
1976	170.5	191.7	144.7	250.8	189.0
1977	181.5	204.9	153.5	283.4	213.4
1978	195.4	227.2	164.0	298.3	232.6
1979	217.4	262.4	176.0	403.1	257.8
1980	246.8	314.0	191.6	556.0	301.8
1981	272.4	352.7	208.2	675.9	345.9
1982	289.1	376.8	224.0	667.9	393.8
1983	298.4	380.0	236.9	628.0	428.7
1984	311.1	385.9	249.3	641.8	445.2
1985	322.2	N/A	264.6	619.5	452.7

Percentage Change

Period					
1960-1970	31.1%	48.9%	20.1%	23.4%	8.8%
1960-1965	6.5	7.4	5.7	6.1	0.8
1965-1970	23.1	38.6	13.6	16.4	7.9
1970-1975	38.6	41.4	24.7	113.7	58.1
1975-1980	53.2	72.8	39.5	136.3	77.9
1970-1980	112.4	144.4	74.0	405.0	181.3
1980-1985	30.6	N/A	38.1	11.4	50.0

Note: 1. Beginning 1978, reflects buying pattern of all urban consumers except homeownership, which reflects urban wage earners and clerical workers for 1983 and 1984

Source: U.S. Department of Commerce, Bureau of Economic Analysis, *Survey of Current Business*, Monthly

index soared by 38.6 percent, only to escalate by 53.2 percent between 1975 and 1980. By 1985 the market basket of items encompassed by the CPI had moved from a 1967 baseline of 100 to more than triple that level. An item priced at $1.00 in 1967 would have cost approximately $3.22 in 1985 if it followed the pattern of the CPI.

The tides of inflation during the 1970s made Americans of all economic classes more and more apprehensive about their capacity to afford the symbols of the good life. Nowhere did this concern achieve more visibility than in the housing domain. The virtual month-to-month escalation in the selling price of new one-family homes, the soaring cost (and uncertainty as to the simple availability) of home heating fuel, the property-tax revolt, and changes in landlord–tenant tensions, epitomized by rent regulation, were real manifestations as well as potent symbols of the dilemmas that confronted Americans and their shelter system.

The insecurity upon entering the 1980s was pervasive. Despite very strong deflationary measures in the early part of the decade, the momentum of price spiraled upward. The index advanced by over 20 percent between 1980 and 1983. While inflation did decelerate markedly during this period, its impact remained monumental. Price stability ultimately reigned by mid-decade, but underlying fears of a price resurgence lingered.

Spearheading the inflationary surge of the 1970s were the two energy shocks of 1973–1974 and 1979. They resulted in a 400-percent increase in the prices of fuel oil and coal between 1973 and 1981, and a near-200-percent rise in the prices of gas and electricity—all of them key to the operating costs of housing. And these were elements which had actually lagged the CPI in the decade of the 1960s. In the post-1973 period, both homeowners and operators of rental facilities alike faced staggering energy-price increments.

Energy components were just a few of the building blocks underlying the base parameters. It is the results—the changes in homeownership and rental costs—which are crucial. The latter are both key inputs into the CPI, as well as reflections of it. These are far from mechanical linkages, and must be viewed in the context of market realities.

First and foremost is the gap that opened up between homeownership and rental prices. The latter, in retrospect, had been a comparative bargain in this measurement context. Even as late as 1983, rent increases since 1967 (137 percent) were substantially below those of the all-items index (198 percent), and less than half of those of homeownership (280 percent).

In contrast, the increases in the homeownership sector since the 1960s were far in excess of general price rises. Even in the low-inflation period of the early 1960s this relationship held true, with the gap widening decisively from 1965 to 1970: while the all-items index increased by 23 percent, the homeownership equivalent moved up by nearly 40 percent. The pattern of deviation between the all-items index and that for homeownership narrowed during the 1970 to 1975 period, but widened precipitously over the next five years, when homeownership increased by nearly three-quarters (72.8 percent). *By the end of the decade of the 1970s, the homeownership buying power of the 1970 dollar had fallen to only 40 cents. Yet the early- and mid-1980 period was one of near parity with inflation. The long inflationary cycle of housing was seemingly redressed by the decline in energy prices and general inflation.*

The profile of rent levels was very different. Despite exposure to most of the factors underlying the cost of homeownership, rents lagged the all-items index—as well as the alternative of homeownership itself. The rental-price rise from 1960 to 1970 was only 20.1 percent—two-thirds that of general-price rises, and barely 40 percent that of homeownership. And this lagging pattern continued through the 1970s; the 74-percent rent increment was half that of homeownership; barely 60 percent of the overall price index.

An intriguing shift, however, took place in the first half of the 1980s, when rents moved slowly ahead of the other price components. Whether this is temporary, merely representing a cost catch-up, is far from clear. Certainly, however, the lagging pattern of rents over the first 20 years covered in Exhibit 10-1 may well explain the lack of investor interest which characterized the area until it was stimulated by the tax changes of 1981, when liberalized depreciation schedules were instituted.

Several technical caveats, however, must be posed in regard to our observations. First, the design of the CPI itself helps to explain part of the owner–rental gap noted above. The CPI assumes a fixed market basket of constant-quality goods and services, and tracks their prices over time. Thus, the shelter components represent consistent-quality residential configurations over time.

In terms of homeownership, the index assumes that current mortgage interest rates were in effect. Therefore, it measured the experience of consumers actually securing a mortgage at the time of the monthly-price survey—and this in a time frame of soaring interest rates; the actual situation of extant homeowners was quite different.

In contrast, the rental index, based on a constant-quality unit a decade-old in configuration, probably did not represent the overall rental pool. As we will examine in Chapter 12, the supply pattern over time is one of deletion of older, cheaper units and the addition of much more expensive, newer ones. Thus, the CPI rental measure more nearly reflects the situation of long-standing tenants in place than of consumers seeking new accommodations.

These disparities account for some of the deviation between homeownership and rental-price behavior as reflected by the CPI. The homeownership conceptualization had long been criticized; in 1983, it was changed to a homeowner–rental equivalent index (Exhibit 10-2 details its 1982 to 1985 behavior). But through the worst period of interest-rate escalation in modern times, the all-items index, as well as the homeownership index, assumed that all Americans experienced rising mortgage costs, though the great majority of homeowners were buffered from the current market realities by fixed-rate, long-term indentures. This was one of the factors underlying the great debate of the late 1970s on the overestimation of inflation by the CPI.

New One-Family House Prices

Americans have long been noted for their love affair with homeownership—a relationship which, at least in the 1970s and early 1980s, was capable of defying inflation and the soaring costs of acquiring homeownership status. As shown in Exhibit 10-3, the median sales price of new one-family homes in the United States moved from $23,400 in 1970 to more than triple that baseline—$84,100 by 1985.

EXHIBIT 10-2

Changed Homeownership Component of the Consumer Price Index: December 1982 to 1985

	Homeowner's Costs	Renter's Costs
December 1982	100.0	100.0
1983	102.5	103.0
1984	107.3	108.6
1985	113.1	115.4

Source: U.S. Department of Commerce, Bureau of Economic Analysis, *Survey of Current Business*, Monthly

EXHIBIT 10-3

Median Sales Price of New One-Family Homes
Sold by Region: 1970 to 1985

Year	United States Total	Region			
		Northeast	*Midwest*	*South*	*West*
1970	$23,400	$30,300	$24,400	$20,300	$24,000
1971	25,200	30,600	27,200	22,500	25,500
1972	27,600	31,400	29,300	25,800	27,500
1973	32,500	37,100	32,900	30,900	32,400
1974	35,900	40,100	36,100	34,500	35,800
1975	39,300	44,000	39,600	37,300	40,600
1976	44,200	47,300	44,800	40,500	47,200
1977	48,800	51,600	51,500	44,100	53,500
1978	55,700	58,100	59,200	50,300	61,300
1979	62,900	65,500	63,900	57,300	69,600
1980	64,600	69,500	63,400	59,600	72,300
1981	68,900	76,000	65,900	64,400	77,800
1982	69,300	78,200	68,900	66,100	75,000
1983	75,300	82,200	79,500	70,900	80,100
1984	79,900	88,600	85,400	72,000	87,300
1985	84,100	101,900	80,100	74,900	92,400
Percent Change					
1970 to 1985	259.4%	236.3%	228.2%	269.0%	285.0%

Source: U.S. Bureau of the Census, *Construction Reports*, Series C-25, "New One-Family Houses Sold and For Sale," Monthly

While this rate of increase (259.4 percent) was far in excess of the overall pace of inflation as measured by the CPI (177 percent), the total impact on the house purchaser was further magnified by the escalator of rising mortgage rates, as will be detailed subsequently.

Moreover, while the shifts of the business cycle, described earlier, were reflected in a boom-and-bust pattern of housing starts, the worst of downturns in the market barely grazed the increments in new home prices. Thus, even during the recession of 1974–1975, the median price of new houses went up by more than 10 percent. *General inflation was a stimulator of housing price even in the face of increased mortgage rates.*

There was a slowing down of year-to-year gains during the early 1980s, but it was far from proportionate to the economic trauma of the time. In part, this may reflect the changing pool of new housing, with custom-built and higher-priced units, at least at the beginnings of a recession, maintaining their sales levels at the expense of more modest facilities. This, however, is far from a total explanation. While the conventional wisdom of recession would suggest price decline, the pattern of general inflation during the 1970s increasingly made housing not merely a source of shelter from the elements—but also from the then-current decline in the value of a dollar. When this imperative was joined by higher levels of marginal taxation through tax-bracket creep, the results were a housing-buying panic, a desperate struggle to enjoy the buffers of ownership. Thus, *in a self-certification of the wisdom of purchase, the very increments in housing prices generated additional desire to own housing.*

And this was a pattern which was shared by every region of the country. While the price gains varied regionally, the direction—with only one significant exception—was upward. Even the Midwest, faced with precipitous declines in its smokestack industries, exhibited only a minor quiver in median sales prices from 1979 to 1980. The final harsh reality of industrial shrinkage, farm setbacks, and oil price deflation, however, was finally revealed by mid-decade declines in Midwest prices.

When the regional patterns are studied in more detail, they tend to reflect the vast demographic shifts which took place in America in the 1970s. The stagnancy of population growth in the Northeast and Midwest was mirrored by relatively low sales-price gains. The comparative vigor of the South and West, in contrast, had as one of its flywheels the enormous flows of migration which took place into those areas.

The sum of these regional variations moved the median sales price of new one-family homes into a much more homogeneous national range than held true in 1970. In that base year, for example, the median sales price of $30,300 in the Northeast was half again as high as in the South, and 25 percent higher than those in the Midwest and West. By 1983, the median price in the Northeast ($82,200) was little more than 10 percent higher than that of the South, and only slightly ahead of the two other regions. Housing prices in the South had increased by two and one-half times, those in the Northeast by only 175 percent.

By the mid-1980s, the pattern of housing prices began to shift again. The economic exuberance and demographic migrations that were fundamental to early changes in regional price had taken new directions. The long relative stagnancy of the Northeast was abruptly reversed. One of the more striking indications was its near-25-percent increase in the median sales prices of new one-family homes from 1983 through 1985. The Midwest, still bedeviled by the issues of the economic difficulties, faltered. Even the South and West lagged the Northeast market leader. And the "rust-bowl" problems were far from limited to the Midwest; they also impacted some of the manufacturing zones of the South, dampening price increments there.

Price shifts for new mobile homes placed for residential use exhibit a generally similar pattern (Exhibit 10-4), except that the West staunchly held its position as price leader. The South, through the mid-1980s, had remained the price laggard. Overall, the rates of mobile-home price increases fell within five percent of those of new one-family homes during the mid-1970s to mid-1980s period.

EXHIBIT 10-4

Average Sales Price, New Mobile Homes Placed for Residential Use, by Region: 1974 to 1985

Year	United States Total	Region			
		Northeast	*Midwest*	*South*	*West*
1974	$ 9,300	$ 9,400	$ 9,300	$ 8,300	$11,600
1975	10,600	10,500	10,700	9,000	13,600
1976	12,300	11,600	11,600	10,600	16,000
1977	14,200	12,900	13,500	12,100	18,100
1978	15,900	14,300	15,100	13,700	20,600
1979	17,600	15,800	16,100	15,600	23,100
1980	19,800	18,500	18,600	18,200	25,400
1981	19,900	19,000	18,900	18,400	25,600
1982	19,700	19,900	20,000	18,500	24,700
1983	21,000	21,400	20,400	19,700	27,000
1984	21,500	22,200	21,100	20,200	27,400
1985	21,800	22,700	21,500	20,400	28,700
Percent Change					
1974 to 1985	134.4%	141.5%	131.2%	145.8%	147.4%

Source: U.S. Bureau of the Census, *Construction Reports*, Series C-20, "Housing Starts," Monthly

Existing Home Price Increases

Resale prices, i.e., sales prices of existing single-family homes, have more potency as gauged by market action than do those of new homes per se. In a typical year, nearly three times more existing one-family homes are sold than new houses.

The pattern of inflation for existing homes has roughly paralleled that of new ones for the United States as a whole (Exhibit 10-5). For new homes, the 1970 to 1985 price increase was 259.4 percent; for existing homes, 227 percent. These are relationships which are relatively constant as we compare regions. The one outstanding exception, again, was the Midwest. The impact of changes of its economic status is reflected in very low resale price growth over time. By mid-decade,

EXHIBIT 10-5

Median Sales Price of Existing Single-Family Homes Sold by Region: 1970 to 1985

Year	United States Total	Region			
		Northeast	Midwest	South	West
1970	$23,000	$25,200	$20,100	$22,200	$24,300
1971	24,800	27,100	22,100	24,300	26,500
1972	26,700	29,800	23,900	26,400	28,400
1973	28,900	32,800	25,300	29,000	31,000
1974	32,000	35,800	27,700	32,300	34,800
1975	35,300	39,300	30,100	34,800	39,600
1976	38,100	41,800	32,900	36,500	46,100
1977	42,900	44,400	36,700	39,800	57,300
1978	48,700	47,900	42,200	45,100	66,700
1979	55,700	53,600	47,800	51,300	77,400
1980	62,200	60,800	51,900	58,300	89,300
1981	66,400	63,700	54,300	64,400	96,200
1982	67,800	63,500	55,100	67,100	98,900
1983	70,300	72,200	56,600	69,200	94,900
1984	72,400	78,700	57,100	71,300	95,800
1985	75,200	89,000	58,800	74,400	95,200
Percent Change					
1970 to 1985	227.0%	253.2%	192.5%	235.1%	291.8%

Source: National Association of Realtors, Economics and Research Division, *Existing Home Sales*, Washington, D.C., Monthly

Midwest resales were still under $60,000, a level dwarfed by the prices elsewhere.

Constant-Quality Price Changes

There are two interlinked phenomena which require additional understanding. One of them is inflation; the other, the changing quality of

EXHIBIT 10-6a

Price Index of Houses Sold in the United States: 1963 to 1984

Year	Price Index of New One-Family Houses Sold, Including Value of Lot					Average Sales Price For	
		Region				Kinds of Houses Sold in 1977 (Estimated from Price Index)	Houses Actually Sold Each Year
	United States	Northeast	Midwest	South	West		
1963	43.2	43.5	45.3	46.6	39.9	$23,400	$ 19,300
1964	43.5	41.3	43.8	47.6	40.8	23,600	20,500
1965	44.4	43.5	45.5	48.1	41.0	24,000	21,500
1966	46.2	46.4	48.1	50.4	42.3	25,100	23,300
1967	47.5	48.1	50.0	51.2	42.7	25,800	24,600
1968	50.0	52.9	53.3	53.4	43.7	27,100	26,600
1969	53.8	57.5	58.2	56.9	47.7	29,200	27,900
1970	55.3	61.5	58.2	58.7	48.8	30,000	26,600
1971	58.3	65.6	60.4	63.3	50.3	31,600	28,300
1972	62.1	70.4	64.2	67.2	53.5	33,600	30,500
1973	67.5	76.1	69.2	71.7	60.1	36,600	35,500
1974	73.8	82.9	74.8	77.4	67.8	40,000	38,900
1975	81.7	89.8	82.5	85.1	76.2	44,300	42,600
1976	88.7	93.6	89.9	91.1	84.6	48,100	48,000
1977	100.0	100.0	100.0	100.0	100.0	54,200	54,200
1978	114.5	111.1	114.3	112.2	118.5	62,100	62,500
1979	130.8	126.1	127.9	128.5	136.5	70,900	71,800
1980	145.2	138.5	135.4	144.3	154.2	78,700	76,400
1981	157.4	149.7	147.2	158.4	164.8	85,300	83,000
1982	161.5	157.3	153.4	164.9	166.4	87,600	83,900
1983	165.5	164.0	150.0	168.0	172.0	89,700	89,800
1984	171.9	181.2	157.5	173.8	171.0	93,200	97,600
1985	176.4	201.2	158.6	178.4	176.1	97,100	100,800

Source: U.S. Bureau of the Census, Construction Reports, Series C-25, *Characteristics of New Housing: 1985*, U.S. Department of Commerce, Washington, D.C., 1985

EXHIBIT 10-6b

Price Index Definition

The data used for computing the price index are obtained from the Census Bureau's Housing Sales Survey. Started in 1963, the survey collects information on the physical characteristics and the transaction prices of new one-family houses sold. This is done through monthly interviews with the builders or owners of a national sample of these houses. The size of the sample is currently about 7,000 observations per year.

The price index is intended to measure changes over time in the sales prices of new one-family houses which are the same with respect to ten important characteristics as the houses sold in the United States in 1977. The ten characteristics used are: floor area, number of stories, number of bathrooms, air-conditioning, type of parking facility, type of foundation, geographic division within region, metropolitan area location, presence of fireplace, and size of lot. Note, however, that houses which are "the same" with regard to these particular characteristics may vary from one time period to the next in a number of ways, such as workmanship, materials, and mechanical equipment. Hence, it should be kept in mind that the price index in this report accounts only for such quality characteristics insofar as they may be correlated with the ten characteristics actually used. The ten characteristics account for approximately 67 percent of the variation in selling price of new one-family houses.

The price index has been structured so that 1977 equals 100.0. The year 1977 was chosen because the most recent quinquennial economic censuses were taken for 1977, and many economic time series are benchmarked to the economic censuses. The index series shown in Exhibit 10-6a is actually a combination of two series. From 1963 to 1973, the index is based on eight characteristics of the houses sold in 1977 (the list of ten, excluding lot size and presence of fireplace). From 1974 on, the index used all ten characteristics. Therefore, changes in lot sizes and the number of houses having fireplaces are not accounted for in the index prior to 1974, unless they were correlated with one or more of the eight characteristics used.

Using a multiple regression procedure which involves these ten basic characteristics, an estimate is made of the average price of the kinds of houses sold in 1977, in terms of what they would have sold for in each of the other time periods.

Since the price index applies to total sales price, it covers not only the cost of labor and materials, but also land costs, direct and indirect selling expenses, and sellers' profits. The index is, thus, conceptually broader in coverage than a cost index. Reflecting the sales price, the price index is affected by all factors which influence movements of house prices—both supply factors, such as wage rates, materials cost and productivity; and demand factors, such as demographic changes, income, and availability of mortgage money.

The price index is computed from actual transaction prices, including value of the developed lot, of houses built for sale and actually sold by merchant or speculative builders. Excluded from the index are houses for which the owner hired a single general contractor to build the house, or acted as his own general contractor, or for which he did some, or all, of the work. A "house sold" is one in which a sales contract is signed at any stage of construction and the month of sale refers to the contract date.

Because the price index is based on fixed proportions of ten characteristics of new houses sold in 1977, movements of the price index may differ greatly from changes in the average sales price of new houses actually sold during each period. Unlike the price index, the average sales price of new houses actually sold may change from one period to the next, not only because of price changes which are independent of quality,

EXHIBIT 10-6b (continued)

Price Index Definition

but also because of shifts in quality; i.e., the proportions of new houses with different characteristics. For example, the price index increased 30.8 percent from 1977 to 1979 in the United States, whereas the average price of new houses actually sold during this period increased 32.5 percent owing to an overall shift towards the construction of larger houses and houses with more amenities.

This comparison may be clearer if one were to think of the price index in terms of the average prices of kinds of houses sold in 1977. The price index indicates that new houses sold in 1977 which had an average sales price of $54,200 would have sold for $70,900 in 1979. However, the actual average price of new houses sold in 1979 was $71,800. The difference of $900, as stated above, may be attributed to the shift towards larger houses with more amenities.

Source: U.S. Bureau of the Census, Construction Report – Series C25, *Characteristics of New Housing: 1985*, U.S. Department of Commerce, Washington, D.C., 1986, p. 53.

America's housing. In order to isolate them, an index computed from the Census Bureau's Housing Sales Survey—an annual survey started in 1963 which measures changes over time in sales prices and physical characteristics—is employed. The price index, as computed by the Bureau and defined in Exhibit 10-6b, is intended to measure the changes over time in the sales prices of new one-family houses which are the same with respect to ten important characteristics as the houses sold in the United States in 1977. As shown in Exhibit 10-6a, the "standardized" house—whose average sales price in 1977 was $54,200—could be purchased in 1963 for barely 40 percent of that figure, or $23,400. By 1985, it had increased in absolute price by almost $43,000—to $97,100. The range of regional variations as shown in the exhibit mirrors that previously discussed.

It is striking, however, to review the data in terms of the relationship between the constant-quality house and those houses actually sold in each year (the far-right columns of Exhibit 10-6a). The standard house, by definition, as of 1977 was the same in price as the houses actually sold in that year—$54,200. But while the former would have sold for $87,600 by 1982, the average sales price of houses actually sold stood at $83,900. *We would suggest that this revealed the decline in quality/amenity of housing which had been imposed on America's new home-buyers as a function of declining housing-buying power in the early 1980s.*

It should further be noted that the relationship between the two indices remained relatively constant through 1979, with the standard house in that year actually exceeded in price by the houses actually sold. In order to maintain constant quality from the 1979 baseline, Americans would have had to pay $16,700 more by 1982 in order to secure parity of quality; instead they chose (or could only afford) to pay an increment of $12,100.

Thus, from 1963 to 1979 there was a general broad improvement in the kinds of new houses sold in America by this rough criterion. This relationship was abruptly ended in 1979. The second oil crisis, and the recession which followed, caused a decline in what had long been an upwards-and-onwards march in the size and quality of America's new housing production.

The comparative income increases that characterized the mid-1980s were reflected almost instantaneously in a surge in housing amenity—as measured by the changes that took place in the price of the standard house versus those actually sold. By 1984, the latter had again surged beyond the constant-quality house and moved even further ahead in 1985. The kinds of housing that Americans buy, and the amenity level of that housing, clearly responded to the depths of the purchasers' pockets—both real and anticipated. The long-term line trend we would suggest, though interrupted by recessions, is one of increasing housing quality and appurtenance.

Demographic Variations

A further perspective on house values and rent levels can be secured via the demographic partitions of the *Annual Housing Survey* (as previously detailed in the "demand" chapters). As a baseline, Exhibit 10-7 first presents the distribution of values per unit (self-reported) for 1970 and 1983, the intra-period changes, as well as the 1983 detailed high-value distribution. In general, the pattern of change paralleled that evidenced by existing-home sales prices (Exhibit 10-5), although the absolute levels of self-reported value lagged the actual sales-price experience. Significantly, the detailed distribution of high-valued ($50,000 or more) units shows a very thin upscale market: only 6.4

EXHIBIT 10-7

Value Per Owner-Occupied Unit
U.S. Total: 1970 to 1983
(Numbers in thousands)

	1970	1983	Change: 1970 to 1983	
			Number	Percent
Specified Owner Occupied	31,726	43,538	11,812	37.2%
Less than $10,000	6,731	633	−6,098	−90.6
$10,000 to $14,999	6,392	721	−5,671	−88.7
$15,000 to $24,999	11,113	2,541	−8,572	−77.1
$25,000 to $34,999	4,444	4,207	−237	−5.3
$35,000 to $49,999	2,050	8,703	6,653	324.5
$50,000 or more	997	26,733	25,736	2,581.3
Median	$17,100	$59,700	$42,600	249.1

1983 Detailed High-Value Distribution

	Number	Percent
Specified Owner Occupied	43,538	100.0%
Less than $50,000	16,805	38.6
$50,000 or more	26,733	61.4
$ 50,000 to $ 74,999	12,217	28.1
$ 75,000 to $ 99,999	7,247	16.6
$100,000 to $149,999	4,500	10.3
$150,000 to $199,999	1,508	3.5
$200,000 to $249,999	637	1.5
$250,000 to $299,999	268	0.6
$300,000 or more	356	0.8

Source: U.S. Department of Commerce, U.S. Bureau of the Census, Current Housing Reports, Series H-150-83, *General Housing Characteristics for the United States and Regions: 1983, Annual Housing Survey: 1983, Part A*, U.S. Department of Housing and Urban Development, sponsor. Washington, D.C.: U.S. Government Printing Office, 1985

percent of owner-occupied units in 1983 had values of $150,000 or more; less than 2.5 percent had values of $250,000 or more.

Median house value by household type is isolated in Exhibit 10-8 for 1976 and 1983. Married-couple families again represented the "premier" demographic sector in general, with those particular couples 35- to 64-years-of-age far out in front of the housing-value parade. Forming the rear contingents were the house values of single-person households and those of other female householders. To the degree that

EXHIBIT 10-8

**Median House Value by Household Type,
U.S. Total: 1976 to 1983**

			Change: 1976 to 1983	
Household Type	1976	1983	Number	Percent
2-or-more-Person Households	$33,400	$62,100	$28,700	85.9%
Married Couple Families	34,300	63,600	29,300	85.4
Under 25 years	25,400	42,300	16,900	66.5
25 to 29 years	31,800	54,700	22,900	72.0
30 to 34 years	37,000	62,200	25,200	68.1
35 to 44 years	38,000	70,200	32,200	84.7
45 to 64 years	34,900	67,000	32,100	92.0
65 years and over	28,100	53,800	25,700	91.5
Other Male Householder	30,000	57,600	27,600	92.0
Under 65 years	31,900	59,700	27,800	87.1
65 years and over	23,100	47,900	24,800	107.4
Other Female Householder	25,900	49,500	23,600	91.1
Under 65 years	26,600	51,200	24,600	92.5
65 years and over	23,300	44,600	21,300	91.4
1-Person Households	23,500	46,500	23,000	97.9

Source: U.S. Department of Commerce, U.S. Bureau of the Census, Current Housing Reports, Series H-150-83, *Financial Housing Characteristics for the United States and Regions: 1983, Annual Housing Survey: 1983, Part C*, U.S. Department of Housing and Urban Development, sponsor. Washington, D.C.: U.S. Government Printing Office, 1985, and earlier editions of this volume

house value is correlated with overall wealth and asset positions, the demographic variation is thus apparent. In addition, as will be shown in Chapter 14, there is also a major linkage to income with the higher-income demographic strata residing in the most expensive shelter.

The same general pattern has been characteristic of the rental sector (Exhibits 10-9 and 10-10). Middle-aged (35- to 44-years-of-age) married couples inhabit the most expensive rental accommodations— single-person and female-householders the least expensive. Demographically inspired shelter-cost variations were a staple of the 1970s and 1980s.

EXHIBIT 10-9

Gross Rent, U.S. Total: 1970 to 1983
(Numbers in thousands)

			Change: 1970 to 1983	
	1970	*1983*	*Number*	*Percent*
Specified Renter Occupied	22,334	29,214	6,880	30.8%
Less than $100	9,167	1,197	−7,970	−86.9
$100 to $149	7,104	1,707	−5,397	−76.0
$150 to $199	3,304	2,364	−940	−28.5
$200 to $299	1,194	7,377	6,183	517.8
$300 or more	265	15,168	14,903	5,623.8
No Cash Rent	1,300	1,401	101	7.8
Median	$108	$315	$207	191.7%

1983 Detailed High-Rent Distribution

	Number	Percent
Specified Renter Occupied	29,214	100.0%
Less than $300	12,645	43.3
$300 or more	15,168	51.9
$300 to $349	3,910	13.4
$350 to $399	3,441	11.8
$400 to $449	2,527	8.6
$450 to $499	1,685	5.8
$500 to $599	1,862	6.4
$600 to $699	848	2.9
$700 to $749	250	0.9
$750 or more	645	2.2
No Cash Rent	1,401	4.8

Source: U.S. Department of Commerce, U.S. Bureau of the Census, Current Housing Reports, Series H-150-83, *General Housing Characteristics for the United States and Regions: 1983, Annual Housing Survey: 1983, Part A*, U.S. Department of Housing and Urban Development, sponsor. Washington, D.C.: U.S. Government Printing Office, 1985

EXHIBIT 10-10

Median Monthly Gross Rent by Household Type,
U.S. Total: 1976 to 1983

			Change: 1976 to 1983	
Household Type	*1976*	*1983*	*Number*	*Percent*
2-or-more-Person Households	$179	$340	$161	89.9%
Married Couple Families	183	349	166	90.7
Under 25 years	166	310	144	86.7
25 to 29 years	192	348	156	81.3
30 to 34 years	193	373	180	93.3
35 to 44 years	195	381	186	95.4
45 to 64 years	184	357	173	94.0
65 years and over	163	308	145	89.0
Other Male Householder	186	371	185	99.5
Under 65 years	188	376	188	100.0
65 years and over	144	243	99	68.8
Other Female Householder	167	312	145	86.8
Under 65 years	168	314	146	86.9
65 years and over	141	278	137	97.2
1-Person Households	142	269	127	89.4

Source: U.S. Department of Commerce, U.S. Bureau of the Census, Current Housing Reports, Series H-150-83, *Financial Housing Characteristics for the United States and Regions: 1983, Annual Housing Survey: 1983, Part C*, U.S. Department of Housing and Urban Development, sponsor. Washington, D.C.: U.S. Government Printing Office, 1985, and earlier editions of this volume

11

Financing Costs:
New Mortgage Realities

It is the cost of money rather than bricks and mortar which is often the principal determinant of housing accessibility for most Americans. Labor costs, for example, typically represent no more than one-quarter of the selling price of new housing. A 10-percent increase in the cost of labor on a $100,000 house, therefore, represents $2,500 ($25,000 x .10). But when financed by a 10-percent mortgage, it translates into only *$250* a year in debt-service costs ($2,500 x .10). By way of contrast, if that same mortgage rate increases from 10 percent to 11 percent, assuming that the mortgage covers three-quarters of the house purchase price, an increase in carrying costs of *$750* a year is generated ($75,000 x .01). Therefore, it is not surprising that, from a consumer's point of view, financing costs may be the primary determinant of affordability.

In a debt-oriented society, the importance of the *nominal price* of an object diminishes compared to the *level of borrowing costs* necessary to support it. Sticker shock is more potent in terms of carrying charges than of list price. The inflationary experience of the 1970s reinforced this tendency; if you can carry it—buy it! This element of consumer response persisted even through the disinflationary years of the 1980s.

This was the mirror image of the predecessor phenomenon. The Great Depression and the deflation it spawned in the 1930s awakened strong conservative fiscal tendencies in the generation which was raised in its wake, an experience which continued to shadow behavior long past World War II.

Increasingly, it has been interest rates, and with them carrying costs, which have determined market action. And American fiscal policy in the early 1980s, after nearly half a century of making special provisions for housing through low mortgage-interest rates, essentially homogenized the financial markets. Mortgage interest rates, therefore, became drastically affected by the mainstream and have become essentially interchangeable with, and subject to, the broad needs of general financing for corporate and governmental use. At times of fiscal plenty, this may not be a problem. But such times are far from universal.

Long-Term Patterns

In Exhibit 11-1 the vagaries of interest rates over time are indicated. From the viewpoint of the consumer, effective interest rates (as defined in the exhibit) are the sum of contract interest rates plus an amount reflecting the amortization of the up-front fees and charges that mortgage brokerage and loan-granting institutions may require.

In this light, it is important to note that the up-front fees have actually increased faster than nominal contract interest rates. In 1976, for example, contract interest rates were at the 8.8-percent level. Initial fees charged were 1.23 percent, representing only 13 percent of con-

EXHIBIT 11-1

Conventional Home Mortgage Loan Terms: National Averages for All Major Types of Lenders[1]

Year	Contract Interest Rate	Initial Fees and Charges	Effective Interest Rate[2]	Term to Maturity	Loan Amount	Purchase Price	Loan-to-Price Ratio
1976	8.88%	1.23%	9.08%	25.1 years	$31,700	$44,000	73.9%
1977	8.82	1.22	9.02	26.2	36,200	49,500	75.0
1978	9.37	1.30	9.59	26.7	41,400	57,100	74.6
1979	10.59	1.50	10.85	27.4	48,200	67,700	73.5
1980	12.46	1.97	12.84	27.2	51,700	73,400	72.9
1981	14.39	2.39	14.91	26.4	53,700	76,300	73.1
1982	14.73	2.65	15.31	25.6	55,000	78,400	72.9
1983	12.26	2.39	12.73	26.0	59,900	83,100	74.5
1984	11.99	2.57	12.40	26.8	64,500	86,600	77.0
1985	11.24	2.51	11.75	26.0	69,900	95,600	75.8

Notes: 1. Savings and loan associations, mortgage bankers, commercial banks, and mutual savings banks

2. Contract rate plus initial fees and charges amortized over 10 years, the assumed average life of a conventional mortgage

Source: Federal Home Loan Bank Board Journal, Monthly

tract interest rates. When amortized over ten years, this produced an effective interest rate of 9.08 percent. In 1985, by way of contrast, contract interest rates were 11.24 percent, while initial fees and charges were 2.51 percent, or more than one-fifth of the nominal contract interest rate.

Nominal contract rates increasingly cloak increased front-end charges. Borrowers may repay their indentures without penalty by law, but face high threshold costs assessed in advance. There is no free lunch—particularly in finance.

The pattern of change during the 1970s and 1980s in effective interest rates needs little elaboration. As shown in the exhibit, interest rates hovered around 9 percent in the mid-1970s, rose to well above 15 percent during the 1982 recession year (as we have earlier noted, this in turn was linked to the lowest level of housing starts since World War II, declined to the 11-percent level by 1985, and to the single-digit level a year later). The mid-1980s' housing boom was spurred by interest rates which, from the viewpoint of a decade earlier, would have been viewed as catastrophic. Given the rates early in the decade, they seemed relatively modest and, most important, stimulated buying. Certainly the halo effect of enormous levels of housing inflation in earlier years aided the revitalization of the market.

Terms to maturity have remained remarkably constant. Indeed, there are few elements of economic import which have shown as little variance over such a considerable time span. And the same stability holds true for loan-to-price ratios, which have stayed close to the 75-percent level. Thus, loan amounts have moved up proportionately to purchase prices. The consumer may require more equity, but with the same ratio to acquisition cost. The typical homebuyer of the early 1970s initiated mortgages on the order of $30,000. By the mid-1980s, they had climbed up to nearly two and one-half times that level. Similarly, typical equity levels in the earlier period were approximately $12,000; by the mid-1980s, they had reached nearly $30,000.

Monthly Fluctuations

The annual averages shown in Exhibit 11-1 tend to obscure the considerable variations which can take place within a year. These are illustrated in Exhibit 11-2, which provides monthly averages for effective interest rates on conventional home mortgages. The peak in the time period shown occurred in May of 1982, during the depths of

EXHIBIT 11-2

National Averages for All Major Types of Lenders:[1]
Conventional Home Mortgage Effective Interest Rates,[2] Monthly

	1978	1979	1980	1981	1982	1983	1984	1985
January	9.15%	10.18%	12.02%	13.57%	15.69%	13.53%	12.23%	12.58%
February	9.18	10.20	12.35	13.94	15.60	13.34	12.23	12.36
March	9.26	10.43	12.75	14.25	15.67	13.17	12.17	12.13
April	9.30	10.49	13.46	14.37	16.00	12.78	12.07	12.09
May	9.37	10.56	14.01	14.49	16.11	12.79	12.15	12.09
June	9.46	10.70	13.14	14.82	15.55	12.63	12.24	11.77
July	9.57	10.89	12.59	15.10	15.60	12.61	12.52	11.45
August	9.70	11.10	12.27	15.45	15.65	12.66	12.69	11.32
September	9.73	11.15	12.37	15.70	15.21	12.81	12.83	11.19
October	9.83	11.25	12.67	15.89	14.83	12.60	12.96	11.28
November	9.87	11.47	13.18	16.37	14.17	12.55	12.88	11.20
December	10.02	11.80	13.48	15.98	13.93	12.42	12.75	11.08

Notes: 1. Savings and loan associations, mortgage bankers, commercial banks, and mutual savings banks
2. Contract rate plus initial fees and charges amortized over 10 years, the assumed average life of a conventional mortgage

Source: Federal Home Loan Bank Board Journal, Monthly

recession, when interest rates topped 16 percent. *Note that as the recession officially ended in November of 1982, mortgage interest rates had already fallen, providing impetus to housing and a rising economy.*

Again, these data should be reviewed in light of Exhibit 8-4. While 1982 was the worst housing-production year in the post-World War II era, housing starts began to show month-to-month gains by the summer of that year. *The linkage of housing, interest rates, and the business cycle is evident.*

In the broad, the phenomenon is particularly highlighted in the "housing blight" years of 1981 and 1982, when peak interest rates stifled the market. But these extremes—peaking as they did at rates unknown since the Civil War—made the *relatively* high interest-rate plateaus of 1983 through 1985 appear to be bargains. Thus, the very positive level of housing production in those years occurred in the face of interest rates which, on a longer historical base, would have seemed overwhelming.

The fight against inflation took its toll. It took nearly six years for interest rates to return to the general levels that they enjoyed in 1979. The much-touted reduction in money costs of 1986 left them somewhat in excess of their equivalent in 1978. But even at these relatively high levels, let us reiterate, America's consumption of housing was re-energized. The housing market of the mid-1980s was one of the more positive elements in the economic landscape.

Price Indices

The long-term change in mortgage interest rates is shown in Exhibit 11-3. Using a 1967 base of 100, contract interest rates had nearly doubled by 1980, peaked at 235.7 in 1982, and then fell back toward the 200-mark by the mid-1980s.

Again, the monthly data give some indication of the intra-year shocks which the housing market must withstand (see Exhibit 11-4). In an industry in which projects not uncommonly may take three to five years to reach maturity, they may be initiated and "penciled out" at

EXHIBIT 11-3

**Consumer Price Index: Contracted
Mortgage Interest Rates, 1970 to 1984
(1967 = 100)**

Year	Contracted Mortgage Interest Rates
1970	132.1
1971	120.4
1972	117.5
1973	123.2
1974	140.2
1975	142.1
1976	140.9
1977	138.5
1978	146.7
1979	165.4
1980	196.1
1981	227.9
1982	235.7
1983	207.1
1984	211.6
1985	discontinued

Source: Bureau of Labor Statistics, *Monthly Labor Review*, Monthly

EXHIBIT 11-4

Consumer Price Index: Contracted
Mortgage Interest Rates, 1979 to 1984, by Month
(1967 = 100)

Month	Year					
	1979	1980	1981	1982	1983	1984
January	155.2	183.8	209.4	245.7	212.0	207.6
February	157.7	187.8	212.3	245.4	211.1	207.7
March	159.2	194.8	216.7	242.3	207.5	205.4
April	160.3	199.8	220.3	244.4	206.0	203.9
May	162.2	202.8	224.9	242.1	202.4	208.4
June	163.1	210.8	227.2	240.2	203.0	209.3
July	164.9	199.6	230.2	239.2	203.8	210.1
August	167.8	192.5	233.3	241.2	205.5	217.4
September	169.7	189.5	239.2	237.5	207.2	218.6
October	172.0	193.0	240.5	232.4	208.8	216.8
November	175.6	198.4	245.3	226.6	208.6	216.9
December	178.4	196.4	245.3	215.9	208.7	217.6

Note: Discontinued after 1984

Source: Bureau of Labor Statistics, *Monthly Labor Review*, Monthly

times like those of the early spring of 1979. The interest-rate levels were then approximately 160 (using 1967 as base 100). But then they may face a selling season with interest rates half again as high. This held in the normally prime sale months of April and May of 1982.

And even these data tend to underestimate the full impact on the consumer's pocket. Total-dollar mortgage-interest *costs* are the product of rates multiplied by the loan amount. Both of these elements, there-fore, must be taken into consideration. As shown in Exhibit 11-5, the consumer price index for contracted mortgage interest *costs* stood at 327.8 in January 1979, i.e., slightly more than triple the level of 1967 (base 100). The price index for contracted mortgage interest rates for that month stood at 155.2 (Exhibit 11-4), i.e., only 55 percent higher than 1967.

After both contracted interest *rates* (245.7) and costs (699.6) peaked in 1982, the levels by 1984 reflected an even wider disparity. The price index for mortgage costs remained well over the 600 level, while interest rates hovered at just over 200. Thus, while interest rates retreated substantially, the actual dollar costs facing new consumers in

EXHIBIT 11-5

**Consumer Price Index: Contracted
Mortgage Interest Cost
(1967 = 100)**

	Year					
Month	*1979*	*1980*	*1981*	*1982*	*1983*	*1984*
January	327.8	453.7	565.9	666.3	624.0	624.1
February	337.9	465.0	566.5	666.6	625.1	617.2
March	344.5	484.1	572.0	656.4	625.7	607.9
April	351.1	500.9	580.9	670.2	625.5	601.6
May	358.9	515.6	598.6	681.4	620.1	615.5
June	366.2	541.5	612.9	690.0	620.8	616.0
July	375.8	514.6	632.6	694.0	622.5	624.9
August	387.4	504.2	643.8	699.6	629.8	658.4
September	397.1	503.6	664.4	686.3	634.2	666.4
October	408.8	521.2	662.5	678.8	634.7	659.3
November	424.2	539.7	667.7	663.4	632.2	657.1
December	436.1	558.7	668.1	633.5	629.4	661.0

Note: Discontinued after 1984

Source: Bureau of Labor Statistics, *Monthly Labor Review*, Monthly

the post-recession mid-1980s remained at a substantially higher plateau—nearly double that of the 1979 pre-recession year—and reflected a sixfold increase in one generation.

Post-Tax and Real Costs

There is no simple approach to ascertaining the "real" costs of financing housing. Not only must effective interest rates be taken into account, but also the dual impacts of tax deductibility and inflation rates. The former, while depending upon the tax brackets and tax-filing postures of individual consumers, serves to reduce actual out-of-pocket costs directly. The latter, indexing the cost of living, serves to mute costs indirectly, i.e., debt is repaid with currency of reduced purchasing power.

In Exhibit 11-6, these two concepts are introduced to derive after-tax and real (inflation-corrected) interest rate equivalents during the tumultuous years from 1976 to 1985. The exhibit begins with the effective interest rates earlier shown. The second column (after-tax

EXHIBIT 11-6

Real Effective Mortgage Interest Rates
National Averages: 1976 to 1985

Year	Effective Interest Rate	After-Tax Effective Interest Rate	Inflation Rate	Real Effective Interest Rate	After-Tax Real Effective Interest Rate
1976	9.08	6.36	5.8	3.28	0.56
1977	9.02	6.31	6.5	2.52	−0.19
1978	9.59	6.71	7.7	1.89	−0.99
1979	10.85	7.60	11.3	−0.45	−3.71
1980	12.84	8.99	13.5	−0.66	−4.51
1981	14.91	10.44	10.4	4.51	0.04
1982	15.31	10.72	6.1	9.21	4.62
1983	12.73	8.91	3.2	9.53	5.71
1984	12.40	8.68	4.3	8.10	4.38
1985	11.75	8.23	3.6	8.15	4.63

Note: Assumes 30 percent marginal tax rate

Source: Bureau of Labor Statistics, Monthly Labor Review, Monthly

effective interest rate) converts them into an imputed post-tax cost, assuming a 30-percent marginal rate of taxation. The after-tax rate to a consumer in this tax bracket is thus equal to 70 percent of the effective rate. The middle column presents the inflation rate, which is measured by year-to-year changes in the all-items CPI. Subtracting this rate from the effective interest and from the after-tax effective interest rates, respectively, establishes the "real" or inflation-corrected equivalents— the final two columns in the exhibit.

There are many variations that could enter into this analysis, not least of them the treatment of front-end charges from a tax point of view, but it does provide at least a baseline perspective on "real" costs. For four of the ten years for which data are provided, after-tax real interest rates for home acquisition were negative; i.e., the overall inflation rate was higher than the after-tax effective interest rate.

A somewhat less-than-definitive pattern emerges when these rates are compared to housing production levels.   While three of the negative-rate years—1977, 1978 and 1979—were very solid housing-start years, one of them—1980—was far from it. Conversely, after-tax real interest rates peaked in 1983 at 5.71 percent and remained at a high threshold the following two years, yet all three of them were very good housing years. Clearly there is far from a uniform relationship.

Regardless of the economic logic involved in the concept of "real" rates, the consumer actually experienced the burden of nominal effective interest rates, i.e., the first columns of Exhibit 11-6. When rates arrived at the giddy heights of 1981 and 1982, they served—at least at that time—to effectively shut off housing demand. While economic arguments can be made on the muting imposed by the tax deductibility of interest rates, the consumer simply did not have the wherewithal—or confidence—to purchase housing. The after-tax real rates may have been negative as they were in 1981, but that was small consolation for those who could not first scale the mountain.

After-tax real interest rates moved up very sharply by the mid-1980s but these, as we have earlier indicated, did not stifle housing demand. To reiterate, consumers' pockets feel the bite of "actual" dollars, not their inflation-corrected analogs. Again, we would repeat as an important halo effect, the earlier inflationary experience. But this experience, in defiance (at least in the short run) of solely economic motivation, indicates the enormous potency of housing ownership within our society.

Despite the changing configuration of households and the much-publicized leisure-society, alternative life-styles that have been advanced, the demand for "a house of one's own" continues unabated.

12

Components of Inventory Change

America's housing dowry has never been fixed. The pool of housing stays continuously in flux. Structures are converted from nonresidential to residential use and vice versa; there are single dwellings which are split into multifamily units at the same time that old rooming houses and single-room occupancies (SROs) are converted into luxury household accommodations. Of equivalent significance, though frequently underestimated in importance, is inventory scrappage, i.e., the number of units which are physically removed from the inventory through demolition or disaster.

Housing differs from many other consumer durables in its longevity. Marketers of appliances, for example, can predict—with a reasonable degree of accuracy—that the half-life of a refrigerator in the United States is somewhere in the order of eight to ten years. While the equivalent parameter for automobiles has changed somewhat over time, its half-life is still within four to seven years.

Housing, at the very least, has a much greater level of potential longevity. A substantial number of very valuable housing units are well past a century in age. Old housing plus new money yields very competitive shelter; housing rehabilitation and improvement in the United States were the fastest-growing elements of the entire construction industry during the 1980s.

On the other side of the spectrum, however, are not only reductions of the inventory for specific-to-the-unit reasons (direct removal), but, equally importantly, through changes in environment and the decline of whole neighborhoods. At its most extreme the latter phenomenon can lead to widespread residential abandonment. Thus, in New York's South Bronx there are buildings which in configuration, age, and initial cost are very comparable to those which command enormous rents in Manhattan. Many of them have been abandoned for more than a generation, in the midst of a city-wide housing shortage.

In Chapter 8, the cycles of annual housing production were given extensive attention. The latter, however, should be set within the other components of change to fully grasp their significance in altering America's housing profile.

Components of Change

The numerical realities of the components of change, i.e., the flows into and out of the housing stock, are summarized in Exhibit 12-1. As of October 1983, the United States inventory comprised 93.5-million housing units—17.6 million, or 23.1 percent, more than a decade before. The increase was the result of a variety of processes. New construction added 16-million units. There was also a net addition (labeled "unspecified units" in Exhibit 12-1) of slightly more than 7-million units through such processes as changes from nonresidential to residential use, conversions of fewer units to more units (epitomized by the increasing prevalence in the 1980s of "granny" flats and equivalents), as well as units returned to the inventory in 1983 which were retrievable losses in the base year. Examples of the latter were 1983 units which in 1973 were condemned for occupancy because of housing-code violations but which were rehabilitated by 1983.

EXHIBIT 12-1

Source of the Inventory: 1973 to 1983
U.S. Total
(Numbers in thousands)

Subject	Total
All Housing Units, October 1983	93,519
All Housing Units, October 1973	75,969
Increase	
Number	17,550
Percent	23.1%
Units Added by New Construction	16,032
Units Lost, Total	5,511
Demolition or Disaster	2,365
Other Means	3,146
Unspecified Units (Net Addition)	7,029

Source: U.S. Department of Commerce, U.S. Bureau of the Census, Current Housing Reports, Series H-150-83, *General Housing Characteristics for the United States and Regions: 1983, Annual Housing Survey: 1983, Part A*, U.S. Department of Housing and Urban Development, sponsor. Washington, D.C.: U.S. Government Printing Office, 1985

Offsetting these gains, however, was a loss of 5.5-million units, 2.4 million through demolition or disaster, and 3.1 million through other means. The latter sector includes residential units changed to nonresidential use, and units removed from the inventory count via condemnation because of violation of local ordinance and housing codes.

In the ten years covered by Exhibit 12-1, new construction and other net additions added 23.1-million housing units to America's overall supply. However, the net increase was reduced to 17.6-million units because of the loss of 5.5-million units from the inventory. Thus, the complexities of demographic change reviewed in Chapters 3 and 4 are fully matched by the intricacies of housing-system change over time. And these are further accentuated or dampened when examined by region.

Newly Constructed Units

The areal flows of new construction, and their impact on regional inventories, have been substantial over time. Americans are far more mobile than holds true for Europeans—and the dynamics of the housing industry reflect it. As shown in Exhibit 12-2, units constructed between 1970 and 1983 represented more than one-quarter (25.7 percent) of the terminal year's total inventory, with both the owner- and renter-occupied sectors reflecting similar shares of "new" units. Thus, by the early 1980s, America's stock of shelter had been bolstered by a vast infusion of new units, with more than one out of four units of post-1970 vintage. By the mid-1980s, the 30-percent level was approached.

When these data are partitioned by region, major differences are apparent. In the South and West, nearly one out of three housing units would have been considered new in 1983, i.e., constructed since 1970. The equivalent in the Midwest was below the national average—one out of five. In the Northeast, however, newly constructed units accounted for barely one in eight of the 1983 total. And this pattern holds basically constant for both the owner- and renter-occupied stocks.

We would suggest, in this context, that some of the regional price differences which occurred since 1983 (Chapter 10)—among them a resurgence in the Northeast relative to the rest of the country—stem not only from the com-

EXHIBIT 12-2

Units Constructed Between 1970 and 1983: Percent of 1983 Total by Tenure and Region
(Numbers in thousands)

	Total Units, 1983	New Construction, 1970–1983	New Construction as a Percent of 1983 Total
U.S. Total			
Total Occupied	84,638	21,766	25.7%
Owner Occupied	54,724	14,534	26.6
Renter Occupied	29,914	7,232	24.2
Northeast Region			
Total Occupied	18,221	2,496	13.7
Owner Occupied	11,009	1,637	14.9
Renter Occupied	7,212	858	11.9
Midwest Region			
Total Occupied	21,618	4,604	21.3
Owner Occupied	14,935	3,111	20.8
Renter Occupied	6,683	1,493	22.3
South Region			
Total Occupied	27,931	9,298	33.3
Owner Occupied	18,825	6,456	34.3
Renter Occupied	9,106	2,842	31.2
West Region			
Total Occupied	16,868	5,368	31.8
Owner Occupied	9,955	3,330	33.5
Renter Occupied	6,912	2,039	29.5

Source: U.S. Department of Commerce, U.S. Bureau of the Census, Current Housing Reports, Series H-150-83, *General Housing Characteristics for the United States and Regions: 1983, Annual Housing Survey: 1983, Part A,* U.S. Department of Housing and Urban Development, sponsor. Washington, D.C.: U.S. Government Printing Office, 1985

parative economic revitalization of the Northeast, but also from the construction shortfall that it suffered during the 1970s and early 1980s.

In general, as we will present in more detail later, new units as they come on-stream within the private-market context tend to be relatively expensive. Therefore, it comes as no surprise, given the linkage of race and income levels, that the occupancy of newly constructed units is skewed toward whites, as compared to blacks (Exhibit 12-3). More than one out of four whites were the beneficiaries of new con-

EXHIBIT 12-3

Units Constructed Between 1970 and 1983, Percent of 1983 Total
by Race and Tenure: U.S. Total
(Numbers in thousands)

	Total Units, 1983	New Construction, 1970 to 1983	New Construction as a Percent of 1983 Total
All-year-round units	91,675	23,686	25.8%
Total Occupied	84,638	21,766	25.7
Owner Occupied	54,724	14,534	26.6
White	49,144	13,258	27.0
Black	4,123	774	18.8
Renter Occupied	29,914	7,232	24.2
White	23,418	6,015	25.7
Black	5,040	905	18.0

Source: U.S. Department of Commerce, U.S. Bureau of the Census, Current Housing Reports, Series H-150-83, *General Housing Characteristics for the United States and Regions: 1983, Annual Housing Survey: 1983, Part A*, U.S. Department of Housing and Urban Development, sponsor. Washington, D.C.: U.S. Government Printing Office, 1985

struction; less than one in five blacks were equivalent beneficiaries, in either the owner- or renter-occupied sectors.

Inventory Removals

Removals from the inventory have an equally potent impact, emphasized by the skew in their distribution. Between 1973 and 1983, 3.8 percent of the total owner-occupied supply as of 1973 had been removed from the inventory. The equivalent for the rental sector was 11.5 percent. *Of the 24.6 million renter-occupied units in 1973, one in nine, or 2.84 million, were removed from the stock during the following decade.* On an average basis, the occupied housing stock of America was drained of 454,000 units per year between 1973 and 1983, a minority of them (170,000 units) owner-occupied; a majority (284,000) renter-occupied.

It is not only the absolute number of losses accruing to the rental sector that is significant. Also relevant is the modest half-life of rental units in the United States which is implied by these data. Assuming a continuance of scrappage (removal) rates comparable to that illustrated in Exhibit 12-4 (11.5 percent per decade in the rental sector; 3.8 percent per decade in the owner sector), it is suggested that the half-

EXHIBIT 12-4

Removals from the Inventory, 1973 to 1983:
Proportion of 1973 Total, by Tenure and Region
(Numbers in thousands)

	Total Units, 1973	*Removals, 1973 to 1983*	*Removals as a Percent of 1973 Total*
U.S. Total			
Total Occupied	69,337	4,540	6.5%
Owner Occupied	44,653	1,700	3.8
Renter Occupied	24,684	2,840	11.5
Northeast Region			
Total Occupied	16,152	944	5.8
Owner Occupied	9,555	211	2.2
Renter Occupied	6,597	733	11.1
Midwest Region			
Total Occupied	18,742	1,163	6.2
Owner Occupied	12,945	468	3.6
Renter Occupied	5,797	694	12.0
South Region			
Total Occupied	21,806	1,743	8.0
Owner Occupied	14,498	744	5.1
Renter Occupied	7,307	999	13.7
West Region			
Total Occupied	12,638	791	6.3
Owner Occupied	7,655	276	3.6
Renter Occupied	4,983	414	8.3

Source: U.S. Department of Commerce, U.S. Bureau of the Census, Current Housing Reports, Series H-150-83, *General Housing Characteristics for the United States and Regions: 1983, Annual Housing Survey: 1983, Part A*, U.S. Department of Housing and Urban Development, sponsor. Washington, D.C.: U.S. Government Printing Office, 1985

life—i.e., the median longevity of the stock—of rental units is a relatively brief forty-five years; that for owner-occupied units, far in excess of a century.

In general, only the relatively modern rental sector of housing in the West had a modest single-digit decade-removal rate (8.3 percent mark). In the other three regions, however, it was in excess of 11 percent. While unquestionably there are limitations on the accuracy of the scrappage rate in general—with units flowing back into the inventory which were earlier counted as removals, as well as in counting procedures—the magnitudes are sufficient to suggest the comparative vulnerability of rental housing.

Displacement as a Function of Removals from the Inventory. Earlier data presented indicated the relative good fortune of whites as compared with blacks (synonymizing that with occupancy of new housing). The racial patterns are reversed as we turn to removals. In Exhibit 12-5 the occupancy of those 1973 housing units which had been removed from the stock by 1983 is shown by both tenure and race. Regardless of tenure, for both owner and renter occupancy, the displacement impact upon blacks was double that of whites.

In the renter-occupied sector, fully one in five units occupied by blacks in 1973 had been taken off the market by 1983. In the average year of the decade for which data are presented, one in fifty black renter households would discover that their unit was removed from the inventory. The equivalent for whites is not trivial, but a much more modest one in one hundred.

EXHIBIT 12-5

Removals from the Inventory, 1973 to 1983: Proportion of 1973 Total, U.S. Total
(Numbers in thousands)

	Total Units, 1973	Removals, 1973 to 1983	Removals as a Percent of 1973 Total
All-year-round units	75,293	5,471	7.3%
Total Occupied	69,337	4,540	6.5
Owner Occupied	44,653	1,700	3.8
White	41,239	1,472	3.6
Black	3,024	214	7.1
Renter Occupied	24,684	2,840	11.5
White	20,224	2,012	9.9
Black	3,938	759	19.3

Source: U.S. Department of Commerce, U.S. Bureau of the Census, Current Housing Reports, Series H-150-83, *General Housing Characteristics for the United States and Regions: 1983, Annual Housing Survey: 1983, Part A,* U.S. Department of Housing and Urban Development, sponsor. Washington, D.C.: U.S. Government Printing Office, 1985

Cost Impact

The processes discussed above not only shape the absolute size of the standing inventory, but also the structure of the costs of occupancy. *In effect, removals systematically delete the supply of low-cost accommodations.*

The median rent of the 1973 inventory was $132. The units removed during the ensuing 10 years had a median 1973 rent of only $98. Thus, as shown in Exhibit 12-6, removals emanate very largely from the bottom of the rental barrel. The dynamics of the market, and governmental efforts, continuously leech out those units which are least valued economically or are the most physically inadequate. More than one in four of the total rental housing units in the country in 1973 (6.5 million out of 24.3 million) had a monthly gross rent of under $100 per month. Almost one in five of these had literally disappeared within a decade. This disappearance was a physical removal from the housing stock. This was not merely a decline in the low-rent inventory as a function of upgrading.

EXHIBIT 12-6

Rental Removals from the Inventory, 1973 to 1983:
Proportion of 1973 Total, U.S. Total
(Numbers in thousands)

Gross Rent	Total Units, 1973	Removals, 1973 to 1983	Removals as a Percent of 1973 Total
Total[1]	24,348	2,778	11.4%
Less than $79	3,811	827	21.7
$80 to $99	2,742	450	16.4
$100 to $149	7,087	780	11.0
$150 to $199	5,561	314	5.6
$200 to $299	2,922	95	3.3
$300 or more	598	30	5.0
No cash rent	1,628	283	—
Median	$132	$98	—

Note: 1. Specified renter occupied

Source: U.S. Department of Commerce, U.S. Bureau of the Census, Current Housing Reports, Series H-150-83, *General Housing Characteristics for the United States and Regions: 1983, Annual Housing Survey: 1983, Part A*, U.S. Department of Housing and Urban Development, sponsor. Washington, D.C.: U.S. Government Printing Office, 1985

While the inventory of low-cost rental units was being depleted, the rental units constructed from 1973 to 1983 had a much higher level of impost (Exhibit 12-7). While the median rent of the overall inventory in 1983 had risen to $315, the median rent for units constructed from 1970 to 1983 was nearly 20 percent higher, or $369. New public-housing starts were at a dribble. Housing the poor in America in the 1980s has been much more dependent upon facilitating the filtration process than may have held true in earlier decades.

The same process is also evident within the owner sector (Exhibits 12-8 and 12-9). Units removed between 1973 to 1983 had a median 1973 value barely half that of the total 1973 inventory ($13,300 versus $24,100). In contrast, units constructed from 1970 to 1983 had a median 1983 value of $74,800. The median 1983 value of the overall owner inventory in comparison was only $59,700.

EXHIBIT 12-7

**Units Constructed Between 1970 and 1983, Monthly Gross Rent:
Proportion of 1983 Total, U.S. Total
(Numbers in thousands)**

Monthly Gross Rent	Total Units, 1983	New Construction, 1970 to 1983	New Construction as a Percent of 1983 Total
Total[1]	29,214	7,185	24.6%
Less than $100	1,197	333	27.8
$100 to $199	4,071	657	16.1
$200 to $299	7,377	1,158	15.7
$300 to $399	7,351	1,902	25.9
$400 to $499	4,212	1,469	34.9
$500 to $599	1,862	744	40.0
$600 to $699	848	338	39.9
$700 or more	895	357	39.9
No cash rent	1,401	226	—
Median	$315	$369	—

Note: 1. Specified renter occupied

Source: U.S. Department of Commerce, U.S. Bureau of the Census, Current Housing Reports, Series H-150-83, *General Housing Characteristics for the United States and Regions: 1983, Annual Housing Survey: 1983, Part A,* U.S. Department of Housing and Urban Development, sponsor. Washington, D.C.: U.S. Government Printing Office, 1985

EXHIBIT 12-8

1973 House Value of Removals from the Inventory, 1973 to 1983
Proportion of 1973 Total
(Numbers in thousands)

House Value	Total Units, 1973	Removals, 1973 to 1983	Removals as a Percent of 1973 Total
Total[1]	35,107	703	2.0%
Less than $5,000	787	113	14.4
$ 5,000 to $ 9,999	2,606	159	6.1
$10,000 to $14,999	4,287	120	2.8
$15,000 to $19,999	5,690	107	1.9
$20,000 to $24,999	5,102	62	1.2
$25,000 to $34,999	8,237	79	1.0
$35,000 to $49,999	5,545	40	0.7
$50,000 or more	2,854	23	0.8
Median	$24,100	$13,300	—

Note: 1. Specified owner occupied

Source: U.S. Department of Commerce, U.S. Bureau of the Census, Current Housing Reports, Series H-150-83, *General Housing Characteristics for the United States and Regions: 1983, Annual Housing Survey: 1983, Part A*, U.S. Department of Housing and Urban Development, sponsor. Washington, D.C.: U.S. Government Printing Office, 1985

The processes shown here are central elements in the continuous upgrading of housing that has taken place in the United States, with rare periods of abatement, for at least a century. In general, it is the least-attractive units which are removed from the stock, and as shown subsequently, those which are physically deficient as well. From the viewpoint of the nation as a whole, this both reflects upon, and serves as a stimulus for, new additions to the inventory that are much more consonant with modern tastes and standards. From the viewpoint of low-cost shelter, however, this is a process which can have a drastic immediate impact upon the least fortunate in our society.

EXHIBIT 12-9

Units Constructed Between 1970 and 1983:   House Value in 1983
Proportion of 1983 Total, U.S. Total
(Numbers in thousands)

House Value	Total Units, 1983	New Construction, 1970 to 1983	New Construction as a Percent of 1983 Total
Total[1]	43,535	10,167	23.4%
Less than $25,000	3,895	278	7.1
$ 25,000 to $ 49,999	12,910	1,734	13.4
$ 50,000 to $ 74,999	12,217	3,103	25.4
$ 75,000 to $ 99,999	7,247	2,370	32.7
$100,000 to $149,999	4,500	1,658	36.8
$150,000 to $199,999	1,508	556	36.9
$200,000 to $249,999	637	227	35.6
$250,000 to $299,999	268	97	36.2
$300,000 or more	356	144	40.4
Median	$59,700	$74,800	—

Note: 1. Specified owner occupied

Source: U.S. Department of Commerce, U.S. Bureau of the Census, Current Housing Reports, Series H-150-83, *General Housing Characteristics for the United States and Regions: 1983, Annual Housing Survey: 1983, Part A*, U.S. Department of Housing and Urban Development, Sponsor. Washington, D.C.: U.S. Government Printing Office, 1985

13

Scale, Condition
and Amenity Level

The changing reservoir of housing in the United States—continuously altered by new starts, conversions and removals from the inventory—has yielded a very substantial upgrading of shelter condition and amenity. By the mid-1980s, the physical profile of America's housing remained the envy of the world. The purpose of this chapter is to document the standing condition of the inventory—the base from which future housing conditions will be gauged.

Structure Size

The freestanding, single-family dwelling (one unit, detached) has been the modular form of shelter in America during the second half of the twentieth century. As shown in Exhibit 13-1, it dominated in absolute scale not only the owner-occupied sector, but also the rental sector. In 1983, detached one-family units accounted for 45.4 million out of 54.7 million owner-occupied dwellings. Only two percent of the owner-occupied stock was in structures with five units or more.

Detached one-family units also stood as the largest structural type within America's rental sector (8.1 million out of 29.9 million units), while attached one-family dwellings exhibited the fastest growth rate over the 1970 to 1983 period. Second, in absolute significance, were structures with two to four units; less than 10 percent of the occupied rental stock (2.8 million out of 29.9 million units) was found in structures comprising fifty or more units.

Large-scale apartment complexes are the exception rather than the rule in America. Small-scale residential environments predominate. However, while structure size remains modest in unit count, individual

EXHIBIT 13-1

Units in Structure, U.S. Total: 1970 to 1983
(Numbers in thousands)

	1970	1983	Change: 1970-1983 Number	Change: 1970-1983 Percent
Owner Occupied, Total	39,886	54,724	14,838	37.2%
1 unit, detached	34,397	45,417	11,020	32.0
1 unit, attached	1,113	2,668	1,555	139.7
2 to 4 units	2,161	2,263	102	4.7
5 units or more	464	1,139	675	145.5
Mobile home or trailer	1,752	3,236	1,484	84.7
Renter Occupied, Total	23,560	29,914	6,354	27.0
1 unit, detached	7,736	8,127	391	5.1
1 unit, attached	794	1,441	647	81.5
2 to 4 units	6,218	7,797	1,579	25.4
5 to 9 units	2,284	3,636	1,352	59.2
10 to 19 units	2,219	3,165	946	42.6
20 to 49 units	1,873	2,173	300	16.0
50 units or more	2,115	2,811	696	32.9
Mobile home or trailer	321	763	442	137.7

Source: U.S. Department of Commerce, U.S. Bureau of the Census, Current Housing Reports, Series H-150-83, *General Housing Characteristics for the United States and Regions: 1983, Annual Housing Survey: 1983, Part A*, U.S. Department of Housing and Urban Development, sponsor. Washington, D.C.: U.S. Government Printing Office, 1985

dwelling units, with only recessionary setbacks, have evidenced sustained growth in size.

Unit-Size Profiles

This is first revealed in the unit-size (rooms per unit) profile shown in Exhibit 13-2. In the 1970 to 1983 period, the owner-occupied inventory as a whole increased by 14.8 million units; this occurred despite an absolute reduction of units with two or fewer rooms. The major gains comprised larger units—composed of seven rooms or more—whose net increment, 7.3 million units, was almost half of the *total* 1970 to 1983 increase.

In the renter-occupied inventory, the changes were much less skewed. There was a decline in the proportion of extreme-sized units, both in the one- and two-room, as well as the five rooms-or-more sec-

EXHIBIT 13-2

Rooms Per Unit, U.S. Total: 1970 to 1983
(Numbers in thousands)

			Change: 1970–1983	
	1970	*1983*	*Number*	*Percent*
Owner Occupied, Total	39,886	54,724	14,838	37.2%
1 Room	90	95	5	5.6
2 Room	279	230	−49	−17.6
3 Room	1,275	1,320	45	3.5
4 Room	5,876	6,626	750	12.8
5 Room	11,394	14,494	3,100	27.2
6 Room	10,720	14,395	3,675	34.3
7 or more	10,251	17,566	7,315	71.4
Median	5.6	5.8	0.2	3.6
Renter Occupied, Total	23,560	29,914	6,354	27.0%
1 Room	994	969	−25	−2.5
2 Room	1,763	1,921	158	9.0
3 Room	5,381	6,853	1,472	27.4
4 Room	7,088	9,392	2,304	32.5
5 Room	4,705	5,927	1,222	26.0
6 Room	2,385	3,074	689	28.9
7 or more	1,294	1,778	484	37.4
Median	4.0	4.0	0.0	0.0

Source: U.S. Department of Commerce, U.S. Bureau of the Census, Current Housing Reports, Series H-150-83, *General Housing Characteristics for the United States and Regions: 1983, Annual Housing Survey: 1983, Part A*, U.S. Department of Housing and Urban Development, sponsor. Washington, D.C.: U.S. Government Printing Office, 1985

tors. It was the three- to four-room category which grew most rapidly; the demographic realities that underlay and supported this transition were earlier presented (see Chapters 3 and 4). Suffice it to note here that the full import of these changes can be realized only in the context of very substantial shrinkages in household sizes. Clearly, the role of the rental sector (at least for the more fortunate) in providing long-term, child-rearing environments has contracted in significance, if not absolute incidence, in light of the increased dominance of large, owner-occupied units.

The number of bedrooms per dwelling unit also serves as an indicator of unit scale (Exhibit 13-3). More than half—46.5 million out of 91.7 million units—of America's all-year-round housing units had three bedrooms or more by 1983. Indeed, the total number of bedrooms by

EXHIBIT 13-3

Number of Bedrooms, U.S. Total, All-Year-Round Housing Units:
1970 to 1983
(Number in thousands)

	1970	1983	Change: 1970–1983	
			Number	Percent
Total Year-Round Units	67,699	91,675	23,976	35.4%
No Bedrooms	1,630	1,790	160	9.8
1 Bedroom	10,681	13,129	2,448	22.9
2 Bedrooms	22,929	30,235	7,306	31.9
3 Bedrooms	23,945	34,689	10,744	44.9
4 or more Bedrooms	8,526	11,831	3,305	38.8
Total Bedroom Estimation[1]	171,004	236,821	65,817	38.5

Note: 1. Assumes units with four or more bedrooms have five bedrooms.

Source: U.S. Department of Commerce, U.S. Bureau of the Census, Current Housing Reports, Series H-150-83, *General Housing Characteristics for the United States and Regions: 1983, Annual Housing Survey: 1983, Part A,* U.S. Department of Housing and Urban Development, sponsor. Washington, D.C.: U.S. Government Printing Office, 1985

the latter year was estimated to be in excess of 236 million. America's bedroom count was virtually identical to its population total! Assuming that most married couples share a bedroom, this suggests that there was an "excess" of up to 50-million bedrooms in America by the early 1980s. This level of abundance probably is still incomprehensible to many societies in the world of the late 1980s.

The Floor-Area Escalator

The house that made Levittown famous in the early 1950s was an 800-square-foot tribute to modesty. By 1965, the *average* floor area of new one-family homes sold in the United States exceeded 1,500 square feet (Exhibit 13-4). By 1984 the average size approached 1,800 square feet. Thus, the typical new one-family home sold in America during the 1980s was more than twice the size of the Levitt forebearer. This was the case despite the reality that almost one out of five new one-family starts in 1984 was an attached, single-family dwelling (see Chapter 8). And this is to say nothing of the upgrading in internal amenity packages.

EXHIBIT 13-4

New One-Family Homes Sold:
Median and Average Square Feet of Floor Area,
U.S. Total: 1963 to 1985

Year	Median	Average
1963	1,365	NA
1964	1,415	1,470
1965	1,495	1,525
1966	1,525	1,570
1967	1,570	1,610
1968	1,605	1,665
1969	1,585	1,640
1970 R	1,400	1,510
1971	1,415	1,575
1972	1,460	1,590
1973	1,540	1,660
1974 R	1,565	1,670
1975 R	1,560	1,660
1976	1,620	1,710
1977	1,630	1,720
1978	1,650	1,750
1979	1,650	1,760
1980 R	1,570	1,700
1981 R	1,560	1,710
1982 R	1,530	1,690
1983	1,580	1,740
1984	1,610	1,790
1985	1,590	1,760

Note: R = recession year

Source: U.S. Bureau of the Census, Construction Reports – Series C-25, *Characteristics of New Housing: 1985*, U.S. Department of Commerce, Washington, D.C., 1986

Thus the reservoir of housing in the United States was being replenished by units of ever-larger size. However, the upward gradient did not proceed without interruption. The 1969-1970 recession was the first setback following the steady gains of the 1960s (Exhibit 13-4). Size renewed its upward movement, with only a temporary stumbling caused by the 1974–1975 recession. New peaks were reached by the late 1970s, but the recessions of 1980 and 1981–1982 halted the size advance. The latter then resumed as the mid-1980s economic expansions took hold.

Thus, the secular size trend has been one of basic increase. Superimposed on this, however, have been business-cycle variations.

The general pattern from the early 1960s through the mid-1980s has been a succession of size peaks coinciding with periods of general economic expansion, interrupted by recession but each surpassing in scale its immediate predecessor.

Housing Condition

Size is merely one criterion of housing quality. Simple measurements of the latter have long evaded researchers. Using extant Census Bureau criteria as a guide, however, it can be concluded that there has been a very substantial upgrading, particularly over the long term. Exhibit 13-5, for example, presents selected measures of housing inadequacy from 1940 to 1983. It is difficult to realize that as late as 1940, 45.2 percent of America's all-year-round housing units lacked some or all plumbing facilities. By 1983, there was a reduction of such deficiencies to 2.4 percent of the total inventory.

While the criteria used for rating housing as dilapidated or needing major repairs have been highly controversial, clearly the shrinkage in the incidence of such units has been dramatic—from 17.8 percent in 1940 to 4.6 percent in 1970. Indeed, even if the categories of "dilapi-

EXHIBIT 13-5

**All-Year-Round Housing Units: Measures of
Housing Inadequacy — U.S. Total, 1940 to 1983**

Measure	1940	1950	1960	1970	1976	1981	1983
Percent lacking some or all plumbing	45.2%	35.4%	16.8%	6.5%	3.4%	2.7%	2.4%
Percent dilapidated or needing major repairs	17.8	9.8	6.9	4.6	NA	NA	NA
Percent substandard: Dilapidated or lacking plumbing	49.2	36.9	18.2	9.0	NA	NA	NA

Sources: U.S. Department of Commerce, U.S. Bureau of the Census, Current Housing Reports, Series H-150-83, *General Housing Characteristics for the United States and Regions: 1983, Annual Housing Survey: 1983, Part A*, U.S. Department of Housing and Urban Development, sponsor. Washington, D.C.: U.S. Government Printing Office, 1985; and earlier decennial census and *Annual Housing Survey* volumes

dated" and/or "lacking plumbing" are aggregated together, by 1970 these substandard units represented less than 9.0 percent of the stock; in 1940 they comprised nearly half (49.2 percent).

The upgrading of America's housing stock has swept across all of its regions. As shown in Exhibit 13-6, units lacking some or all plumbing facilities have declined in every regional and metropolitan category from 1970 to 1983. By the terminal year, only 1.9 percent of the Northeast's housing units, and 1.2 percent of the West's, did not have an adequate quota of such facilities. However, the South still lags the rest of the nation, particularly in its rural (nonmetropolitan) and suburban (outside central cities) contexts. In general, failure to meet this standard is much more of a problem in rural areas (outside SMSAs) than in central cities. Nationally, in central cities, only 1.2 percent of the units are deficient, while in rural areas it is 5.0 percent.

EXHIBIT 13-6

All-Year-Round Housing Units, Lacking Some or All Plumbing Facilities, by Region and SMSA Status: 1970 and 1983
(Numbers in thousands)

Region	Total 1970	Total 1983	Inside SMSAs Total 1970	Inside SMSAs Total 1983	In Central Cities 1970	In Central Cities 1983	Not in Central Cities 1970	Not in Central Cities 1983	Outside SMSAs 1970	Outside SMSAs 1983
United States										
Total	4,398	2,233	1,494	750	716	328	778	422	2,904	1,483
Northeast	576	371	363	214	192	141	171	73	212	157
Midwest	1,069	463	399	163	216	84	183	79	670	299
South	2,395	1,174	544	253	197	61	347	192	1,851	921
West	358	225	187	120	110	42	77	78	170	106
Percent of Total All-Year-Round Units										
United States										
Total	6.5%	2.4%	3.3%	1.2%	3.2%	1.2%	3.3%	1.2%	13.4%	5.0%
Northeast	3.6	1.9	2.8	1.4	3.1	2.1	2.5	0.9	6.5	3.7
Midwest	5.7	2.0	3.3	1.1	3.6	1.3	3.0	0.9	10.3	3.6
South	11.5	3.8	4.7	1.5	3.2	0.8	6.4	2.1	19.9	6.9
West	3.0	1.2	2.0	0.8	2.6	0.7	1.5	0.9	6.6	2.6

Source: U.S. Department of Commerce, U.S. Bureau of the Census, Current Housing Reports, Series H-150-83, *General Housing Characteristics for the United States and Regions: 1983, Annual Housing Survey: 1983, Part A,* U.S. Department of Housing and Urban Development, sponsor. Washington, D.C.: U.S. Government Printing Office, 1985

The Home Heating Revolution

As the costs of energy soared upward until the early 1980s, the pattern of fuel use became an increasingly vital issue. But well before our own era there were equally important—if not more pressing—elements, concerning the ease, convenience, cleanliness and labor inputs required to keep winter at bay. The data presented in Exhibit 13-7 provide insight into these matters. As late as 1950, it was coal or coke which was the single most-common home heating fuel: more than a third (34.6 percent) of America's occupied housing units secured its heating from

EXHIBIT 13-7

Heating Fuels for Occupied Housing Units:
U.S. Total, 1950 to 1983
(Numbers in thousands)

	1950	1960	1970	1976	1983
Occupied Units, Total	42,826	53,024	63,445	74,005	84,638
House Heating Fuel:					
Utility Gas	11,387	22,851	35,014	41,219	46,700
Fuel Oil, Kerosene	9,686	17,158	16,473	16,451	13,031
Electricity	283	933	4,876	10,151	15,684
Bottled, Tank, or LP Gas	787	2,686	3,807	4,239	3,869
Coal or Coke	14,828	6,456	1,821	484	432
Wood or Other Fuel	4,855	2,460	1,060	998	4,245
None	999	478	395	463	677

Percent Distribution

	1950	1960	1970	1976	1983
Occupied Units, Total	100.0%	100.0%	100.0%	100.0%	100.0%
House Heating Fuel:					
Utility Gas	26.6	43.1	55.2	55.7	55.2
Fuel Oil, Kerosene	22.6	32.4	26.0	22.2	15.4
Electricity	0.7	1.8	7.7	13.7	18.5
Bottled, Tank, or LP Gas	1.8	5.1	6.0	5.7	4.6
Coal or Coke	34.6	12.2	2.9	0.7	0.5
Wood or Other Fuel	11.3	4.6	1.7	1.3	5.0
None	2.3	0.9	0.6	0.6	0.8

Source: U.S. Department of Commerce, U.S. Bureau of the Census, Current Housing Reports, Series H-150-83, *General Housing Characteristics for the United States and Regions: 1983, Annual Housing Survey: 1983, Part A*, U.S. Department of Housing and Urban Development, sponsor. Washington, D.C.: U.S. Government Printing Office, 1985; and earlier decennial census and *Annual Housing Survey* volumes

such sources. Gas accounted for slightly more than one-quarter (26.6 percent), with fuel oil, kerosene, etc., commanding a 22.6-percent share. Electricity played a very minor role, with only 0.7 percent of America's housing units utilizing it as energy for heating.

By 1983—a quarter of a century later—gas had assumed a dominant role: 55.2 percent of all housing units employed it for heat. Oil, which peaked in utilization in 1960 (32.4 percent), had fallen to 15.4 percent, far below even its 1950 share. Large declines had been experienced by the most primitive forms of heating: coal, coke, wood, and other fuel. Such sources had heated nearly half (44.9 percent) of America's occupied housing units in 1950. By 1976 they were down to the 2.0-percent level. But the second energy crisis of 1979 wrought even further change: wood and other fuel experienced a resurgence. By 1983, the latter heated more than 4.2 million homes, up from less than one million in 1976.

Electricity showed the biggest proportionate gain, surpassing fuel oil as the second most-common heating fuel, and approaching a share of almost one out of five occupied units (18.5 percent) by 1983. This shift was substantially the result of patterns of new construction. As shown in Exhibit 13-8, almost 50 percent of new privately owned, completed-since-1975, one-family houses in America were heated by electricity. By 1985, oil heat was installed in only three percent of newly completed, one-family dwellings.

Amenity Levels

The cost premium of new inventory additions, detailed in the preceding chapter, was not only a consequence of size, but also levels of amenity. Particularly significant, as shown in Exhibit 13-8, are number of bathrooms and central air conditioning. In 1970, 52 percent of newly completed one-family homes had 1.5 bathrooms or less. By 1985, 78 percent had two or more bathrooms, and this increase in facilities took place at a time of sharp demographic reductions in the number of potential users per unit.

Central air conditioning was once a relative luxury. As late as 1970, two-thirds of newly completed, one-family dwellings were sold without it. Despite new energy-cost thresholds, by 1985 70 percent of

EXHIBIT 13-8

Percent of New Privately Owned, Completed One-Family Houses with Various Characteristics: U.S. Total, 1970 to 1985

Characteristic	1970	1975	1980	1985
Bathrooms	100%	100%	100%	100%
1 or less	32	24	18	13
1.5	20	17	10	11
2	32	40	48	48
2.5 or more	16	20	25	29
Heating Fuel	100%	100%	100%	100%
Electricity	28	49	50	49
Gas	62	40	41	44
Oil	8	9	3	3
Other	1	2	5	4
Central Air Conditioning	100%	100%	100%	100%
With	34	46	63	70
Without	66	54	37	30
Parking Facilities	100%	100%	100%	100%
Garage	58	67	69	70
Carport	17	9	7	5
No garage or carport	25	24	24	25
Bedrooms	100%	100%	100%	100%
2 or less	13	14	17	25
3	63	65	63	57
4 or more	24	21	20	18

Note: Data beginning 1975 show percent distribution of characteristics for all houses completed (includes new houses completed, houses built-for-sale completed, contractor-built and owner-built houses completed, and houses completed for rent). Data for 1970 cover contractor-built and owner-built, houses for rent for year construction started, and houses sold for year of sale. Percents exclude houses for which characteristics specified were not reported.

Source: U.S. Bureau of the Census, Construction Reports – Series C-25, *Characteristics of New Housing: 1985*, U.S. Department of Commerce, Washington, D.C., 1986

one-family completions included central air conditioning. It had almost attained the status of basic necessity.

Through the 1980s, then, a continuous infusion of resources into the nation's housing stock took place. The shelter infrastructure of America has been vastly upgraded; the rapidly paced growth of the inventory has been marked by substantial improvements in its physical attributes. The process of upgrading, however, contributed to increasing costs. These are particularly important as they are matched to consumers' income resources.

IV

Market Relationships

14

Market Barometers:
Demand–Supply Interrelationships

The interaction between *demand* (expressed in household counts modified by economic capacities and social desires) and *supply* (and its physical and economic parameters) is the generator—and the very definition—of the housing market. Patterns of demand may emanate from life-style desires and aspirations, but their physical realization depends upon the capacity of the supply system to accommodate them. Thus, the availability of cost-competitive residential accommodations both reflects and shapes the profiles of demand.

It is the market arena that matches the population of households to the housing stock. The functioning of the market—its allocation of shelter to consumers—is measured by a limited set of variables. The "sensors" presently available are not abundant in number, nor are they entirely comprehensive in terms of coverage. Nonetheless, they act as basic barometers gauging the functioning of the broader market.

In this chapter, three major variables will be examined. *Vacancy rates* (a measure of the slack capacity of the market) are the quotients of vacant, available housing units divided by the total available supply. Changes in such rates over time gauge the relative absolute changes in the supply of housing versus the effective demand for it. *Persons per room* (a measure of internal housing density or crowding) is the quotient (at the individual unit scale) of household size divided by unit size (in rooms). This provides an index of the *fit* (quantity of space) of a household to its housing accommodations. *Income-cost/price/value relationships* relate the cost of consuming housing to resource (income) availability.

These are coarsely meshed nets. No matter how benign the relationships which they capture, there are always households and groups in desperate shelter straits. Their use, however, provides a framework

187

which utilizes standard, regularly collected data, and offers the potential for trend analysis.

Population, Households, and Inventory Growth

The first task before examining the market barometers is a brief recapitulation of the broader trends of growth in population, households, and housing units. The basic data in this regard are collected in Exhibit 14-1. Between the July 1 benchmarks of 1970 and 1983, the population of the nation increased by 25.5-million people, or 12.5 percent. During the same 13-year span (but estimated as of March of the respective years), the number of households expanded by 20.5 million, or 32.3 percent. Thus, for every individual added to the population, there was an addition of nearly one household.

Problems of comparability arise from further variations within the basic data accounts. The *Annual Housing Survey* employs October 31 for current measurements, and April 1970 (the decennial census) as the baseline. Consequently, the housing-unit totals are tallied over a slightly longer time frame (13.5 years) in this analysis. The 24-million-unit increase (33.4 percent) in the supply of all-year-round housing units overstates the differential—3.5 million (24.0 million, minus 20.5 million)—with household growth. This inconsistency can be miti-

EXHIBIT 14-1

Population, Households, and Housing Unit Change:
U.S. Total, 1970 and 1983
(Numbers in thousands)

	1970	1983	Change: 1970–1983	
			Number	Percent
Population[1]	203,810	229,348	25,538	12.5%
Households[2]	63,410	83,918	20,508	32.3
Occupied Housing Units	63,445	84,638	21,193	33.4
All-Year-Round Housing Units[3]	67,699	91,675	23,976	35.4

Notes: 1. Resident population as of July 1
           2. As of March of the respective years
           3. April 1, 1970 to October 31, 1983

Source: See preceding chapters

gated by employing occupied-housing units from the *Annual Housing Survey* as a surrogate for independent household tabulations. As a result of extending the accounting period six months, another 700,000 households (21.2 million versus 20.5 million) are secured, and the household–housing unit differential narrows (24-million housing units versus 21.2-million households).

Nonetheless, over the 1970 to 1983 period, the basic trend lines hold. Thus, the rate of growth of the housing supply (35.4 percent) was substantially in excess of the pace of growth of households (33.4 percent, or 32.3 percent), as well as the rate of population growth (12.5 percent).

A thirteen-year analytical span may tend to give the impression of smooth trend lines. As detailed previously, however, abrupt annual fluctuations mark supply additions as represented by housing starts. And it is vacancy rates which measure the relative balance between effective market demand and supply. We stress the qualifier of "effective market demand" here. At any one time, there may be significant latent need, but it typically must wait upon income competency or effective cost-reduction.

Vacancy Rates

The use of vacancy rates in measuring market performance has a legislative heritage. For example, in many instances the justification for rent control is predicated on the basis of a legislative determination of vacancy rates. The rationale usually is as follows. If the rate falls below a specified level, it is deemed that a housing emergency exists; supply is inadequate to meet housing need (or demand), and thus a malfunctioning market puts consumers at an extreme disadvantage. With little slack capacity in the inventory, occupants have limited mobility; therefore, the market fails to provide an adequately balanced pricing mechanism. There may be no inhibition to raising rents when the supply is scarce; hence, public regulation is justified via this logic.

Vacancy-Rate Derivation

The derivation of both owner- and renter-vacancy rates for 1970 and 1983 is presented in Exhibit 14-2, along with the basic composition of the vacant inventory for the respective years. As noted earlier,

EXHIBIT 14-2

Vacancy Totals and Vacancy Rate Determination:
U.S. Total, 1970 and 1983

Vacancy Totals

Vacancy Category	1970	1983
Vacant Year-Round Units	4,254,000	7,037,000
For Sale Only	501,000	955,000
For Rent Only	1,666,000	1,906,000
Rented or Sold, Not Occupied	345,000	1,005,000
Held for Occasional Use	998,000	1,459,000
Other Vacant	744,000	1,712,000

Vacancy Rate Determination

$$\text{Vacancy Rate} = \frac{\text{Vacant (For Sale or Rent)}}{\text{Occupied} + \text{Vacant (For Sale or Rent)}}$$

Owner

1970 $\text{Vacancy Rate} = \dfrac{501,000}{39,886,000 + 501,000} = 1.2\%$

1983 $\text{Vacancy Rate} = \dfrac{955,000}{54,724,000 + 955,000} = 1.7\%$

Renter

1970 $\text{Vacancy Rate} = \dfrac{1,666,000}{23,560,000 + 1,666,000} = 6.6\%$

1983 $\text{Vacancy Rate} = \dfrac{1,906,000}{29,914,000 + 1,906,000} = 6.0\%$

Source: U.S. Department of Commerce, U.S. Bureau of the Census, Current Housing Reports, Series H-150-83, *General Housing Characteristics for the United States and Regions: 1983, Annual Housing Survey: 1983, Part A*, U.S. Department of Housing and Urban Development, sponsor. Washington, D.C.: U.S. Government Printing Office, 1985

the vacancy rate is the quotient of the number of vacant, available housing units (owner or renter, respectively) divided by the sum of the total number of occupied units (owner or renter, respectively) and vacant available units. (Thus, the denominator represents the total available supply.)

Vacancy Rate Trend Line

A basic perspective on vacancy-rate behavior is shown in Exhibits 14-3 and 14-4, with the latter providing more detailed quarterly data.

EXHIBIT 14-3

Vacancy Rates, U.S. Total, by Area and Type: 1960, 1965, 1970 and 1975 to 1985

Area	1960	1965	1970	1975	1976	1977	1978	1979[1]	1979[2]	1980	1981	1982	1983[3]	1984[3]	1985[3]
Rental Units															
United States	8.1	8.3	5.3	6.0	5.6	5.2	5.0	5.0	5.4	5.4	5.0	5.3	5.5	6.3	6.7
Inside SMSAs[4]	7.0	8.0	4.9	6.1	5.7	5.3	5.2	5.0	5.4	5.2	4.8	5.0	5.3	6.1	6.4
In central cities[4]	(NA)	8.1	5.3	6.6	6.2	5.7	5.6	5.3	5.7	5.4	5.0	5.3	5.7	6.8	6.6
Not in central cities[4]	(NA)	7.8	4.3	5.4	5.1	4.6	4.7	4.7	5.1	4.8	4.6	4.6	4.8	5.3	6.2
Outside SMSAs[4]	10.3	8.8	6.4	5.7	5.1	5.2	4.5	4.9	5.4	6.1	5.7	6.2	6.3	6.7	7.3
Northeast	4.9	5.6	2.7	4.1	4.7	5.1	4.8	4.0	4.5	4.2	3.7	3.7	3.7	3.9	3.4
North Central	8.3	7.2	5.8	5.7	5.6	5.1	4.8	5.1	5.7	6.0	5.9	6.3	6.1	6.3	6.2
South	9.5	9.0	7.2	7.7	6.4	5.7	5.5	5.8	6.1	6.0	5.4	5.8	7.3	8.7	9.1
West	11.0	11.9	5.6	6.2	5.4	5.0	4.8	4.9	5.3	5.2	5.1	5.4	4.4	5.3	6.8
Homeowner Units															
United States	1.3	1.5	1.0	1.2	1.2	1.2	1.0	1.1	1.2	1.4	1.4	1.5	1.6	1.7	1.6
Inside SMSAs[4]	1.3	1.6	1.0	1.3	1.2	1.0	1.0	1.1	1.1	1.3	1.4	1.5	1.6	1.5	1.5
In central cities[4]	(NA)	1.5	1.1	1.4	1.4	1.2	1.3	1.2	1.4	1.4	1.6	1.8	1.8	1.7	2.0
Not in central cities[4]	(NA)	1.5	0.9	1.3	1.1	1.0	0.8	1.0	1.0	1.3	1.3	1.4	1.5	1.4	1.3
Outside SMSAs[4]	1.4	1.6	1.1	1.1	1.2	1.4	1.2	1.1	1.2	1.4	1.3	1.5	1.6	1.9	1.7
Northeast	1.0	1.0	0.8	1.0	1.0	0.9	0.8	0.9	1.0	1.1	1.1	1.0	0.9	0.9	0.8
North Central	1.2	1.2	1.0	1.0	1.0	0.9	1.0	1.1	1.2	1.6	1.4	1.6	1.6	1.5	1.5
South	1.6	2.0	1.2	1.5	1.6	1.7	1.3	1.1	1.1	1.3	1.3	1.6	1.9	2.1	1.9
West	1.4	1.9	1.1	1.5	1.2	0.9	1.0	1.3	1.3	1.6	1.7	1.9	1.9	1.9	1.9

Notes: 1. Rates as presented in the published *Housing Vacancy Survey Annual Report* for 1979.
2. Revised rates in 1979 and subsequently due to expanded methodology to improve reliability.
3. Data are fourth quarter rates.
4. Not directly comparable; for 1975 and subsequently, SMSAs defined as of 1970; prior to 1975, based on 1960 Census definition.

Source: U.S. Bureau of the Census, Current Housing Reports, Series H-111, *Vacancy Rates and Characteristics of Housing in the United States: Annual Statistics.* Washington, D.C.: U.S. Government Printing Office, Annual

EXHIBIT 14-4

**Rental and Homeowner Vacancy Rates for the United States:
1960 and 1965 to 1985**

Year	Rental vacancy rate				Homeowner vacancy rate			
	First quarter	*Second quarter*	*Third quarter*	*Fourth quarter*	*First quarter*	*Second quarter*	*Third quarter*	*Fourth quarter*
1985	6.3	6.2	6.8	6.7	1.8	1.9	1.8	1.6
1984	5.6	5.5	6.0	6.3	1.6	1.7	1.7	1.7
1983	5.7	5.5	5.8	5.5	1.4	1.5	1.6	1.6
1982	5.3	5.1	5.3	5.5	1.4	1.6	1.5	1.6
1981	5.2	5.0	5.0	5.0	1.3	1.3	1.5	1.4
1980	5.2	5.6	5.7	5.0	1.3	1.4	1.4	1.4
1979[1]	5.1	5.5	5.7	5.4	1.1	1.1	1.2	1.3
1979[2]	4.8	5.0	5.2	5.0	1.0	1.1	1.1	1.1
1978	5.0	5.1	5.0	5.0	1.0	0.9	1.0	1.1
1977	5.1	5.3	5.4	5.1	1.3	1.3	1.1	1.0
1976	5.5	5.8	5.7	5.3	1.2	1.2	1.3	1.2
1975	6.1	6.3	6.2	5.4	1.2	1.2	1.4	1.2
1974	6.2	6.3	6.2	6.0	1.2	1.1	1.2	1.3
1973	5.7	5.8	5.8	5.8	1.0	0.9	1.1	1.2
1972	5.3	5.5	5.8	5.6	1.0	1.0	0.9	1.0
1971	5.3	5.3	5.6	5.6	1.0	0.9	1.0	1.0
1970	5.4	5.4	5.3	5.2	1.0	1.0	1.1	1.1
1969	5.6	5.7	5.5	5.1	1.0	1.0	1.1	1.0
1968	6.1	6.2	5.9	5.4	1.1	1.1	1.2	1.2
1967	7.3	6.9	7.0	6.2	1.4	1.3	1.4	1.3
1966	8.3	7.4	7.4	7.7	1.5	1.5	1.4	1.3
1965	8.5	8.2	7.8	8.5	1.7	1.5	1.6	1.5
1960	8.0	8.0	8.3	8.4	1.2	1.3	1.3	1.3

Notes: 1. 1979 revised rates
          2. Rates as published in 1979 before revisions in processing were employed

Source: U.S. Department of Commerce, U.S. Bureau of the Census, Current Housing
Reports, *Housing Vacancies*, Series H-111, quarterly

The pattern over the 1960 to 1985 period reveals a sustained, abrupt decline in vacancy rates in the last half of the decade of the 1960s, from a total rental vacancy rate in 1965 of 8.3 percent to 5.3 percent by 1970. The process of change since then has been more erratic. An increase to 6.0 percent by 1975 was followed by reductions until the late 1970s/early 1980s, and then a steady increase from 1981 through

1985. By the latter date, the rental vacancy rate (6.7 percent) was higher than at any time since the mid-1960s. In the broad, a rapid expansion of the rental inventory in the 1980s led to a significant market oversupply during the mid-decade years.

There are also significant regional variations within these overall trend lines. The Northeast historically has had rental vacancy rates less than half those of the West, and barely 60 percent those of the nation. While regional rates converged in the 1970s, the historic differentials returned by the mid-1980s.

The metropolitan–nonmetropolitan rental vacancy rates have evidenced shifting patterns of divergence. Nonmetropolitan areas historically had the highest level of vacancies; but during the 1970s, their rates fell below those of metropolitan territories, representing a reversal of demand pressures as America's settlement patterns spread out. But by the mid-1980s, the long-term pattern had resumed.

Throughout the period under discussion, vacancies in the owner-occupied sector have been very low. Most newly built owner dwellings (particularly detached, single-family units) are presold. And, typically, owners of older units do not move until their houses are sold. But during the 1980s the rates have increased somewhat, accentuated by the number of speculatively built condos and co-ops.

The analysis of vacancy rates across the macro-geographic partitions indicates, at least in very broad measure, that the expansion of supply has been adequate to meet the growth in demand. Or, reversing the causal sequence, it can be suggested that the supply expansion has been such as to facilitate household formation to unprecedented levels.

Within this positive sweep, however, there are many exceptions. In central cities, for example, substantial vacancy-rate variations may occur, with demand exceeding supply in select neighborhoods, while less desirable areas may be so weak as to generate inventory losses (abandonment). Mid-Eastside Manhattan and the South Bronx stand, respectively, as prototypical examples within New York City—realities which are obviously obscured when the aggregate central-city indicators are studied.

Vacancy rates, at best, indicate only the match of broad supply–demand modules. They provide little insight into the adequacy of physical housing accommodations for their occupants. To secure at least a general grasp of the latter concern, it is necessary to examine the intersection of unit and household-size indicators.

Overcrowding: Internal Unit Density

One aspect of market "fit" is the quantity of housing delivered to individual households as measured by overcrowding. The degree to which overcrowding exists provides some indication of the adequacy of the supply as compared to the physical needs of households. And certainly this barometer has shown substantial positive results throughout recent history. The shrinkage in household size—a slow-growing population rapidly dividing into burgeoning numbers of households—coinciding with increasing unit sizes, and an overall housing inventory expansion in excess of household formations, has generated a diminished level of overcrowding and rising quantities of housing per occupant.

While this phenomenon is certainly not new (analytically, it represents the shape of the last three decades), the pace of improvement during the 1970 to 1983 period has been substantial. The data in Exhibit 14-5 reveal, for both owner- and renter-occupied facilities, the profile of the number of persons per room for the United States as a whole, as well as within several geographic subsets.

The criterion of overcrowding has tended to grow more stringent as expectations rise and earlier goals are surmounted. While in the 1950s it was viewed as 1.51 or more persons per room, by the 1970s the standard had been elevated to 1.01 or more persons per room.

The thirteen years from 1970 to 1983 witnessed a virtual two-thirds reduction in the proportion of owner-occupied units with 1.01 or more persons per room (6.4 percent to 2.3 percent). A smaller, but very substantial, decline was experienced in the renter-occupied sector (10.6 percent to 5.6 percent). This general pattern is consistent and pervasive in each of the geographic subsets shown in the exhibit.

In a complementary development, more than 50 percent of both owner- and renter-occupied facilities across all geographic partitions had .50 persons or less per room by 1983. The consumption of increasing quantities of housing space continued as a major dynamic through the 1980s.

It is significant to note in this context that the incidence of overcrowding in central cities falls below that in nonmetropolitan areas. The problem has not been extinguished by any means, but clearly the order of impact has decreased substantially. By 1983, for example, only 2.1 percent of all central city, renter-occupied housing units had 1.51 or more persons per room.

EXHIBIT 14-5

Persons Per Room, Percentage Distribution, Owner- and Renter-Occupied Units: U.S. Total by Geographic Area, 1970 and 1983

| | Total | | Inside SMSAs | | | | Outside SMSAs | |
| | | | In Central Cities | | Not in Central Cities | | | |
	1970	1983	1970	1983	1970	1983	1970	1983
Owner Occupied Total	100.0%	100.0%	100.0%	100.0%	100.0%	100.0%	100.0%	100.0%
.50 or less	53.0	64.6	54.8	66.4	49.5	64.8	55.5	63.2
.51 to 1.00	40.6	33.1	39.0	31.2	44.4	33.5	37.4	33.8
1.01 to 1.50	5.2	1.9	5.0	1.9	5.0	1.4	5.5	2.5
1.51 or more	1.2	0.4	1.1	0.4	1.0	0.3	1.7	0.5
Renter Occupied Total	100.0%	100.0%	100.0%	100.0%	100.0%	100.0%	100.0%	100.0%
.50 or less	45.0	56.0	46.1	54.7	44.8	57.4	43.0	56.4
.51 to 1.00	44.4	38.4	43.7	38.9	46.3	38.0	43.6	38.1
1.01 to 1.50	7.3	4.0	7.1	4.4	6.4	3.2	8.7	4.2
1.51 or more	3.3	1.6	3.1	2.1	2.4	1.4	4.7	1.2

Source: U.S. Department of Commerce, U.S. Bureau of the Census, Current Housing Reports, Series H-150-83, *General Housing Characteristics for the United States and Regions: 1983, Annual Housing Survey: 1983, Part A*, U.S. Department of Housing and Urban Development, sponsor. Washington, D.C.: U.S. Government Printing Office, 1985

Even allowing for some level of population undercount, the basic trend lines have now been established. The overcrowding concerns of a generation ago have largely disappeared. The primary focus has shifted to cost.

Rent/Value/Cost-Income Ratios

Two alternative concepts of basic demand–supply interactions have been noted. One suggests that the rapid expansion of supply has stimulated and facilitated the process of household formation, in effect serving to escalate demand. The alternate interpretation envisions inventory additions struggling to maintain parity with ever-burgeoning demand, as the nation's population resettles itself into ever smaller household configurations. This distinction, however, is artificial. The reality is more of interacting forces than a one-way linkage. And this dynamic receives an additional impetus as other variables are entered into the equation: income capacities, occupancy costs, and levels of inflation—the major economic parameters.

Rental Costs and Income

Despite the nominally excess supply of housing units created from 1970 to the mid-1980s (over and above the growth of both population and household numbers), costs soared. America's renters spent more of their income in order to secure housing. Summary data in this regard are shown in Exhibit 14-6. Median gross rent increased by 191.6 percent between 1970 and 1983; median incomes of renter households grew by a much more modest 96.8 percent. In turn, the 20 percent gross rent–income ratio (the proportion of income allotted to shelter) in 1970 shifted to 29 percent by 1983. And this was a pattern which pervaded all regional and geographic partitions, as shown in both Exhibits 14-6 and 14-7.

Certainly, these simple tabulations could serve to suggest a "crisis" within the rental sector. An alternative interpretation is also possible. The greater consumption of housing can imply that housing costs were low, encouraging increased demand. This is reflected by increased rates of household formation. If "real" costs rose, they should have inhibited this key factor. Incomes were stressed by a greater consumption of

EXHIBIT 14-6

Renter Households, Income and Rent Relationships:
U.S. Total, 1970 to 1983

	1970	1983	Change: 1970–1983 Number	Change: 1970–1983 Percent
U.S. Total				
Median Gross Rent	$ 108	$ 315	$ 207	191.7%
Median Income	$6,300	$12,400	$6,100	96.8%
Median Rent/Income Ratio[1]	20%	29%	9%	45.0%
Northeast Region				
Median Gross Rent	$ 110	$ 316	$ 206	187.3%
Median Income	$6,900	$12,400	$5,500	79.7%
Median Rent/Income Ratio[1]	20%	29%	9%	45.0%
Midwest Region				
Median Gross Rent	$ 110	$ 286	$ 176	160.0%
Median Income	$6,700	$11,800	$5,100	76.1%
Median Rent/Income Ratio[1]	20%	28%	8%	40.0%
South Region				
Median Gross Rent	$ 93	$ 304	$ 211	226.9%
Median Income	$5,400	$12,400	$7,000	129.6%
Median Rent/Income Ratio[1]	20%	27%	7%	35.0%
West Region				
Median Gross Rent	$ 119	$ 362	$ 243	204.2%
Median Income	$6,500	$13,500	$7,000	107.7%
Median Rent/Income Ratio[1]	22%	30%	8%	36.4%

Note: 1. Published Ratio

Source: U.S. Department of Commerce, U.S. Bureau of the Census, Current Housing Reports, Series H-150-83, *General Housing Characteristics for the United States and Regions: 1983, Annual Housing Survey: 1983, Part A*, U.S. Department of Housing and Urban Development, sponsor. Washington, D.C.: U.S. Government Printing Office, 1985

housing space and amenity, but this reflected the greater priority given housing by consumers.

Detailed Rent–Income Ratios

But the use of simple measures of centrality can obscure as much as enlighten. Analysis requires a grasp of the dispersion or spread of data, the relative importance of the extremes. In Exhibit 14-8, the distribution of gross rent–income ratios is presented. In 1970, slightly less

EXHIBIT 14-7

Rent-Income Ratios by Region and Geographic Area: 1970 to 1983

	Total		Total		In Central Cities		Not in Central Cities		Outside SMSAs	
	1970	1983	1970	1983	1970	1983	1970	1983	1970	1983
United States Total	20%	29%	21%	29%	21%	31%	20%	28%	19%	27%
Northeast	20	29	20	29	20	30	19	27	20	29
Midwest	20	28	20	29	21	31	19	26	19	27
South	20	27	21	28	22	29	20	27	18	26
West	22	30	23	31	24	32	22	30	20	28

Source: U.S. Department of Commerce, U.S. Bureau of the Census, Current Housing Reports, Series H-150-83, *General Housing Characteristics for the United States and Regions: 1983, Annual Housing Survey: 1983, Part A*, U.S. Department of Housing and Urban Development, sponsor. Washington, D.C.: U.S. Government Printing Office, 1985

than 40 percent of America's renters were paying 25 percent or more of their incomes for rent; by 1983 the equivalent figure was 57.9 percent. Indeed, in central cities the proportion at the latter point of time exceeded the 60-percent level.

As stated earlier, the change in rent–income ratios basically relates to two different pools of renters—one at the baseline in 1970, the other as of 1983. And as earlier discussed, there had been a consistent withdrawal of more affluent tenantry into homeownership. Thus, while rents increased relatively modestly, the pool of renters represented an increasingly less affluent proportion of American households. Regardless of the causal factors at work, the pressures that evolved were evident.

The singular stress of rent on income as a function of household configuration is also key to appropriate insight into the market. Data on this point for 1983 are shown in Exhibit 14-9. (In order to secure measures by household demographics, a median-rent to median-income ratio had to be constructed on the basis of *group* rent and income medians. In the preceding exhibits, the median rent–income ratio represents the median of the distribution of individual household rent-income ratios.) While the median-rent to median-income ratio for all households stood at 30.5 percent in 1983, the married-couple household median was considerably lower—23.4 percent. But this was a sector which throughout the decade of the 1970s had rapidly fled rental housing.

EXHIBIT 14-8

Rent-Income Ratios by Geographic Area: 1970 to 1983

| | Total | | Inside SMSAs | | | | | | Outside SMSAs | |
| | | | Total | | In Central City | | Not in Central City | | | |
	1970	1983	1970	1983	1970	1983	1970	1983	1970	1983
Specified Renter Occupied	100.0%	100.0%	100.0%	100.0%	100.0%	100.0%	100.0%	100.0%	100.0%	100.0%
Less than 10%	9.8	3.9	8.9	3.5	9.3	3.4	8.3	3.7	13.0	5.4
10 to 14%	19.3	10.1	18.9	9.7	18.5	9.2	19.6	10.3	21.0	11.9
15 to 19%	18.4	13.9	18.6	13.5	17.6	12.3	20.3	15.2	17.6	15.1
20 to 24%	12.9	14.2	13.2	14.3	12.7	13.7	14.2	15.0	11.6	14.0
25 to 34%	14.3	20.7	14.6	20.8	14.5	20.5	14.7	21.1	13.1	20.4
35 to 49%		14.4		14.7		15.0		14.3		13.1
50% or more	25.3	22.8	25.7	23.6	27.3	26.0	23.0	20.3	23.7	20.1
Median	20%	29%	21%	29%	21%	31%	20%	28%	19%	27%

Note: Upper 1970 limit was 35% or more

Source: U.S. Department of Commerce, U.S. Bureau of the Census, Current Housing Reports, Series H-150-83, *General Housing Characteristics for the United States and Regions: 1983, Annual Housing Survey: 1983, Part A,* U.S. Department of Housing and Urban Development, sponsor. Washington, D.C.: U.S. Government Printing Office, 1985

EXHIBIT 14-9

Median Rent as a Percent of Median Income:
U.S. Total, 1983

Household Type	1983 Median Income	1983 Median Monthly Gross Rent	1983 Median Annual Gross Rent	1983 Median Annual Rent as a Percent of Median Income
Total Households	$12,400	$315	$3,780	30.5%
2-or-more-Person	14,200	340	4,080	28.7
Married Couple	17,900	349	4,188	23.4
Under 25	14,300	310	3,720	26.0
25 to 29	19,400	348	4,176	21.5
30 to 34	19,700	373	4,476	22.7
35 to 44	20,200	381	4,572	22.6
45 to 64	19,100	357	4,284	22.4
65 and over	12,400	308	3,696	29.8
Other Male	14,000	371	4,452	31.8
Under 65	14,400	375	4,500	31.3
65 and over	8,500	316	3,792	44.6
Other Female	8,500	312	3,744	44.0
Under 65	8,300	314	3,768	45.4
65 and over	9,700	278	3,336	34.4
1-Person	9,900	269	3,228	32.6

Source: U.S. Department of Commerce, U.S. Bureau of the Census, Current Housing Reports, Series H-150-83, *Financial Characteristics of the Housing Inventory of the United States and Regions: 1983, Annual Housing Survey: 1983, Part C*, U.S. Department of Housing and Urban Development, sponsor. Washington, D.C.: U.S. Government Printing Office, 1985

Only the very young (under 25 years of age) and mature (65 years of age and over) married couples had ratios exceeding 25 percent.

It is the other household configurations, particularly those which are female-headed, that must surrender the largest proportions of their incomes for rents. The "other female" category, which includes many single-parent families, had a median-rent to median-income ratio of 44 percent in 1983. And as shown in Exhibit 14-10, this is a phenomenon which has demonstrated progressive deterioration over time. While all rental household types have seen housing costs exert greater fiscal pressures, it is the female-householder sector whose rent burden has grown most markedly.

EXHIBIT 14-10

**Renter Households, Median Rent as a Percent of Median Income:
1973 to 1983**

Household Type	1973	1979	1981	1983
2-or-more-Person	19.6%	24.1%	26.7%	28.7%
Married Couple	18.2	20.0	22.2	23.4
Under 25	19.8	21.3	24.0	26.0
25 to 29	17.4	19.0	20.6	21.5
30 to 34	17.0	18.6	21.4	22.7
35 to 44	17.1	19.0	21.2	22.6
45 to 64	16.4	19.1	20.7	22.4
65 and over	29.6	27.8	30.7	29.8
Other Male	21.0	28.3	31.1	31.8
Under 65	20.7	28.1	30.9	31.3
65 and over	28.0	31.0	33.6	44.6
Other Female	26.9	37.2	40.9	44.0
Under 65	26.6	38.3	41.9	45.4
65 and over	31.0	32.4	34.3	34.4
1-Person	30.70	30.2	31.4	32.6

Sources: U.S. Department of Commerce, U.S. Bureau of the Census, Current Housing Reports, Series H-150-83, *Financial Characteristics of the Housing Inventory of the United States and Regions: 1983, Annual Housing Survey: 1983, Part C,* U.S. Department of Housing and Urban Development, sponsor. Washington, D.C.: U.S. Government Printing Office, 1985; and previous editions of this volume for the respective years

Thus, the demographic sectors on the lower rungs of the income ladder, as detailed in Chapter 6, have the heaviest shares of income which must be allocated to shelter costs. And they play an increasing role within the rental market. American households of means have largely shifted to ownership.

Ownership Relationships

An endemic debate on the trends in affordability of pre- and post-inflation homeownership has been a staple of the housing field. Exhibits 14-11 through 14-15 provide some of the key data relating to this broad issue. The first of these compares the median sales prices of new one-family housing with median family incomes, deriving the sales price (value) to income ratio. The pattern is one which has altered quite markedly over time. At the beginning of the 30-year cycle shown,

EXHIBIT 14-11

Median Sales Prices of New One-Family Houses Sold and Median Family Income, United States: 1954 to 1985

Year	Median Sales Price	Median Family Income	Ratio of Sales Price to Income
1954	$12,300	$ 4,173	2.95
1955	13,700	4,421	3.10
1956	14,300	4,783	2.99
1959	15,200	5,417	2.81
1963	18,000	6,249	2.88
1964	18,900	6,569	2.88
1965	20,000	6,957	2.87
1966	21,400	7,532	2.84
1967	22,700	7,933	2.86
1968	24,700	8,632	2.86
1969	25,600	9,433	2.71
1970	23,400	9,867	2.37
1971	25,200	10,285	2.45
1972	27,600	12,116	2.48
1973	32,500	12,051	2.70
1974	35,900	12,836	2.78
1975	39,300	13,719	2.86
1976	44,200	14,958	2.95
1977	48,800	16,009	3.05
1978	55,700	17,640	3.16
1979	62,900	19,661	3.20
1980	64,600	21,023	3.07
1981	68,900	22,388	3.08
1982	69,300	23,433	2.96
1983	75,300	24,549	3.07
1984	79,900	26,433	3.03
1985	84,100	27,735	3.03

Sources: U.S. Bureau of the Census, Department of Commerce, *Construction Reports,* "New One-Family Houses Sold and For Sale," Series C-25 (Washington, D.C.: U.S. Government Printing Office, Monthly); U.S. Bureau of the Census, Department of Commerce, Current Population Reports Series P-60, *Money Income and Poverty Status of Families and Persons in the United States: Annual* (Washington, D.C.: U.S. Government Printing Office, Annual)

the ratio was approximately 3.0, i.e., the median sales price was triple that of median family income. It descended to a low of 2.37 in 1970 (in part, undoubtedly, as a result of a surge of subsidized housing becoming available at that time). It reached its high of 3.20 in 1979, the last year of the homeownership binge of the 1970s. But by the mid-1980s, the ratio had returned to the same levels as prevailed in the mid-1950s.

EXHIBIT 14-12

Owner Households by Household Configuration, U.S. Total: Income and House Value Relationship, 1983

Household Type	1983 Median Income	1983 Median House Value	1983 House Value/ Income Ratio
Total Households	$24,400	$59,700	2.4
2-or-more-Person	27,400	62,100	2.3
Married Couple	29,100	63,600	2.2
Under 25	19,900	42,300	2.1
25 to 29	27,100	54,700	2.0
30 to 34	30,300	62,200	2.1
35 to 44	33,700	70,200	2.1
45 to 64	32,300	67,000	2.1
65 and over	16,100	53,800	3.3
Other Male	24,300	57,600	2.4
Under 65	26,200	59,800	2.3
65 and over	15,600	47,900	3.1
Other Female	15,900	49,500	3.1
Under 65	16,700	51,200	3.1
65 and over	13,400	44,600	3.3
1-Person	10,400	46,500	4.5

Source: U.S. Department of Commerce, U.S. Bureau of the Census, Current Housing Reports, Series H-150-83, *Financial Characteristics of the Housing Inventory of the United States and Regions: 1983, Annual Housing Survey: 1983, Part C*, U.S. Department of Housing and Urban Development, sponsor. Washington, D.C.: U.S. Government Printing Office, 1985

Thus, the ratio has traversed a long cycle—decreasing in the 1960s, rising in the 1970s, only to return in the 1980s to the levels of three decades earlier.

Within this pattern, it is important to focus on the realities of owner-occupied units by household type. Again, simple measures of centrality—median income and median house value—provide more insight when appropriately partitioned by household configuration (Exhibit 14-12). While the data are not directly comparable to those presented in Exhibit 14-11, they do indicate the variations, as a function of income-related household configurations, to the housing market. The data parallel very closely the rental counterparts discussed in Exhibit 14-9. It is the elderly- and female-headed households that exhibit the greatest level of imbalance between income and their house values.

EXHIBIT 14-13

Median House Value to Income Ratio, U.S. Total:
1976, 1981 and 1983

Household Type	1976	1981	1983
2-or-more-Person	2.1	2.4	2.3
Married Couple	2.0	2.3	2.2
Under 25	2.0	2.2	2.1
25 to 29	2.0	2.1	2.0
30 to 34	2.1	2.2	2.1
35 to 44	1.9	2.2	2.1
45 to 64	1.9	2.1	2.1
65 and over	3.3	3.6	3.3
Other Male	2.1	2.5	2.4
Under 65	2.0	2.4	2.3
65 and over	2.6	3.3	3.1
Other Female	2.8	3.3	3.1
Under 65	2.8	3.2	3.1
65 and over	3.3	3.7	3.3
1-Person	4.6	4.8	4.5

Source: U.S. Department of Commerce, U.S. Bureau of the Census, Current Housing Reports, Series H-150-83, *Financial Characteristics of the Housing Inventory of the United States and Regions: 1983, Annual Housing Survey: 1983, Part C*, U.S. Department of Housing and Urban Development, sponsor. Washington, D.C.: U.S. Government Printing Office, 1985

And this is a pattern which has persisted over time, as shown in Exhibit 14-13.

The adequacy of simple value-to-income ratios for gauging market dynamics is limited. Certainly, direct shelter costs as a share of income stand as a measure of somewhat greater potency. Exhibit 14-14 presents the relevant data in this context.

What is unanticipated is the modest scale of housing-cost burdens for homeowners when the focus is on the total pool of ownership units. As of 1983, selected monthly housing costs (the sum of mortgage payments, property taxes, insurance, utilities, and garbage collection) as a percentage of income for units with a mortgage stood at 20 percent. For units owned free and clear, selected housing costs represented only 13 percent of income. While these percentages do represent increases from the levels of a decade earlier, they have been increasing far more

EXHIBIT 14-14

Owner-Occupied Units, Select Housing Costs as a Percent of Income:
U.S. Total, 1974, 1977, 1979, 1981 and 1983
(Numbers in thousands)

	1974	1977	1979	1981	1983
Specified Owner Occupied	36,154	38,754	41,336	43,293	43,535
Units with a Mortgage	22,959	24,889	26,446	27,917	27,758
(Percent)	63.5%	64.2%	64.0%	64.5%	63.8%
Units Owned Free and Clear	13,195	13,865	14,891	15,376	15,777
(Percent)	36.5%	35.8%	36.0%	35.5%	36.2%
Selected Monthly Housing Costs (Median)					
Units with a Mortgage	$209	$283	$337	$402	$463
Units Owned Free and Clear	$ 72	$102	$116	$143	$166
Selected Monthly Housing Costs as a Percent of Income (Median)					
Units with a Mortgage	17%	19%	19%	19%	20%
Units Owned Free and Clear	11%	12%	12%	12%	13%

Sources: U.S. Department of Commerce, U.S. Bureau of the Census, Current Housing Reports, Series H-150-83, *General Housing Characteristics for the United States and Regions: 1983, Annual Housing Survey: 1983, Part A,* U.S. Department of Housing and Urban Development, sponsor. Washington, D.C.: U.S. Government Printing Office, 1985; and previous annual additions for the respective years.

modestly than rent-income ratios (Exhibit 14-10). For most extant American homeowners in the mid-1980s, at least as interpreted via the *Annual Housing Survey,* housing costs certainly did not appear to be excessive.

Much of this was a residual from the pre-inflation years of the 1970s, with costs—at least in part—still reflecting the economic parameters of an early era. However, the market reality confronting new purchasers has been quite different. A measure of affordability of existing homes for the median American family for each year from 1970 to 1985 is shown in Exhibit 14-15. Much of the cyclicity previously discussed is evident in the trends in the various data entries. *Significantly by 1986, when monthly principal and interest (P + I) payments required to carry the purchase of the median-price, existing, single-family home fell to their lowest level ($588) since 1980, they were still far higher than the median total housing costs paid by the overall pool of U.S. owner-occupied units (Exhibit 14-14).*

EXHIBIT 14-15

Housing Affordability: U.S. Total, 1970 to 1986

Year	Median-Priced Existing Single-Family Home	Mortgage[1] Rate	Monthly Principal and Interest Payment	Payment as Percent of Income	Median Family Income	Qualifying[2] Income	Affordability[3] Index
1970	$23,000	8.35%	$140	17.0%	$ 9,867	$ 6,697	147.3
1971	24,800	7.67	141	16.5	10,285	6,770	151.9
1972	26,700	7.52	150	16.2	11,116	7,183	154.8
1973	28,900	8.01	170	16.9	12,051	8,151	147.9
1974	32,000	9.02	206	19.2	12,902	9,905	130.3
1975	35,300	9.21	232	20.2	13,719	11,112	123.5
1976	38,100	9.11	248	19.9	14,958	11,888	125.8
1977	42,900	9.02	277	20.7	16,010	13,279	120.6
1978	48,700	9.58	330	22.4	17,640	15,834	111.4
1979	55,700	10.92	422	25.7	19,680	20,240	97.2
1980	62,200	12.95	549	31.3	21,023	26,328	79.9
1981	66,400	15.12	677	36.3	22,388	32,485	68.9
1982	67,800	15.38	702	35.9	23,433	33,713	69.5
1983	70,300	12.85	616	29.9	24,580	29,546	83.6
1984	72,400	12.49	618	28.2	26,433	29,650	89.1
1985	75,500	11.74	609	26.2	27,940	29,243	95.5
1986 (June)	82,300	10.21	588	24.7	28,625	28,226	101.4

Notes: 1. Mortgage rate is the effective rate on loans closed on existing homes as determined by the Federal Home Loan Bank Board.
2. Qualifying Income is based on current lending requirements of the Federal National Mortgage Association using a 20-percent downpayment.
3. Index equals 100 when median family income equals qualifying income.

Source: National Association of Realtors, Economics and Research Division, *Existing Home Sales*, Washington, D.C., Monthly

Despite this, by the mid-1980s, with recovery from the devastating 1980–1982 recessions, housing affordability improved markedly. In the midst of the recession, the median family income in the United States was less than 70 percent of the income level required to qualify for a mortgage to purchase the median-priced, existing, single-family home (Exhibit 14-15); by 1986, the median income exceeded 100 percent of the qualifying figure.

The housing market conditions in the mid-1980s began to approach those of the single-family boom years of 1977–1979. The expansionary phase of the business cycle had again developed in concert with improved homeownership market conditions. Indeed, the latter was increasingly viewed as the locomotive—with the business cycle the caboose.

15

Housing to Come: Markets Dynamics and Issues

The prospects and issues raised by America's housing market dynamics are complex. Forecasting their exact scale, shape and variation is an uncertain art form. Nonetheless, we would like to suggest some parts of the picture to come.

America's Shelter: The Single-Family Unit

America's shelter of choice has been the detached, single-family home. Despite the fiscal battering imposed by economic cycles and high costs, this remained an unshakable rock—the desire for freestanding, single-family units proved impregnable and constant. While the recession of the early 1980s brought condominiums and multifamily units into the limelight, their share of market receded with prosperity. We see little on the landscape that will alter this relationship. The emerging demographics, with their dominance of middle-age, should ensure an unparalleled competence to secure this dwelling selection.

The Upscale, Repeat Buyer

The prime center of the housing market will be the upscale, repeat buyer. These will be the households who have bought the attached condominiums of the recent past, and/or modest, freestanding housing as their resources expanded. They will graduate to buyers of choice rather than of necessity. Upscale, seasoned, repeat buyers will dominate the 1990s.

Taxation and Homeownership

The tax "revolutions" of the 1980s—manifested in the 1981 and 1986 tax acts—led, respectively, to a rental housing boom and a rental housing bust. Income-producing residential real estate's future will remain tied to the parameters of America's tax codes, but increasingly will be limited by the new demographics.

The homeownership dynamic was barely grazed by "revolutions" past. It remained a dominant part of the American social fabric. Indeed, the mid-decade tax change enhanced homeownership's role as the premier middle-class tax shelter. The long-standing homeownership ethic will not be measurably weakened by American tax code vicissitudes in the future.

Communications Technology and Residence

The sweep and proliferation of communications technology enhance the role of the primary residence as a focal point for entertainment and as the key physical setting for consumption. High-tech media rooms (with projection TVs, VCRs, and cable linkages) have rendered quaint the old TV room and have posed yet another threat to the theater industry. And this is just one illustration of the technological ingenuity which is reinforcing the role of residence. While we are somewhat more conservative than some commentators in terms of the potential of the new electronic "cottage industries" (employment at home while information commutes), it is nevertheless a very real factor further enhancing the residence role.

Primary Life-Style Focus

As some of the preceding factors suggest, housing will be reinforced as the primary target of consumer spending. Life-style elements—of bedroom suites incorporating "spas" rather than a stall shower, of kitchens with a high-tech presence—provide the potentials for enhancing the square footage of housing beyond utilitarian demographic requirements. The average size and amenity levels of housing units—assuming the cooperation of the American economy—will enter the threshold of a new frontier.

Baby Boom Segmentation: Bypassed Consumers

The baby boom has never been, nor will it ever be, a monolithic whole. The leading edge of the generation, which rode the housing-inflationary cycle of the 1970s, will have far more housing-capital accumulation than its rearguard contingents. In addition, the participants in the "new" economy will have far higher income potentials than those imprisoned in the old. And there will be demographic sectors of less-than-affluent financial capacity—single-parent families among them. Not everyone will be able to secure adequate accommodations on the "express" housing train. From a demographic point of view, however, growth in the latter group's number should diminish.

The Window of Opportunity: Social Housing

America's middle class is here to stay. The shrinkage that may take place in its scale will be upward- rather than downward-bound. Yet, there will be a portion of America's households for whom shelter, even at its most basic level, becomes more and more unattainable. Its extreme has been mirrored in the growth of the homeless; it is and will be far broader than this group alone. There are no easy answers to the problem. But there will be a window of opportunity evolving, given the diminished level of future household formation. The supply system will have excess capacity and will probably overbuild. This may present the "underhoused" with increased filtering opportunities at the very least. But unparalleled opportunities will be available for governmental efforts taking advantage of slack production capacity. The industry, given resources, will turn to this target of necessity.

Redressed Generational Inequities

As we move deeper into the third economic/housing era, both inter- and intragenerational shelter inequities have been at least partially redressed. The 1970s witnessed a financial tug-of-war between generations. When interest rates on CDs (Certificates of Deposit) peaked at 16 percent and more, a powerful flow of funds emerged. It moved from the relatively youthful baby boomers, borrowing for housing, to their typically more mature creditors, particularly the elderly, who had accumulated savings and resided in housing with minimal, if any, outstanding debt. This substantially diminished in the face of the more modest interest rates of the mid-1980s.

Within the baby boom itself there is not only segmentation, but also questions of intragenerational shelter inequities. By the beginning of the 1980s, a substantial housing advantage had been gained by the older, first-wave, members of this generation. They had the opportunity of boarding the housing-ownership train at a time of modest prices and carrying costs, and subsequently rode—and benefited from—the inflationary run-up in house values.

In contrast, the younger baby-boom latecomers saw their housing buying power diminish. The conjunction of inflated shelter prices and high mortgage interest rates was devastating. Fears of their being left behind in the station—missing the homeownership train—were omnipresent.

But the mortgage reality that emerged by the mid-1980s worked for the generation in the broad. While the accumulated housing equity advantage of the more mature boomers remained unique, their mortgage-rate advantages were tempered. Inflation rates in housing, with the exception of a very few dynamic markets, substantially abated. The massive wave of "refinancing" which took place during the mid-1980s helped redress the intra-baby boom generation mortgage-cost inequities, while it also permitted the older boomers to trade up.

Future Financial Uncertainties

Housing's favored credit position, a result of bank and thrift industry (savings and loan associations, and savings banks) regulation, has disappeared. Eliminated were the directives for the thrifts to invest most of their assets in housing. The thrifts had been permitted to pay higher interest rates to depositors than could commercial banks. This meant that a relatively assured supply of "cheap" capital directed primarily to housing was mandated by law. Deregulation pulled the plug.

A new homogenized financial structure, with lending for housing merely one of its components, had been created. But it incorporated a far greater level of secondary financial entities. The mortgage became an enormously sophisticated instrument, fully capable of floating on the international financial sea.

The product is a huge rationalized marketplace. Without question, it yields the consumer more mortgage availability than would otherwise be the case. But in its very homogenization, and worldwide interdependence, the risk of massive shifts in costs and terms (down-payment requirements, length of mortgage, and the like) becomes potentially more ominous.

When we turn to mortgage markets to come, therefore, we face not only the uncertainties of the business cycle, but also the relatively uncharted profile of a new financial reality: from neighborhood savings and loan to global financial markets. The mid-1980s housing boom was carried out via this new system. Will it perform as well in a future which may be defined by a more stringent worldwide economic/financial environment?

The Savings Crisis and Resolution

America has been in a demographic–savings crisis during the 1980s. The result has been a necessity to borrow increasing amounts from abroad in order to maintain the patterns of consumption—not least of all in housing—that seemingly define America and its maturing baby boom generation.

The demographic problem emerged when the baby boom moved en masse to the 25- to 44-years-of-age sector—the time of peak consumption and prime borrowing. The borrower ranks swelled just at a time when the prime saver group (45 years of age and over) showed little growth. This demographic "mismatch" will persist through the beginning of the 1990s.

We have projected sharp shifts in future housing demand: slow growth in household formation and with it a declining potency of starter housing, countered by an enormous demand for upscale, trade-up units. The savings realities, coupled with lower gross housing demand, give a promise for an easier tomorrow as we move into the 1990s. Assistance will be on the way as a function of a much more positive demographic balance, assuming the baby boom as it ages will reflect, at least in part, the income patterns and savings behavior of previous generations.

The New Housing Geography

The scale of gentrification which has been taking place in America's cities is highly controversial. What is evident, at least, is that it typically has been linked to relatively youthful adults at the early stages of the household life cycle. As we view the demographic shape of things to come, either America's cities will have to fortify their pulling power, or whatever the scale of gentrification past may have been, it will diminish in the future. Demographic maturing and a familial focus suggest suburbia and exurbia, not central city settlement patterns.

The major locational imperative will be the continued dominance of housing within reasonable range of employment opportunities for multi-worker households. The central city's physical setting should be fortified by this—but the suburban employment matrix is growing with such rapidity that the latter's future hegemony seems assured.

Selected Bibliography

Brereton, Peter E. "Housing Prosperity's Bellwether." *Mortgage Banking* 43 (February 1983): 10–14.

Browne, Lynn E. "From Boom to Bust in the Housing Market." *New England Economic Review* (May/June 1982): 28–50.

Case, Fred E. "Creative Financing Instruments." *Real Estate Appraiser and Analyst* 48 (Spring 1982): 45–58.

Clemhout, Simone. "The Impact of Housing Cyclicality on the Construction of Residential Units and Housing Costs." *Land Economics* 57 (November 1981): 609–623.

Colton, Kent W., and Seiders, David F. "Financing the Housing Needs of the 1980s: Highlights of the Report of the President's Commission on Housing." *Federal Home Loan Bank Board Journal* 15 (July 1982): 2–12.

De Leeuw, Frank, and Ozanne, Larry. "The Impact of the Federal Income Tax on Investment in Housing." *Survey of Current Business* 59 (December 1979): 50–61.

Downs, Anthony. "The American Dream of an Affordable House: As the Image Recedes." *Across the Board* 18 (December 1981): 58–63.

_____. "The Real Estate Revolution." *American Demographics* 4 (June 1982): 20–23.

_____. "Too Much Capital for Housing?" *Brookings Bulletin* 17 (Summer 1980): 1–7.

Eichler, Ned. *The Merchant Builders*. Cambridge, MA: MIT Press, 1982.

Eilbott, Peter. "Condominium Rentals and the Supply of Rental Housing." *Urban Affairs Quarterly* 20 (March 1985): 389–399.

Esaki, Howard, and Wachtenheim, Judy A. "Explaining the Recent Level of Single-Family Housing Starts." *Federal Reserve of New York Quarterly Review* 9 (Winter 1984/1985): 31–38.

Feins, Judith, and Lane, Terry Saunders. *How Much for Housing?* Cambridge, MA: Abt Books, 1981.

Freund, James L. The Housing Market: Recent Developments and Underlying Trends." *Federal Reserve Bulletin* 69 (February 1983): 61–69.

Friedman, Joseph, and Weinberg, Daniel H., ed. *The Great Housing Experiment*. Beverly Hills, CA: Sage Publications, 1983.

Goetze, Rolf. *Rescuing the American Dream: Public Policies and the Crisis in Housing*. New York: Holmes and Meier, 1983.

Grieson, Ronald E., ed. *The Urban Economy and Housing.* Lexington, MA: Lexington Books, 1983.

Guttentag, Jack M. "Recent Changes in the Primary Home Mortgage Market." *Housing Finance Review* 3 (July 1984): 221–255.

Hayden, Dolores. *Redesigning the American Dream: The Future of Housing, Work, and Family Life.* New York: Norton, 1984.

Hendershott, Patric H., and Ling, David C. "The Likely Impact of the Treasury Tax Reform Plan on Housing." *Federal Home Loan Bank Cincinnati Quarterly Review* (1985): 9–14.

Hendershott, Patric H., ed. "Taxes, Mortgage Instruments, and Housing. Some Simulation Results." *Public Finance Quarterly* 10 (April 1982): 131–280.

Hoben, James F. "Affordable Housing: What States Can Do." *Urban Land* 42 (April 1983): 20–23.

Howenstine, E. Jay. *Attacking Housing Costs: Foreign Policies and Strategies.* New Brunswick, NJ: Rutgers University, Center for Urban Policy Research, 1983.

Huth, Mary Jo. "The Relationship Between Selected Household Characteristics and Housing in the United States." *Journal of Urban Affairs* 4 (Winter 1982): 33–47.

Johnson, M. Bruce, ed. *Resolving the Housing Crisis: Government Policy, Decontrol and the Public Interest.* Cambridge, MA: Ballinger, 1982.

Kendig, Hal L. "Housing Tenure and Generational Equity." *Aging and Society* 4 (Summer 1984): 249–272.

Lee, Dwight R. "Why the 1970s Housing Boom Had to End." *Real Estate Review* 14 (Summer 1984): 88–92.

Mallach, Alan. "The Fallacy of Laissez-Faire. Land Use Deregulation, Housing Affordability, and the Poor." *Washington University Journal of Urban and Contemporary Law* 30 (Spring 1986): 35–72.

Montgomery, Roger, and Marshal, Dale Rogers, ed. *Housing Policy for the 1980s.* Lexington, MA: Lexington Books, 1980.

Myers, Dowell. "Wives' Earnings and Rising Costs of Homeownership." *Social Science Quarterly* 66 (June 1985): 319–329.

Newman, Sandra, and Reschovsky, James. *Federal Policy and the Mobility of Older Homeowners: The Effects of the One-Time Capital Gains Exclusion.* Ann Arbor, Michigan: University of Michigan, 1985.

Schechter, Henry B. "Economic Squeeze Pinches the Future of Housing." *Journal of Housing* 37 (April 1980): 192–196.

Smith, Wallace F., ed. "Housing in America." *Annals of the American Academy* 465 (January 1983): 9–148.

Stegman, Michael A. *Housing Finance and Public Policy.* New York: Van Nostrand Reinhold Co., 1986.

Sternlieb, George, and Hughes, James W. *America's Housing: Prospects and Problems.* New Brunswick, NJ: Rutgers University. Center for Urban Policy Research, 1980.

———. "The Evolution of Housing and Its Social Compact." *Urban Land* 41 (December 1982): 17–20.

———. "The Housing Locomotive and the Demographic Caboose." *American Demographics* 6 (March 1984): 22–23 + .

———. *"Demographics and Housing in America."* Population Bulletin Vol. 41, No. 1, January 1986.

Tuccillo, John, et al. "Homeownership Policies and Mortgage Markets, 1960 to 1980." *Housing Finance Review* 1 (January 1982): 1–21.

United States. Congress. House. Committee on Banking, Finance, and Urban Affairs. Subcommittee on Housing and Community Development. *Future of the Housing Industry and Federal Housing Policy: Hearings. July 15–October 15, 1981.* 97th Congress, 2nd session, 1982.

———. *Housing—A Reader.* Washington, DC: U.S. Government Printing Office, 1983.

United States. Congress. House. Committee on Banking, Finance, and Urban Affairs. Subcommittee on Housing and Community Development. *Making*

———. *Making Affordable Housing a Reality: Hearing, June 24, 1984,* 98th Congress, 2nd session, 1984.

United States. Department of Housing and Urban Development. Office of Policy Development and Research. *Families and Housing Markets: Obstacles to Locating Suitable Housing.* Washington, DC: U.S. Government Printing Office, 1980.

United States. Federal Home Loan Bank Board. Office of Policy and Economic Research. *A Strategic Management Approach to the Housing Crisis: Making the Solution Fit the Problem,* by Arthur Sharplin. Washington, DC: U.S. Federal Home Loan Bank Board, 1983.

Index